By Amy Ellis Nutt

BECOMING NICOLE

BECOMING NICOLE

The TRANSFORMATION
of an AMERICAN FAMILY

AMY ELLIS NUTT

RANDOM HOUSE | NEW YORK

Copyright © 2015 by Amy Ellis Nutt

Published in the United States by Random House,
an imprint and division of Penguin Random House LLC, New York.

RANDOM HOUSE and the HOUSE colophon are
registered trademarks of Penguin Random House LLC.

Grateful acknowledgment is made to Viking Books for Young Readers, a division
of Penguin Random House LLC, for permission to reprint an excerpt from
Cat, You Better Come Home by Garrison Keillor, copyright © 1995 by Garrison
Keillor. Reprinted by permission of Viking Books for Young Readers, a division of
Penguin Random House LLC.

Photo of the Maines family on the beach is © Kelly Campbell. All other photos are
courtesy of the Maines family.

ISBN 978-0-8129-9541-1
eBook ISBN 978-0-8129-9542-8

Printed in the United States of America on acid-free paper

randomhousebooks.com

987654321

First Edition

Book design by Barbara M. Bachman

For Kelly, Wayne, Jonas, and Nicole

What we have not had to decipher, to elucidate by our own efforts, what was clear before we looked at it, is not ours. From ourselves comes only that which we drag forth from the obscurity which lies within us, that which to others is unknown.

—Marcel Proust, *Time Regained*

The stream of continuing creation flowed through his blood, and he could go on and on changing forever and ever.

He became deer, he became fish, he became human and Serpent, cloud and bird. In each new shape he was whole, was a pair, held moon and sun, man and wife inside him. He flowed as a twin river through the lands, shone as a double star in the firmament.

—Hermann Hesse, "Pictor's Metamorphoses"

Omnia mutantur
("All things are changed")

—Ovid, *Metamorphoses*

Contents

III. GENDER MATTERS

IV. BREAKING BARRIERS

Mirror Image

THE CHILD IS MESMERIZED. TAPPING HIS TOES AND SHUFFLING HIS small sandaled feet in a kind of awkward dance, he swirls and twirls, not in front of the camera, but in front of the window in the shiny black oven door. It's just the right height for a two-year-old. Wyatt is bare chested and wears a floppy hat on the back of his head. A string of colorful Mardi Gras beads swings around his neck. But what has really caught his attention, what has made this moment magical, are the shimmering sequins on his pink tutu. With every twist and turn, slivers of light briefly illuminate the face of the little boy entranced by his own image.

"This is one of Wyatt's favorite pastimes—dancing in front of the window of the stove," says the disembodied voice behind the video camera. "He's got his new skirt on and his bohemian chain and his hat and he's going at it. . . . Wave to the camera, Wy."

Maybe Wyatt doesn't hear his father. Maybe he's only half-listening, but for whatever reason he ignores him and instead sways back and forth, his eyes never leaving his own twinkling reflection. Finally, the little boy does what he's asked—sort of. He twists his head around slightly and gazes shyly up at his father, then lets out a small squeal of delight. It is a child's expression of intense happiness, but Wayne Maines wants something else.

"Show me your muscles, Wy. Can I see your muscles?" he prompts the son.

Suddenly Wyatt seems self-conscious. His eyes slide slowly from his father's face and settle on something—or nothing—on the other side of the kitchen, just out of camera range. He hesitates, not sure what to do, then, ignoring his father again, turns back to the oven window and strikes a pose. It's a halfhearted pose, really: With his two little fists propped under his chin, he flexes his nonexistent muscles. He knows he's not giving his father what he wants, but he also can't seem to break the spell of his reflection.

"Show me your muscles. Over here. Show them to me."

Wayne is getting frustrated.

"Show Daddy your muscles, like this. Over here. Wyatt. Show me your muscles."

At last, the appeals have their desired effect. Wyatt turns again toward his father, hands still under his chin, arms still against his sides, and looks up at him. But that's it. That's all Wayne Maines is going to get. With a look of part defiance, part apology, the little boy turns back to the oven window.

"All right. That's enough," the disappointed father says and clicks the camera off.

BEFORE LOVE, BEFORE LOSS, before we ever yearn to be something we are not, we are bodies breathing in space—"turbulent, fleshy, sensual," Walt Whitman once wrote. We are inescapably physical, drawn to the inescapably human. But if we are defined by our own bodies, we are entwined by the bodies of others. An upright, moving human being is endlessly more fascinating to an infant than any rattle or plaything. At six months, babies can barely babble, but they can tell the difference between a male and a female. When a feverish infant rests its head on its mother's chest, her body cools to compensate and brings the child's tem-perature down. Place the ear of a preemie against its mother's heart and the baby's irregular heartbeat finds its right rhythm.

As we grow and mature and become self-conscious, we are taught that appearances—who we are on the outside—aren't nearly as impor-tant as who we are on the inside. And yet beauty beguiles us. Human beings are unconsciously drawn to the symmetrical and the aesthetic. We are, in short, uncompromisingly physical, even self-absorbed. The philosopher and psychologist William James once wrote that man's "most palpable selfishness" is "bodily selfishness; and his most palpable self is the body." But man does not love his body because he identifies himself with it; rather, "He identifies himself with this body because he loves *it*."

And if he does not love his body, what then? How can you occupy a physical space, *be* a body in space, and yet be alienated from it at the same time?

There are dozens of videos of Wyatt Maines and his identical twin brother, Jonas, in the first years of their lives, growing up in the Adiron-dacks of New York and then in rural Maine. Adopted at birth, they are the only children of Kelly and Wayne Maines, and they are lavished with love and attention, the video camera catching everything from the ordinary to the momentous. They splash at each other in the bathtub, plop in rain puddles together, and unwrap presents side by side on Christmas morning. Kelly never wanted the boys to fight over their pres-ents. Anything one gets, the other gets, too, right down to the candles on their shared birthday cake. When they turn one year old there are two candles, one for each boy. When they turn two, four candles. Kelly also believed in exposing them to traditional playthings as well as atypical toys. So at birthdays and Christmases both receive big yellow dump trucks, roller-skating Barbie dolls, and motorized Dalmatian puppies.

In the beginning, with their bowl-cut hairstyles, dungarees, and flan-nel shirts, it was virtually impossible to tell them apart, except that Wyatt's face was ever so slightly rounder. But there *were* differences, and

Kelly and Wayne noticed them soon enough. Wyatt was the one who every morning, in his diaper and with a pacifier in his mouth, stood next to his mother in front of the TV and imitated her Pilates moves. Usually he'd do the exercises while holding a Barbie doll, often giving it a shake so its long blond hair swished this way and that, sparkling in the morning sunlight. At other times, he'd unsnap his onesie, letting the sides hang down, as if it were a kind of skirt.

Kelly and Wayne could tell Wyatt was moodier than Jonas; he would occasionally lash out at his brother as if frustrated just by his presence. There was something else, too. At night, when she bathed the boys, Kelly would catch Wyatt staring into the long mirror hanging on the inside of the bathroom door. As she pulled off Jonas's clothes and plunked him into the tub, she'd notice Wyatt standing naked and transfixed in front of the mirror. What did the two-year-old see? Himself? His identical twin brother? It was impossible to know, and impossible to ask Wyatt, of course. But often it seemed as if the little boy was puzzled by his reflection, unsure of the image staring back. There was some inscrutable pain behind his eyes. He seemed tense and anxious, as if his heart was in knots and he didn't know how to untie them.

We are all born with traits, characteristics, and physical markers that allow others to identify us, to say, "He's a boy" or "She's a girl." None of us, however, is born with a sense of self. By the age of two, children recognize themselves in a mirror, but so do chimpanzees and dolphins. Even the humble roundworm can distinguish its body from the rest of its environment via a single neuron. But of our "who-ness" or "what-ness"— our essence—there is no single place in the brain, no clump of gray matter, no nexus of electrical activity we can point to and say, Aha, here it is, here is my self, here is my soul.

All those questions about who and what we are: They were still in the future when Kelly and Wayne first brought their boys home from the hospital. The parents looked on their identical twin sons as wholly unexpected gifts. Unable to have biological children, they felt they were living out their own version of the American dream, courtesy of two perfect little specimens of male *Homo sapiens*. Wayne, in particular, yearned for the day when he could buy his boys their first hunting rifles, their first fishing rods, their first baseball gloves. That was the way it had always been done in his family, and he would continue the tradition.

Who we are is inseparable not only from who we think we are, but from who others think we are. We are touched and loved, we are appreciated or dismissed, praised or scorned, comforted or wounded. But before all else, we are seen. We are identified by others through the contours and colors and movements of our bodies. In his 1903 treatise *The Souls of Black Folk*, W.E.B. Du Bois, the African American author and intellectual, wrote about a double consciousness, a two-ness, of the "Negro" race, "this sense of always looking at one's self through the eyes of others, of measuring one's soul by the tape of a world that looks on in amused contempt and pity." He believed the history of African Americans in the United States was the history of a kind of "strife,—this longing to attain self-conscious manhood, to merge his double self into a better and truer self. . . . He simply wishes to make it possible for a man to be both a Negro and an American, without being cursed and spit upon by his fellows."

Dignity, self-respect, the right to be treated as an equal, that's what everyone wants. But Du Bois knew that those who are alienated from the community of man because of color (or, one might add, because of sexual orientation or gender) have a much harder path, because the alienated, the differentiated, the misfits of society must bear the burden of a single unspoken question on the lips of even the most polite members of society:

"What does it feel like to be a problem?"

Beginnings

But the Lord said to Samuel, "Do not consider his appearance or his height. . . . The Lord does not look at the things people look at. People look at the outward appearance, but the Lord looks at the heart."

—1 SAMUEL 16:7

CHAPTER 1

Identical Twins

A T SIX MONTHS IN UTERO, WYATT AND JONAS MAINES ARE FULLY formed. In a sonogram performed in a medical office near Northville, New York, on the afternoon of July 7, 1997, one of them is hunched over, the individual vertebrae visible in the shadow of the fetus's arched spine. The imaging technician uses an arrow to point out the head, then the trunk, then the legs. A tiny hand hovers in space, relaxed in the amniotic fluid, its minuscule fingers moving ever so slightly, as if practicing a piano piece. Forty-five seconds into the video, the technician points to the vaguely outlined shadow of one of the twin's genitalia and types onto the screen "Still a boy!!!" It's the tech being funny, of course. Both fetuses emerged from a single egg, they have the exact same DNA, and they're identical male twins. How could one of them *not* still be a boy?

By the time Wayne and Kelly finally held their newborn sons in their arms three months later, the couple had been married five years. For three of those years Kelly suffered through multiple miscarriages as well as months of tedious and painful fertility treatments. Everything changed in early 1997, though, when she got a phone call from her cousin Sarah, a sixteen-year-old she barely knew. The teenager said she was "in trouble" and didn't want to have an abortion. But she was also too young to raise a child on her own. Would Wayne and Kelly consider a private adoption?

Kelly's own upbringing in the Midwest was anything but traditional. The roots of her family, as much as she knew them, began on the limestone bluffs on the north bank of the Ohio River in the town of Madison, Indiana. Founded in 1809, about halfway between Louisville, Kentucky, and Cincinnati, Ohio, Madison had its heyday as a river town in the mid-nineteenth century. It was also an important first stop on the Underground Railroad and as early as the 1820s was home to a thriving community of free blacks. In 1958 it was the fictional location for author James Jones's quaint Midwestern hometown when Hollywood filmed his autobiographical novel, *Some Came Running,* there. According to legend, the star of the film, Frank Sinatra, was so worried about being stuck in a "hick" town during shooting he persuaded his buddy Dean Martin to take a supporting role.

Kelly's grandfather was a paddleboat captain in Madison at a time when steamboats still plied the waters, delivering goods to towns up and down the Ohio. He took his first wife there, but divorced her to marry Kelly's grandmother, the oldest of nine and barely a teenager when her own father abandoned the family. A short time later she began working in a glove factory to help support her mother and siblings, and at age nineteen married Kelly's grandfather, partly out of love, partly as an escape from the drudgery of caring for so many children. The couple soon moved to Indianapolis, where Kelly's grandfather got a job with the Mayflower Moving Company, and Kelly's grandmother raised three girls and a boy. Her grandparents were both of German descent and their values and mannerisms reflected their heritage. They were matter-of-fact, honest to a fault, and no-nonsense. Kelly grew up learning expressions such as "There are no pockets in a shroud," meaning you can't take your money with you, and "It beats hens pecking on a rock," used when she saw something she could barely believe.

None of the women in the family cottoned to the popular notion that men were superior, or that "ladies" should follow certain rules or behave in socially acceptable sorts of ways. Which may be why Kelly and others in her family could be so frank about their origins, saying they'd come into the world in what some people once called the "bastard way." For Kelly and her relatives, it was just the way it was. Roxanne, her biological mother, told Kelly her father was likely a one-night-stand. Kelly was only two in 1963 when Roxanne asked her sister Donna to adopt her baby girl.

For Donna, a woman with a quick mind and aspirations of a career, life was largely one of frustration. Under other circumstances she would likely have become a doctor or lawyer. When she was growing up, college was not something many parents wanted, or cared about, for their daughters. Donna worked for a time at a travel agency and, years later, after the kids were out of the house, enrolled in nursing school and earned straight As. If you want something bad enough and work hard at it, you can get it—that was a lesson Kelly learned from Donna. Motherhood was not the role that fit Donna best. Still, despite the fact she already had a daughter, she took in Roxanne's baby girl. "I'm like the second dog you get when the first one is driving you crazy," Kelly would say, laughing. The house was always clean and there was always food on the table. Dinner was at five o'clock sharp and you'd better be there on time.

Donna loved her children—two boys eventually joined the two girls—but she also worked long hours and didn't have much time, or energy, for affection. It didn't seem to matter to Kelly and her siblings. They knew they had a place to lay their heads every night, and for the most part that was enough. When Kelly was in her twenties and thirties Roxanne would occasionally call and apologize for giving her up for adoption, but Kelly, without rancor and in all honesty, told her she didn't need to say she was sorry. She'd done the right thing, Kelly told her. The children Roxanne had tried to raise all had difficult lives at best.

Kelly left home at seventeen, the summer before her senior year of high school. She surfed couches for a while in Indiana and lived for a bit with her grandmother, where she graduated from high school early. But she had no idea what to do next. Like her mother before her, Kelly didn't think college was possible. Kelly ended up living for a time with her father, whom Donna had divorced when Kelly was eleven. She made a few friends, worked different jobs, and generally had a good time. For the next few years she traveled around the country, earning her way as she went, ending up in California when she was in her early twenties. Kelly kept thinking there was more she wanted from her life than simply working blue-collar jobs and living paycheck to paycheck.

She picked up her education where she'd left off and began to take a few courses at Golden West, a community college in Huntington Beach. She wasn't in a rush, until one Saturday night, the boyfriend of one of Kelly's friends hatched a plan to steal some drugs from a local dealer. Afterward, when Kelly learned what he'd done, she was furious. It was a watershed moment for the twenty-four-year-old. Sharing an apartment, working low-earning jobs, partying on the weekends—she'd never thought of this as her life, really. It was always a stage, a phase, something she knew she'd grow out of. And she did. Fast.

The meandering was over. She needed to think beyond the present and plan for the future. Concentrating on her college courses, she received enough credits for an associate's degree in art from Golden West, though she never formally graduated. A short time later she followed up on an ad for a full-time position at an environmental consulting firm. During her interview she admitted she had no experience in cartography— a prerequisite—but, she added, there was nothing she couldn't draw. She got the job and before long was pulling down $30,000 a year.

The firm had a small branch in Chicago, and eventually Kelly found herself at another crossroads. She could go on for her bachelor's degree in Southern California, or she could move back to the Midwest and be nearer to her family without giving up her job. There was so much she'd already learned from her colleagues, not only about the environmental business, but about what it meant to be a professional. The decision was made: She would head east.

Not long after the move, her bosses, recognizing her intelligence and capabilities, asked her to learn more about underwater wells and waste

management. That's what led her to attend a five-day educational enhancement event in Findlay, Ohio, in July 1989—and to Wayne Maines.

The seminar was held at the local community college and was taught
by a former fireman who had been badly burned years earlier in a chemical fire. The days were excruciatingly long and included donning full
hazmat suits. There were only about a dozen students taking the course,
and at the end of each day they stumbled, exhausted, into the nearest
watering hole to kick back, cool off, and relax. On one of those evenings,
Kelly and Wayne, who was director of the Institute for Safety and Health
Training (now the Safety and Health Extension) at West Virginia University, found themselves playing pool and talking late into the night
about business, politics, and the course they were taking. They were
both products of small towns, and they felt unusually comfortable with
each other. She liked that he was talkative, sweet natured, and self-
assured. He liked her blue eyes, her easy laughter, and her honesty. By
the end of the week, when Wayne headed back to West Virginia and
Kelly to Chicago, they agreed to get together again as soon as possible.
Thus began a year of weekend traveling for both of them, at the end of
which Kelly moved into a two-bedroom duplex in Morgantown, West
Virginia, with Wayne.

THERE WAS NO MISTAKING Wayne Maines for anything but pure American boy. He was born in 1958 and grew up in the village of Hagaman,
New York, about forty miles northwest of Albany. According to the 1840
state *Gazetteer*, Hagaman's Mills (the name it was founded under in the
late 1700s) was home to one church, one tavern, one store, one gristmill,
one sawmill, one carpet factory, and "about 25 dwelling houses." Today
the village is slightly more populated—about twelve hundred people
sprinkled over a mile-and-a-half slice of land—but the habits and values remain old-fashioned and rural. Not until Wayne was five did the
Maines family have running water. They had a well for freshwater and
an outhouse. In the winter their heat came courtesy of a kerosene stove.

Wayne's bedroom was above the living room, and the grate on his floor looked directly down onto the stove and the television right next to it. All Wayne had to do was make a subtle adjustment to the TV's position before he went to bed and he could lie on the floor of his room and peek through the heating grate to watch *Rowan & Martin's Laugh-In*, without his parents knowing.

Wayne's father, Bill, worked in a carpet mill in Amsterdam, New York, and later commuted thirty miles each way to Saratoga for a job at General Foods. He also liked to frequent the local taverns and racetracks. Tall and slender, Bill Maines briefly played semipro baseball but a heart attack at age forty-four curtailed his ability to work full-time for the rest of his life.

Wayne's mother, Betty, worked different jobs over the years to keep the family fed. She cleaned an upscale beauty shop on weekends, waited tables, and sold Avon products. For a couple of years she worked the second shift at a leather mill that made Spalding footballs. Every day after school, on his way home, Wayne would take a path that dipped behind the factory where his mother would have just begun the second shift. Usually he'd call up to her and ask, "Mom, what do you want me to fix for dinner?" More often than not she'd yell back that she'd already made something and left it on the counter. All he needed to do, she said, was put it in the oven and fix a vegetable for himself, his brother, and his sister. The conversation always ended the same way, with Betty Maines smiling down at Wayne and saying, "I love you. See you in the morning."

As a product of small-town America, Wayne grew up with small-town values, especially devotion to family and respect for country. For Wayne, the lessons learned from his father were simple and, he figured, sturdy enough to last a lifetime: Make your first punch count, don't ever quit on your team, never point a gun at someone unless you're prepared to use it, try to return things in better condition than when you borrowed them (cleaned, oiled, and tuned up), and never, ever drink while playing cards.

While growing up, for several summers Wayne worked as a barker for a traveling carnival along with his brother, Bill, and toured up and down the Northeast. At one stop in Huntington, New York, when he was fifteen, Wayne was working a game booth beside a ride called the Zipper. A simple cable on an oval boom pulled about a dozen cars around the largely vertical ride. One night, a bolt attached to the door of one of the cars came loose, and as the boom whipped the cars up, the door with the loose bolt blew open and two teenage girls were flung from their seats. Hearing the screams, Wayne rushed to try and catch one of the girls as her body sailed through the air, but she hit the ground hard and broke her neck, dead on impact. The other teenager landed in a sand pit and was badly injured but survived.

Wayne had seen death before. He was a hunter. But he'd never witnessed someone killed in an accident, and especially someone so young and in such a senseless way. He'd always felt he had control over the world immediately around him, and when he didn't like something or felt it wasn't right for him, he was able to change it or move on. But the helplessness he felt in not being able to do anything for that girl was new to him. He knew he couldn't have run faster or gotten to her any sooner. Sometimes things happened and there was no questioning why or what if. Still, for many years afterward he couldn't get the image of that girl's mangled body out of his mind.

Wayne's only identity crisis occurred when he graduated from high school and enlisted in the air force. Joining the military was an honorable tradition in the Maines family. It was also practical. No one in the family had a college degree. In the air force he could learn a trade, so he signed up to be trained as a dental assistant. While stationed in Fairbanks, Alaska, Wayne worked for an oral surgeon. The man was an officer, voluble and opinionated. He was also a snob. One day he stopped in the hallway where Wayne and several other technicians and nurses were hanging out on break. The doctor said he had a question for Wayne.

"Who's the vice president of the United States?"

Wayne paused, embarrassed, then told the doctor he didn't know.

The surgeon turned to the physician beside him and said, loud enough for everyone to hear: "See, I told you so."

Told him what? Wayne wondered. That he was some kind of dumbass who probably didn't even know the name of the vice president of the United States? Well, he didn't. So what? He didn't know what the two doctors had been talking about before they'd stopped, and at nineteen years old he was too young—and too low in rank—to ask. But he probably blushed down to his boots. He was humiliated in front of a half dozen people for no other reason than for some arrogant surgeon's amusement. At that moment Wayne promised himself he'd never again be caught in a position where someone could make fun of him because of something he didn't know. He'd always felt confident being a good ole boy from a blue-collar family. The Maineses never tried to make themselves appear to be something they weren't. But Wayne was no longer satisfied just being a kid from rural upstate New York. Before his four-year hitch in the air force was up, he'd decided when he got out he would enroll in college on the GI Bill.

Pragmatic, like the woman he would later marry, Wayne first studied for his associate's degree at a community college near home, then made a huge leap into the unknown when he applied to, and was accepted at, Cornell University. He was in his midtwenties, and it wasn't easy being older than everyone else in college, or being just about the only promilitary conservative on a liberal Ivy League campus in the 1980s, but by the time Wayne was awarded his bachelor of science degree in natural resources in 1985, he was ready for more. Five years later, he'd earned a master's degree and doctorate, both in safety management, from West Virginia University. That's where he was living when he met and fell in love with his future wife.

Not quite three years later, Wayne and Kelly were married in Bloomington, Indiana, in a small ceremony at the Fourwinds Lakeside Inn. Kelly wore a white tea-length dress and a wide-brimmed hat. Wayne wore a tuxedo. He was so relaxed the day of the wedding he played a round of golf and took a nap beforehand. They honeymooned in Georgia, first at the Okefenokee National Wildlife Refuge, where they camped out at the headwaters of the Suwannee and St. Mary's rivers, then spent a few days on Jekyll Island before finishing their trip in Savannah. When they returned, they briefly settled back into life in West Virginia, then decided to move to Northville, New York, to be closer to Wayne's parents and the rural life he loved.

KELLY HADN'T SEEN HER cousin Sarah since she was a baby. She was the daughter of Kelly's cousin Janis, whose mother, Donna, raised Kelly and Janis under the same roof. When a teenage Janis got pregnant (Sarah was her second child), the pattern of family dysfunction looked to be a harsh hereditary burden. Like Roxanne, Janis had multiple husbands and boyfriends and didn't raise her own children. Sarah was brought up by her biological father and grandmother in Montana and later, as a teenager, lived with her mother in Tennessee. She was smart and artistic, but also stubborn and reckless. Still, she imagined going to college, perhaps even becoming a veterinarian. Getting pregnant at sixteen had not been part of the plan, but dashed expectations were a familiar family trope.

Wayne and Kelly had transformed their lives through sheer force of will, and both had already achieved more than their parents had. They'd been willing to accept the risks that came from moving outside their cultural comfort zones, not to mention others' expectations. So if Sarah's unexpected phone call gave them the chance to have a family, well, then, they would take it. Maybe there was a kind of cosmic logic to Kelly not being able to bear children of her own. Maybe this was a balancing of the scales. She'd been ready to move on with her life when the fertility treatments didn't work. Then came Sarah's phone call. Kelly believed in fate. Maybe she was the right person at the right time to usher a child into the world who otherwise would have been set adrift in a family with a legacy of chaos.

It didn't take long for Wayne and Kelly to decide they wanted the baby. Part of Kelly also identified with Sarah, and she knew better than anyone the importance of getting the teenager and her unborn baby out of her family's toxic environment as soon as possible. So when it was clear Sarah would bear their child, Kelly and Wayne asked her to come live with them until it was time to give birth. She was four months pregnant when she moved into the house in Northville in April 1997. Kelly and Wayne wanted to make sure Sarah was comfortable and had the right food and medical attention, but Kelly also wanted to help Sarah get her life together. She encouraged her to apply for her driver's license and study for a general education diploma.

By this time, Wayne was commuting fifty miles every day to a job as the corporate director of health, safety, and training at a chemical company in Schenectady, and he often daydreamed about the baby that was soon to be his. A sonogram had revealed it was going to be a boy, and Wayne imagined all the things he'd be doing with his first male child—playing catch, shooting baskets, firing deer rifles.

That's pretty much what Wayne was thinking about when his cellphone rang one spring afternoon as he was driving home from work. It was Kelly, and she was shouting. He could hear Sarah yelling in the background. Oh my God, what's wrong? he immediately thought.

"It's two! It's two!"

"What two?"

"Twins!" Kelly screamed. "We're having twins!"

It almost seemed too good to be true. Kelly, who'd had multiple miscarriages, had always wanted two children, and now they were getting their instant family. After the initial shock and wonderment wore off, Wayne thought: Oh, no, two college freshmen at the same time! He was thrilled about having a baby, even two babies, but he also knew all the concerns about being an expectant father had just doubled. As a safety expert, he didn't like surprises. He liked plans, analyzing a situation, and assessing all the risks and consequences. Now everything had to be rethought.

For months they had been preparing for one infant. How much

harder, Wayne wondered, would it be to take care of two? Everything was swirling around in his head as he found himself swept up in a kind of giddy anxiety. He took a deep breath and pushed the worries to the back of his mind. By the time Wayne reached home and embraced Kelly, he was smiling, thinking not about the added expenses but about the double joy: two baseball gloves, two basketballs, two rifles for his two baby boys!

CHAPTER 2

My Boys

On an unseasonably warm autumn afternoon, October 7, 1997, at 12:21, Wyatt Benjamin came into the world, born in the county of Fulton, in the city of Gloversville in upstate New York. Ten minutes later he was joined by Jonas Zebediah. Both babies were five pounds, two ounces, and two weeks early. Wayne and Kelly were present in the delivery room. Doctors had induced labor at about nine in the morning and Sarah had refused pain medication, so Kelly and Wayne, dressed in surgical gowns, held her hands as the babies emerged. It was both terrifying and exhilarating. Sarah had difficulty delivering the placenta and lost quite a bit of blood. It was strange, but Kelly felt like she was intruding and yet at the same time as though she was exactly where she was supposed to be. As one infant emerged and then the other, they were placed into Kelly's and Wayne's arms. It felt surreal to hold them, Kelly thought. They each had wispy dark hair, the softest pink skin, and tiny little squeals.

There was no family significance to either name. Jonas Kover was the name of Wayne's favorite college professor at Fulton-Montgomery Community College in Johnstown, New York. Wayne liked the old-fashioned name Zebediah, which was his vote for the other baby, but Kelly pre-vailed with the slightly more traditional Wyatt.

Three days later, Kelly, Wayne, and Sarah left the hospital with the twins, but only after the nursing staff made sure the new parents knew how to feed and change their babies. When it was Wayne's turn, he sucked in his breath and tried to settle his nerves. Okay, I can do this, he said over and over to himself as he prepared to give them each a bottle. Slowly, he lifted each infant, remembering to cradle their heads in his hand, then coaxed them to suck.

"Don't worry," the nurse said. "They won't break."

That's when it hit Wayne: He was really a father now. These two little boys would rely on him and Kelly for the rest of their lives. After feeding each, Wayne carefully placed one and then the other over his shoulder to burp. Nervously he patted their little backs.

"We're going to have so much fun together," he whispered in his boys' ears. "We're going to go hunting and fishing and I will teach you everything I know."

"My boys," Wayne said over and over. Wayne loved the sound of those words, and he said to Kelly not long after their births, "They are your boys now, but someday they will be my boys." He wasn't being mean, he explained. It was just his way of saying it's every dad's dream to bond with his sons, especially as they grow from children to teenagers to young men. There were certain rites of passage that he wanted to help them through, certain "guy" things, even silly things, such as arguing about sports, that he, not she, would probably be doing with them. That was how father-son relationships worked, he said.

Kelly was thinking about more immediate things. A week after the babies were born, she drove Sarah to Albany the night before her flight back home to Tennessee. It was only an hour's drive, but Kelly thought it would be good for both of them if they had a chance to talk before parting. As ebullient as she felt over her babies, she couldn't help feeling a sense of dread for Sarah, sending her back to an unstable mother and an uncertain life in the South. She hoped she and Wayne had been able to offer a little bit of perspective on all that she could do with her life if she just got herself out of Tennessee one day. In Albany, Kelly took Sarah out to dinner, and the two shared stories and a few laughs. Then Kelly thanked the teenager for the incredible gift she'd given her.

"You're free now to go live the life you want," she said. "We can have a relationship and you can be a part of the twins' lives, if you want that for yourself."

Driving back to Northville, Kelly was filled with mixed emotions. She worried about how Sarah would fare, but she also felt relieved that she and Wayne could finally begin their journey parenting two beautiful boys. At the same time, she knew she had to anticipate contingencies. Things could change quickly, and she needed to be ready for whatever was thrown at her. Sarah didn't talk about wanting to keep the babies, but Kelly felt the need to steel herself against the possibility anyway. If it came to that, Kelly would deal with it. Once those babies were placed in her arms, they were hers and Wayne's, and she would do everything humanly possible to make sure it stayed that way.

CHAPTER 3

Finally Ours

TEN MONTHS AFTER THE TWINS WERE BORN, ON AUGUST 21, 1998, a revised birth certificate for each infant was filed, this time with their new last names: Jonas Zebediah *Maines* and Wyatt Benjamin *Maines*.

The boys quickly put on weight and were healthy and happy. Kelly stayed at home with the babies while Wayne continued to work as the corporate safety director at the plant in Schenectady. It was a hefty commute, but there was very little traffic on Route 30, the main artery connecting Northville and Schenectady, so it was usually just Wayne and the deer for fifty miles or more.

The company had four plants in New York at the time, and nearly two dozen overseas. With a total number of employees between four hundred and five hundred, it was doing about $800 million a year in sales. The plants manufactured chemicals involved in the production of various industrial and commercial products—they were caustic ingredients few others wanted to make. The company did not have a very good safety record. Wayne's job was to get it back in compliance, which he did in short order. Under his watch, the injury rate plummeted to just two or three per one hundred workers.

Wayne was the company's first professional safety officer, and much about the plant remained redolent of times long gone. The men's locker room, for instance, was still a gang shower with no privacy. These were towel-snapping, tobacco-chewing workers and if, for instance, you were gay, this wasn't the kind of place you'd feel comfortable coming out.

The day Wayne began his new job he walked into his office and found its previous occupant had plastered the walls with graphic centerfold photos from *Hustler* magazine—all of them laminated. Wayne was aghast, even more so when a safety supply sales representative, a woman, walked into the office to say hello.

"Please, please don't come in here," Wayne said, trying to prevent the woman from seeing the pornographic pictures. "I'm so sorry."

Wayne did not immediately endear himself to the down-home employees of the company, including management. It took time to change the culture, and Wayne knew that he'd have to lead by example. At the same time, he wanted others to know that even though he came from the outside, he also was one of them. The first time Wayne wrote a permit for a welding job in a place where the workers had to climb into a tank that had once been full of caustic formaldehyde and flammable liquids, he told them, "I'm coming in with you." They said he didn't have to do that. Wayne told them he knew, but he was coming anyway. He wasn't going to let them risk everything just so he could write out safety permits in the comfort of his office. He needed to understand the dangers firsthand, and one of the immediate payoffs was that his credibility among the employees shot way up.

Away from work, Wayne and Kelly busily restored the nineteenth-century farmhouse they had bought in Northville, a village located in the town of Northampton, New York, about sixty miles north of Albany in the foothills of the Adirondacks. Northville rests on the cusp of the Great Sacandaga Lake, and when the village was established in 1788, Northampton was known as Fish House because of a large fishing camp on the lake. Today Northville is a village of barely a thousand residents, and fishing remains a recreational mainstay of the area. Northville was the setting for a 1997 two-part episode of *The X-Files* in which agents

Scully and Mulder discover a UFO at the bottom of the Great Sacandaga. The town's real-life residents were proud of their *X-Files* connection, but they also were comfortable being ordinary. It was a conservative family town, and that's what Wayne and Kelly loved about it.

Six months after the twins were born, Sarah's mother, Janis, began calling regularly, something she'd rarely done before. She also seemed overly chatty. Kelly was suspicious that Janis was angling for something, and it quickly became clear what it was. She'd recently remarried, an Englishman this time, and after living in Great Britain for a while had returned to Tennessee. In one of those early phone calls she told Kelly, "We're going to be best friends." Then she said that her daughter Sarah was living with a man who was doing drugs. When Janis called yet again, this time to say she thought the biological father of the twins wasn't the man listed on the birth certificate but someone else who was now in jail, Kelly got off the phone and turned to Wayne.

"I think she's trying to take the kids. I'm getting passports."

It would take eighteen months for Kelly to get those passports, but when she did, she felt reassured she and Wayne could flee the country with their babies on a moment's notice.

A few days later Janis called again. She had a proposition to make, she told Kelly.

"Why don't we keep one of the twins?"

Kelly cut Janis off.

"Nope, that's not how it works," she told her. "These babies are not going to be split up. If you want them, you take both of them, or you take neither."

It was a threat Kelly felt comfortable making. There was no way Janis would take both. She'd already had four children. Two infants would be way too much work. Kelly was right. Janis backed off.

ON MAY 17, 1998, KELLY and Wayne sat in the front row of a courtroom in Northville with the seven-month-old twins in their laps.

"Okay, who are we going to do first?" the judge asked.

"How about Jonas?" Kelly answered.

"I'm pleased to say we have two adoptions at the same time," the judge announced. "We want to make sure we are identifying you as the parents in court. . . . We also want to identify the children, that they are, in fact, the right children. That's essentially why we're here."

The adoption almost hadn't happened, or at least was almost postponed. A couple of days earlier, red blotches had appeared on Wyatt's face, arms, legs, and torso. Kelly thought it might be chicken pox, and if it was he'd have to be kept home for several days. The date for the adoption would be postponed, and any delay was just more time to worry. Now, the day before it was all going to be official, she found herself rushing Wyatt to the doctor's office, afraid not only that he was sick but that another roadblock was going to delay the babies' legally being hers. The pediatrician quickly noticed the "slapped cheek" look of the rash and diagnosed fifth disease, a common childhood virus. It is contagious, but by the time a rash appears the infection is over. There was nothing to worry about.

Inside the courtroom, the judge looked at Kelly and Wayne. "Raise your right hands," he said. "What are your names?"

"Kelly Maines and Wayne Maines."

"Sir, who are you holding?"

"Jonas."

"Ma'am, who are you holding?"

"Wyatt."

"Are these your signatures on the papers?"

"Yes."

"You are married, is that correct?"

Kelly and Wayne nodded.

"I've done this before and there is a difference between males and females," the judge said, trying to make a joke. "When I ask a date, it's a lot easier to get it from the woman. What day were you married?"

Kelly answered: "May 16, 1992."

"I'm signing the order of adoption, and you'll each get a copy of this and we'll send it to the appropriate agencies and they'll send you a new birth certificate. That takes care of Jonas. Congratulations."

Kelly's mother, Donna, and Wayne's father and mother, along with a smattering of other people in the courtroom, clapped. The judge then added his signature to a second document.

"That makes it official for Wyatt as well. Congratulations to you. I know this is a special day for you, and it was a very pleasant one for us. We're adjourned."

Wayne and Kelly posed for photographs holding the babies with the judge between them. Then the judge posed with both babies, holding each in the crook of an arm and smiling broadly for the camera. At home, dessert and champagne awaited the family's celebration. Written in red icing atop a chocolate cake were the words: FINALLY THEY'RE OURS!

A sense of relief overwhelmed Kelly and Wayne. They wouldn't need those passports. Now they could just concentrate on being the parents of two normal, healthy baby boys.

IT WAS CLEAR FROM the beginning that there was an almost physical bond between the two babies. They seemed to always want to be in close proximity to each other. In the first year of their lives, they spent a lot of time snuggled together in a playpen in the living room. When they began to crawl they'd take naps with the two family dogs, Ethyl, a Doberman/Rottweiler mix, and Emit, who was mostly German shepherd. Usually the two dogs would growl and snap at each other, and both infants would mimic them, grunting just like Ethyl and Emit.

But as they grew into toddlers, Wyatt loved everything Barbie, while Jonas loved everything *Star Wars*, *Power Rangers*, and Dwayne "The Rock" Johnson. He spent hours making his own imaginative action figures out of clay, then liked to smash them with makeshift weapons.

Wyatt tended to take out his frustration on Jonas; Jonas took his out on his toys. From an early age, Jonas was more of an interior child, with an unusual gentleness.

You can hear the differences between the twins in two law enforcement videos taken when they were barely four years old. One after the other, they stand in front of a makeshift measuring stick (both of them are three and a half feet tall) sponsored by the New York Masonic Safety ID program, which keeps files of key statistics on children in case they ever go missing. On the video the twins, who are in preschool, are asked individually about their school, their friends, where they ride their bicycles, and where they'd go if they were hiding from someone. Jonas says he'd hide behind a tree in the front yard; an excited Wyatt explains he'd climb to the top of the roof. Wyatt's best friend is Leah. Jonas's best friend is Mommy and Daddy. When asked his nickname, Wyatt answers: Wyatt Zebediah Maines. Jonas isn't sure, so the interviewer prompts him, "What does Mommy call you?"

"Angel."

The biggest difference between the boys could be seen in the characters they chose to play when they acted out stories. Jonas was always the "boy" character and Wyatt the "girl" character. He loved playing Cinderella, Dorothy from *The Wizard of Oz*, Wendy from *Peter Pan*, and Ariel from *The Little Mermaid*.

In fact, Wyatt was obsessed with Ariel, a beautiful, red-haired mermaid who is also voluptuous, in a Disney sort of way, with just a hint of cleavage above her bikini top and yet nary a suggestion of sexual anatomy. Part human, part fish, Ariel, with her shiny green scales, is decidedly a mermaid below the waist. But above it, with her long hair and luscious red lips, she is all girl.

Ariel's problem, however, is that she lives in one world, under the sea, even as she yearns to be in another, on land. As she gazes at her image in a mirror beneath the waves, she feels comforted by the top half of her reflection. It's the bottom that doesn't make sense. Because she yearns to be a girl, a human female, she wants nothing more than to escape her mermaid's tail, which is why, against her father's wishes, she swims to the surface whenever she can to watch the humans aboard passing ships. When ships are wrecked in storms, Ariel collects the artifacts left behind—a teapot, dinner plates, a man's pipe, and a sewing thimble—and spirits them away to a secret cave. For her, the most ordinary items used by humans are objects of beauty, because they symbolize something she is not but badly wants to be.

"Oh my gosh, have you ever seen anything so wonderful in your life?" she exclaims about a fork, even as everyone around her tries to tell her, "It's better/Down where it's wetter."

Ariel had a kind of hypnotic power over Wyatt. He watched *The Little Mermaid* DVD incessantly and imitated Ariel's long, flowing hair by running around the house with a red shirt halfway over his head trailing behind him.

One day, shortly before the twins turned three, Wayne stood in one of the bathrooms, hammering. Using Kelly's design, he was renovating the room in a classic deer camp motif, complete with a vanity mirror bordered by fishing lures. Little Wyatt toddled in to see what his father was up to. For a minute or so he just stood there, quietly watching, then left. A few minutes later he was back, this time with his own toy hammer, and he began to bang on the wall with it just like his dad. Wayne gloried in the father-and-son moment, one of the few he'd had with Wyatt since he was born. He wanted to slow it all down, to savor it.

"Do you want a snack?" he asked his son.

Wyatt nodded and the two took a break. Wayne sat on the side of the antique bathtub. Wyatt stood next to him. Both nibbled on animal crackers. Suddenly, Wayne noticed his son's expression darken. Wyatt looked up at his father.

"Daddy, I hate my penis."

Jolted out of his reverie, Wayne tried to take in the words his precious son had just uttered. Then he reached down, scooped up the young boy, and hugged him fiercely. He kissed away the tears in Wyatt's eyes. He kissed the tip of his nose, his cheeks, his lips, all the while fighting back his own tears.

"It's okay," he whispered. "Everything's going to be okay. I love you very much."

Wayne pressed Wyatt's head against his shoulder, trying to comfort the boy even as his own chest heaved with emotion. The next moment, Jonas was in the bathroom, too, hugging his father's leg. One twin was never very far from the other.

"What's the matter, Daddy?" Jonas asked.

Wayne slumped down onto the floor, his back against the bathtub, and took his twin boys into his arms, hugging and kissing one and then the other, over and over.

"It's okay," he whispered to Wyatt and Jonas, stroking both boys' hair. "Everything's going to be okay."

CHAPTER 4

Gender Dysphoria

To Kelly, Wyatt wasn't strange, and he certainly wasn't sick. He was just "different"—that's how she explained it to friends and family, and to Wayne. She knew most others didn't understand, especially Wayne. She'd seen her husband sitting reading the newspaper while Wyatt skipped around in his tutu, a hand-me-down from his friend Leah. Wayne pretended not to see him. He didn't look up. He didn't want to look up.

Kelly was learning to do things pretty much on her own for both boys, but especially Wyatt. He clamored to wear the same colorful clothes as Leah, and rather than wear the flannel shirt his mother bought him to match Jonas's, he would go bare chested. Kelly felt it was cruel to keep dressing Wyatt in clothes he hated, so she made the decision, without Wayne's input, to shop every now and then for something less masculine for Wyatt to wear.

The first time Kelly walked into the girls' clothing section of Target she felt weird. Anyone who knew the family knew she often bought the twins their clothes there. And here she was, shopping for one of her sons in the girls' department. She forged ahead anyway. The children weren't yet in school; who did it hurt for Wyatt to wear pink and purple? It was hard enough just getting him to wear shirts and pants. She looked for a girl's shirt that wasn't too frilly and not too feminine, but preferably pink, and when she found it she knew it would be a lot easier to dress Wyatt in the morning. She'd have to get over what other people might think or say when they saw Wyatt in his pink shirt. She decided it was their problem, not hers. And it certainly wasn't Wyatt's.

Wayne didn't approve, but he also didn't stop Kelly—not that she'd have listened to him anyway.

"Why do you have to indulge him?" Wayne would ask.

"He's trying to tell us something," Kelly would say. "He's showing us who he is, and we've got to help him figure it out."

All Wayne wanted was to have a "normal" family, just like everyone else. Everyone else doesn't have a normal family, Kelly told him. She hadn't had one, and maybe that's why she wasn't crushed, like Wayne, when Wyatt turned out to be different. Kelly didn't know what a perfect family looked like, so she had no expectations. She had no threshold for disappointment, no picture in her mind or her heart that Wyatt wasn't living up to. But Wayne did have a picture from his own happy child-hood, and as far as he was concerned, every time Wyatt dressed up in girls' clothes he made a mockery of it.

"Wyatt, you don't want to wear those shoes," Wayne would say when Wyatt appeared in a pair of Kelly's heels.

"Yes, I do."

"No, you don't."

"Yes, I do."

"You don't really want to be a girl."

"Yes, I do."

That's how the conversations—if you could call them that—went. Wyatt wearing a dress; Wayne wanting Wyatt to act more like a boy. Around and around they went, with Wyatt just as stubborn and deter-mined and convinced he was correct as Wayne was. And each time her husband and child had one of these back-and-forth exchanges, Kelly knew Wayne was fighting reality.

One evening, when the twins were about three years old and had been tucked in for the night, Kelly sat down at the computer in the living room and typed five words into the search engine:

"Boys who like girls' toys."

It was both a question and a statement of fact. For Kelly, it was also a beginning. She scrolled through science articles, online forums, and medical sites. She read about homosexuality, transsexualism—wasn't that what drag queens were?—and something called transgender. She read for hours. Her first thought was, well, maybe the girls' toys and clothes and behavior meant Wyatt was gay. But sexual orientation was the same thing as attraction, and that seemed almost crazy to imagine, at least in a three-year-old. Transsexualism certainly wasn't right, either, since that seemed mostly about adults who undergo surgery to change from being male to female or vice versa. As for being transgender, the Merriam-Webster dictionary defined it as "of or relating to people who have a sexual identity that is not clearly male or clearly female."

Well, that was sort of like Wyatt. One of his best friends in pre-K was Cassandra, and she taught him all the girly things he wanted to know. For instance, a girl doesn't dry her hands at the sink in the back of the classroom with brown paper towels. Oh no, Cassandra told him, a girl gracefully shakes her hands, fast, like they're on fire. Cassandra was the girliest girl Wyatt knew. She had long hair that fell all the way down her lower back. She even had long nails and wore nail polish. It was true Wyatt loved to play with dolls, but he was also very physical. He could throw a ball even better than Jonas, and he often wrestled around on the ground with his brother.

Gender, Kelly read, was the belief that you're male or female. It was something innate, not something you had to think about or tell other people about, unless those other people treated you like one gender when you felt you were the other. Kelly didn't remember ever having such self-conscious thoughts when she was a child.

The articles flew by, she took notes, and she kept searching, that night and the next and the next night after that, until the words she was using in her searches got downright ridiculous: "Boys who like pink," "Boys who have bowl haircuts and wear shirts on their heads, but have male toys and like wrestling."

She kept coming back to that one word, "transgender." Gender is about having the physical characteristics of a male or female. Gender identity, she read, is something else—and it has nothing to do with having a penis or a vagina, and everything to do with how a person *feels*. Did Wyatt feel like he was female? Most people who are born with the anatomy of a male also identify as male, and most born with the anatomy of a female identify as female. But not everyone. Some people grow up feeling like the gender opposite of the one they were born into. Others have physical characteristics of both genders. Kelly didn't pretend to understand it all, not by a long shot, but "transgender" sounded more like Wyatt than anything else.

She kept reading. Although a sense of self is innate and established by the age of four, some children express dissatisfaction with their birth gender as early as two years old. Those who do, and in whom the dissatisfaction persists, are said to have gender identity disorder. The diagnosis was changed to gender dysphoria in 2013 in the fifth edition of the *Diagnostic and Statistical Manual of Mental Disorders*, or DSM-V, maintained by the American Psychiatric Association. Gender dysphoria is the state of unease that results when a person's sexual anatomy doesn't match up with his or her inner sense of gender. This was more than just a shift in language by the APA, it was a watershed moment akin to the elimination of homosexuality from the DSM-II in 1973.

In the DSM-V, the general diagnostic criteria for gender dysphoria lists eight traits or behaviors a child must manifest for at least six months, including:

- A strong desire to be of the other gender or an insistence that one is the other gender (or some alternative gender different from one's assigned gender).

- In boys (assigned gender), a strong preference for cross-dressing or simulating female attire.

- A strong preference for cross-gender roles in make-believe play or fantasy play.

- A strong preference for the toys, games, or activities stereotypically used or engaged in by the other gender.

- A strong dislike of one's sexual anatomy.

There must also be present "clinically significant distress" or an impairment in functioning. This last indication is important partly because of what it doesn't say but implies. The distress transgender people feel when their anatomy is in conflict with their gender identity is different from the distress, for example, of a depressed person. In the latter case, the distress is part and parcel of the condition of depression, but that's just not the case with transgender people. If there is an inner distress it arises from knowing exactly who they are, but at the same time being locked into the wrong body and therefore being treated by others as belonging to one gender when they really feel they are the opposite. The dysfunction arises not from their own confusion, but from being made to feel like freaks or gender misfits. Kelly shuddered when she thought of the torment other kids were capable of inflicting on someone like Wyatt. All in all he was a happy child, but when he wasn't, it almost always had to do with being a "boy-girl," which is how he referred to himself.

Out of the blue, he'd ask Kelly, "When do I get to be a girl?" or "When will my penis fall off?" The questions almost seemed natural, as if it was just a matter of time before he became a girl. If Kelly could only see into Wyatt's brain. Did he believe he'd emerge as a "she" from this boy chrysalis stage he was in, like a human butterfly? Maybe Wyatt really did believe that some babies were born female, some male, and some could change from male to female when they were still young. He was impatient, though, and that's where the unhappiness seemed to come from, from wanting to push the process he thought must be as natural as caterpillars transforming into butterflies.

Wayne wanted to be close to both his sons, but he couldn't get his mind around Wyatt's gender-bending behavior, so he retreated—to the woods to cut down trees, to the gym to work out his frustrations, to the pool or the lake to swim until he was exhausted. He wanted to be a good parent, but he didn't know how to deal with Wyatt's situation, whatever it was.

Every holiday season, Wayne mailed a letter along with the family's Christmas card to friends and relatives. He liked writing the letter. He was proud of his wife and—for the most part—his two boys, and writing the letter gave him time not only to reflect on the past year but to take pleasure in all that he and his family had accomplished and learned. But by Christmas 2000 Wayne was finding it harder to compose the annual missive. How to explain to people—people he loved and admired but who might lack a depth of understanding—about his Wyatt. That he was just a little bit different, but in every other way normal.

> 2000: Wyatt is still very dramatic. He loves to dress up, play music and wrestle with daddy. . . . For Christmas he wants Yellow Barbie. Jonas is a bit taller than Wyatt. We are not sure why, it is difficult to get him to eat anything but cookies. He still loves his Teletubbies, reading books and helping daddy. For Christmas he wants a fishing game.

Two years later, not much had changed, except perhaps the intensity of the differences between the five-year-old boys:

> 2002: Wyatt is creative, kind and obsessed with girls. . . . He plays "dress-up" and acts out numerous stories. . . . His girlfriend is Leah.

It was easier to describe Jonas:

> Jonas is very analytical. He also never stops talking or moving. His favorite things are action figures, puzzles, the computer and of course pirates.

Wyatt's favorite things? Coloring, dolls, computer games and puzzles. His favorite story was Ariel.

Feeling stymied at work and realizing there was limited upward mobility, Wayne began to look around for other jobs. In the spring of 2003, with the children in pre-K, an opportunity presented itself: an offer from the University of Maine in Orono, where he would eventually become the executive director of safety, health services, transportation, and security. It wasn't a huge bump up in terms of money, but a job at an academic institution was prestigious and appealed to Wayne's love of learning. It would be hard for him to leave the area where he grew up, but he couldn't turn down the position. Kelly wasn't thrilled. She loved living in the village of Northville, with the sun-swept views over the lake. One of her closest friends was Jean Marie, Leah's mother. Leah also had a brother, Wolfgang, whom they called Wolfie, who was a good friend of Jonas's. Originally from Long Island, New York, Jean Marie was funny, outgoing, and uninhibited. Even with four kids running around, Kelly felt comfortable and relaxed with her in a way that she did with few others. The kids especially liked to act out the books Kelly and Jean Marie read to them, or pretend they were characters from one of their favorite TV shows. Kelly was usually the one who put together the costumes, and Jean Marie provided the sound effects.

The move wasn't going to be easy for the twins, either. Jonas loved playing in the woods behind the house, and Wyatt enjoyed skipping through the big colorful garden with the stepping-stones that bore the imprints of the twins' tiny hands and etchings of lady bugs and butterflies. Kelly's mother, Donna, had recently come to live with them, in an apartment attached to the house, but she wouldn't be going with them to Orono. She and Wyatt had become particularly close. Together they'd dress up Barbie and comb her long locks or watch *The Little Mermaid*. Sometimes Wyatt would help Grandma Donna water the flowers in the garden. He always felt like a princess there, in his own special kingdom. On the plus side, in Orono the family would be part of a university town, which Kelly hoped would be more inclusive. Maybe it would even help her figure out what she needed to do for Wyatt.

In the meantime, Kelly continued to think about gender. One night, as she was watching the TV news, a story came on about a couple in New York City who had allowed their young son to go to school dressed as a girl. The parents were reported to the police and arrested, and the child, at least temporarily, was taken away from them. Kelly was a hyper-vigilant mother, so she was keenly aware of all the ways her children could be wrested away. She'd let Wyatt grow his hair out and occasionally wear a feminine shirt or blouse, which meant that Wayne and Kelly sometimes found themselves getting into awkward conversations with strangers. If they were eating out someone might comment on the twins and ask, "How old are your son and daughter?"

"Oh, they're four," Kelly would say, not bothering to correct the questioner.

When they were at McDonald's they usually let the kids tumble around in the play area. When it was time to leave Kelly or Wayne would have to call out, "Wyatt, Jonas, it's time to go!" That's when Kelly and Wayne would notice the puzzled looks on other parents' faces. Kelly ignored them. For Wayne, though, every public encounter with a stranger's confusion jabbed at him. People weren't just judging Wyatt; they were judging him and Kelly.

What does it matter? Kelly would say. It isn't anyone else's business, and we don't have to explain our situation every time we meet someone. Who cares?

But it did matter, and he did care.

One night, before the move, the Maineses were invited over by Jean Marie and her husband, Roscoe, to see the improvements they'd made on their house. Wayne and Roscoe were cut from the same cloth—they both grew up loving sports, hunting, and enjoying what they called "rustic carpentry"—building things without the need for absolute precision. Wyatt was playing with Leah when the two of them tumbled downstairs, giddy and flushed and both wearing dresses, heels, earrings, and full makeup. Everyone laughed, even Wayne, but it was a tight laugh, and it caught in his throat. Roscoe invited Wayne out on the porch for a beer.

"What am I going to do?" he said to Roscoe.

They both knew what he was talking about.

Roscoe looked at Wayne, not sure what to say, and took a swig from his beer.

"I don't know, Wayne. I don't know."

"Kelly thinks I'm a jerk, but I just don't know what to do."

The two men were quiet, unable to think what more they could say to each other. Wayne's pain and confusion were palpable, but they were Wayne's to bear, and as he stood there next to Roscoe he let the cool night air wash over him.

CHAPTER 5

Down East

"DOWN EAST" IS HOW MANY PEOPLE REFER TO MAINE, ALTHOUGH to Mainers, down east is more specifically the coastal sections of rural Hancock and Washington counties, from Penobscot Bay on the west to the Canadian border on the east, with the Atlantic Ocean defining the southern side of the region. Spiritually or culturally, down east means you are never far from the sea, with islands, peninsulas, coves, and bays giving the jagged coast of Maine its distinctive character. The origin of the term "down east" dates to the time of the sailing ships. When traveling from Boston to Maine, in a northeasterly direction, ships were often rewarded with a wind at their backs, which meant they were sailing downwind. Likewise, on their return trip to Boston, these same ships would often be sailing upwind, which is why Mainers often say they're "going up to Boston," though geographically Boston is about fifty miles to the south of Maine's southern border.

A New England ethos runs deep here. Generations of the same families have refused to be dislodged by bad weather, bad business, or bad fortune. Mainers make do, no matter what, and it's not hard to understand why. Battered by the push and pull of ancient glaciers, beaten by the wind and weather, the coast of Maine is as ornery and stubborn as the people who settled it. Generations of the same families populate the rural cemeteries and the property records of Maine, where anyone not born in the state, no matter how long they've lived here, is referred to as being "from away."

With 95 percent of Mainers identifying as Caucasian, only Vermont is whiter, and even though Orono is a college town, it is still 93 percent Caucasian. In other ways, though, Orono is a peculiar hybrid. Straddling both land and water, it lies at the mouth of the Stillwater, a tributary of the Penobscot River. The Stillwater breaks away from the larger river twelve miles to the north and drains back into the Penobscot downstream. Marsh Island was created when it was encircled by the two rivers. Orono occupies part of the island and part of the mainland—the University of Maine is one of the only colleges in the country located entirely on an island that is not also a state or a city—and its founding predates the American Revolution. Orono was named for the chief of the Penobscot Indians, the same Indians the Europeans eventually pushed out of Orono's rich fishing and hunting grounds. After the Revolution, lumber mills dominated the town, and while they no longer do, Orono is very much a product of pragmatism and reinvention, a place where very little is ever thrown out and everything is capable of being repurposed, including its stores. A sign for the Orono Pharmacy & Ice Cream Parlor hangs from a rusty pole out front, even though the Ice Cream Parlor is long gone. So is the video store that replaced it, as well as the walk-in medical clinic that replaced the video store. Now the front of the pharmacy is inhabited by Layla's Bazaar, an international grocery store.

Despite a few urban highlights, including the Sunkissed Tanning Salon, the town has retained a rural character. When the farmers market opens in the warm weather, many customers arrive by canoe or kayak. Part of Marsh Island, where the university sits, is open every year to bow hunters in search of white-tailed deer, and along Orono's thirty-nine miles of roadway grow a hundred varieties of shade trees, Norway maple, eastern white pine, red oak, green ash, and black locust. American elm trees still line the byways of Orono, as well as serviceberry trees, so named by New England's first settlers, who planned their funeral services around the timing of the tree's bloom, because it signaled the ground had thawed enough for graves to be dug.

The Maineses' new house in Orono was a four-bedroom with cedar sides, a three-hundred-foot-long driveway, and a one-stall barn. The front yard was heavily wooded with oak, spruce, and hemlock that were so close to the house, Kelly said, she felt she was suffocating. Eventually, Wayne cut a few down, not because of Kelly's complaints, but because *he* suddenly decided they were crowding the house.

With six acres of mostly woodland, there was a lot for the twins to explore. Wayne cut down forty trees to build a one-room log cabin for the kids. Kelly bought a zip line for the backyard and in the winter fashioned a bobsled run that stretched from the back deck down the stairs and across the yard to the edge of the woods. The kids seemed to adjust well, but Kelly wasn't happy. The house was too boxy. It was too dark inside from all the shade trees; it was overrun by ants, and the water pipe to the well was cracked. But the home wasn't too far from town or school or Wayne's new job as safety director at the university, so even though Kelly complained she knew they weren't going anywhere else anytime soon.

With the boys about to begin the first grade, the family decided to hold a "Get to Know the Maineses" party for the neighborhood. It was a cool, cloudy autumn day as guests streamed into the house. Kelly was still in the kitchen fixing platters of food, but with the party starting Wayne went looking for the two boys. He found Jonas in the den, then Wyatt appeared at the top of the stairs, smiling down excitedly at his father. There he was, his parents' sweet, irrepressible, chestnut-haired boy—wearing his favorite pink princess dress from Toys R Us.

"Wyatt, you can't wear that!"

Wayne's harsh tone cracked through the party chatter, and Wyatt's little body jerked, then froze. Kelly, who heard her husband's strained voice from the kitchen, knew something was wrong and rushed out.

"What's the matter?" she asked.

"Wyatt cannot—"

"What did you say to him?!"

Kelly followed her husband's eyes to the top of the stairs. One of Wyatt's tiny hands grasped the banister; the other clutched a glittery wand. On his face was fear and confusion.

"Are you going to let him wear *that*?" Wayne asked.

Kelly didn't answer. Instead, she raced up to Wyatt, hot tears now streaking his face, took him by the hand, and led him back into his bedroom. It was, she knew right then and there, the worst moment of her life. It wasn't so much the reaction of the people at the party, who were mostly stunned into silence—that was Wayne's issue—but rather the hurt her son was experiencing, and for no good reason other than that he wanted to wear his princess dress to the family's party. How could she explain to him that he'd done nothing wrong when his father had just scolded him? She didn't think she was ready for this, and yet she knew it was just the beginning.

"This isn't really the right time," Kelly gently told Wyatt, persuading him it would be better, for now, to wear pants and a shirt.

"I can't be myself," Wyatt said, a mixture of sadness and anger in his voice. "Jonas gets to wear what he wants. Why can't I?"

Kelly knew it was true, and that it wasn't fair.

"Let's just try to get to know people first," she said.

Still dazed, Wayne remained downstairs, enveloped in a kind of concussive quiet. The world where he was a father and husband in an ordinary, hardworking, middle-class family had just blown up. He stood there stunned, unable to hear whatever was going on around him, as if deafened by the psychological explosion. Was everyone at the party looking at him right now? He felt strangely alone, and, worse, unmasked. As if the hunter, the fisherman, the air force veteran, and the Republican had all been stripped away and the only thing left was the father—but father of what and of whom? Yes, he was a happily married man and the parent of two beautiful boys, but it was also true he was embarrassed by one of them—and he'd just broken that little boy's heart.

Nothing seemed to help Wayne make sense of Wyatt, not his small-town background, not his time in the military, and certainly not all that education. How could Wyatt and Jonas be identical twins and be so different? There was no question Jonas was pure boy, and his very existence seemed to put the lie to Wyatt's insistence he was female.

Wayne had shared his fears, confusion, and anger with no one, not even Kelly. She knew he was disappointed in Wyatt and even angry, but he held it inside and instead continued to put distance between himself and the family—working late during the week, running and swimming and exercising for hours at a time, doing chores outside that allowed him to be alone with his thoughts. There was a stubbornness to Wayne and also, at times, an inability to see beyond the walls of his own experience. Kelly had learned that lesson up close. One day, early in their relationship but before they were married, Wayne announced he was going hunting. Kelly thought, how nice, he's going to go off and do his male thing, so she made him a sandwich and kissed him goodbye. When he came home in his dirty camouflage fatigues, a deer was splayed inside his Chevy Chevette, its nose on the dashboard and its feet sticking out the back. Kelly was aghast.

"What's that in your pocket?" she asked, noticing a rather large bulge at Wayne's waist. He pulled out the deer's heart and proffered it to Kelly.

"Oh my God!"

Kelly couldn't believe what she was looking at. What had her husband done? What kind of person was he? Actually, Wayne had properly gutted the deer in order to preserve its meat to bring home to be cooked, and the heart was particularly delectable to hunters and meat eaters. Flooded with all the wrong images, however, Kelly was suddenly furious with her husband and took off in her car. She drove for three hours—all the way from Morgantown, West Virginia, to Pittsburgh and back—trying to calm down. When she finally returned home, Wayne had cleaned up, but he told her they needed to talk, to work this out, because hunting was important to him—it was part of who he was. She told him she just hadn't been prepared for exactly what that meant. She was fully capable of seeing beyond her own experiences and she knew she'd have to adjust. She just wanted him to know that it had been upsetting to her and that in the future, there would be no dead deer in the house. Period.

KELLY WASN'T SOMEONE WHO needed to have a lot of close female friends, but those she did have, she confided in. One of them was Chris, whom she met when she took the kids swimming at a local pool. Chris was homey, down-to-earth, and very matter-of-fact. She had four kids of her own, one the same age as the twins. Another friend and neighbor Kelly often talked to about Wyatt was Allison, who also had children the same age. On Friday afternoons, Kelly and Allison would unwind at the breakfast bar in Kelly's kitchen, drinking Cosmos and eating veggie snacks, because they were both watching their weight. Allison was a kind of sounding board for Kelly, especially when she complained about Wayne. Everything was so complicated with him, she told her friend. He just didn't understand, or want to understand, Wyatt, and he was so shut down she'd pretty much given up even trying to talk to him about their child.

"Have you ever thought about divorce?" Allison once asked Kelly.

"Oh God, no," she replied. "I'd never think of asking for one. I'd be scared he'd get custody of the twins."

In truth, sometimes Kelly *was* afraid Wayne would leave her because she was "allowing" Wyatt to act like a girl. When he went out on one of his long bike rides, she thought maybe he wouldn't come home. More than that he would leave her, though, she was afraid he would take Jonas and Wyatt. The bottom line was, she couldn't count on Wayne. She also wasn't about to run away or hide or rant or cry, either. She just needed to be a good mother to Wyatt. And right now she wasn't sure how. What she was sure of was that Wayne wasn't helping. No matter what she said to him, even if it was just wondering out loud if maybe Wyatt was gay, she knew what Wayne's answer would be: "No, that's not it," he'd say, and then turn back to what he was doing.

Despite his inability to talk with Kelly, divorce wasn't in Wayne's vocabulary, although he sometimes worried *she* would leave *him*. Wayne was also trying to make sense of Wyatt, in his own way, but mostly he was hoping these were all things his son would simply outgrow. He didn't want to think about his son being gay. It was fine if the sons of other fathers were gay, because he had no problem working with gay people or his children having gay friends. He just didn't want that for his son. It would be too hard his whole life, and Wayne was afraid he wouldn't know how to be the kind of father Wyatt would want—or need.

CHAPTER 6

Things to Be Careful Of

APRIL 1, 2003

Dear Wyatt's Diary,

Today Wyatt shared his secret thoughts with me.
He is a very nice person. I love being his mommy.

WYATT DIDN'T HAVE A NAME FOR IT, FOR THE FEELING, SO TO the question "Who are you?" his answer was simple: "A boy who wants to be a girl," or "I'm a girl in a boy's body," or, more simply, "I'm a boy-girl." That's what Wyatt often told his mother and anyone else who asked. And if those "others" were first graders—and they sometimes were—they didn't seem to care that his answer was slightly equivocal. If there was trouble at school, it was with kids outside his class, like a few of the second graders, who sometimes called him "girly." That wasn't so bad, really, except that he knew they said it to him to be mean.

Wyatt's pre-K teacher, Mrs. Jenks, wrote on his evaluation: "Wyatt is a delight! His dramatics will surely have him on the stage in the future! It is interesting to watch Wyatt's competitive side, which he displays mostly with his brother, rather than the other children."

Being twins and spending so much time together, it was natural the boys would be competitive. But there was something else at work. It wasn't that Jonas didn't accept his brother being different. That's all Jonas knew, so he never thought there was anything unusual about Wyatt's behavior. Liking girl things was simply who Wyatt was. When Jonas introduced a friend to Wyatt, he'd say, "Here's my brother. He likes to put a shirt on his head like it's hair and plays with Barbie dolls." And sometimes Jonas would even play with Barbie, too, at least until he got bored.

At other times, however, the differences in their personalities erupted in fights, usually with Wyatt lashing out at Jonas. When Kelly or Wayne separated them and asked Wyatt why he was so angry, he'd tell them he didn't know. And he really didn't seem to know, because it would happen so suddenly. Looking at Jonas, he saw himself, but also "not" himself. The cognitive dissonance must have rankled. It was as if his own image mocked him at every turn. Wyatt didn't know why he and Jonas both looked like boys but only he felt like a girl. Once, when Wyatt was asked yet again why he had hit his brother, he finally gave an answer: "Because he gets to be who he is and I don't."

Four months later Mrs. Jenks added to her report. "I hope that the boys soon learn to be happy and comfortable with themselves as *individuals,* so they can also rejoice in one another's successes and accomplishments rather than competing for the same attention. They are a beautiful pair with so much to offer and to discover about themselves! So much fun and excitement ahead!"

In Orono, the boys were put in separate classes in the first grade, but otherwise they spent most of their waking hours together, and their closeness, even with the occasional fights, was unmistakable. Their main play activity, nearly every day, was acting out TV shows or stories they saw, heard, or read. They'd play the Three Little Pigs, then a bit later, Teen Titans. Everything became fodder for a story, and stories were what they immersed themselves in.

The first real organized sport Wayne and Kelly got the kids involved in was soccer. One cool fall morning, Wyatt seemed particularly distracted out on the pitch. Dressed in his little shorts and shirt, he just stood in the middle of the field while the two muddy teams swirled chaotically around him. When he did get involved, it was simply to push someone else out of the way. When Wayne, who was coaching, saw this happen he grew irritated. He didn't want the behavior of his children to affect the play of the team, so he pulled Wyatt from the game. Frustrated, angry, and unhappy, Wyatt took off running across the field, through the school parking lot, and right out into the street. Wayne sprinted after him, and Jonas after his father.

"Wyatt! Stop!"

There was a car heading directly for his son.

"STOP!"

Wyatt came to a halt, right in the middle of the street. A second later, Wayne grabbed him by the arm and swung him back onto the sidewalk, then practically dragged both boys into the back of the car.

"Don't ever do that!" he kept saying to his sons, as he got in the backseat with them.

Wayne was frightened, and he wanted his children to understand why: that what Wyatt had done was very, very dangerous. Neither boy had ever seen their father this angry. And they'd certainly never been yelled at quite like this before. They were quiet and scared.

"You could have gotten hit by a car, Wyatt. Daddy was very worried. I love you both, and I don't ever want you two to get hurt."

The twins' safety was paramount for both parents, so much so that they enrolled the boys in tae kwon do just so they could develop the skills they'd need to physically defend themselves. Wyatt's safety was particularly important, Kelly realized, because he could become an easy target for harassment. Kelly's concerns about Wyatt meant she was always on alert for stories in the news about other children like him. She'd have preferred to avoid the ones about transgender people being physically attacked, but she felt it was her obligation to know exactly what Wyatt might one day have to face.

In October 2002, just after Wyatt and Jonas turned five, a grisly news story out of California's Alameda County made headlines. Gwen Araujo, a seventeen-year-old from the town of Newark, had attended a party at a schoolmate's house on the night of October 3, then seemed to disappear into thin air. Two weeks later, one of the partygoers drove with the police out to a remote part of the Sierra Nevada foothills to point out a shallow grave. Gwen, who had been born male, had engaged in sexual activities with several men in their twenties in the weeks leading up to her murder. Suspecting Gwen was male at birth, these men cornered her at the October 3 party, stripped her naked, strangled her with a rope, and beat her skull in with a frying pan. Her last words were, "Please don't. I have a family."

Stories like these made Kelly anxious. Before the kids visited their friends' homes, she checked out the parents and made sure they understood about Wyatt's unusual personality and behavior. Then she'd watch over the kids to make sure nothing untoward happened.

As the twins moved from kindergarten to first grade, Kelly knew she needed to speak to the teacher about Wyatt. More important, she needed to make sure the teacher would accept him for who he was—and wasn't.

"Wyatt is a little different," she told the teacher when they met early in the school year. "He really likes girls' things and we're okay with that—and you're okay with that, too, right?"

She was. Kelly felt relieved. First school hurdle cleared.

One of Wayne's friends was surprised by her own son's reaction to Wyatt. The two families had spent time together on a weekend trip to Boston and on the way back, Wayne's friend asked her own two sons, who were similar in age to Jonas and Wyatt, what they thought of the "Maines boys."

"Mom, you mean the Maines kids. They have a boy and a girl," one of the sons said.

"No, they have twin boys."

The woman's children insisted: Wyatt was a girl. Finally the husband asked, "Do you remember when you went to the bathroom together? Didn't Wyatt have a penis?"

There was a long pause, then one of the sons answered.

"I know that boys have penises and girls don't, but Wyatt is a girl, and she just happens to have a penis."

Later in the year Wyatt composed and illustrated a "safety" book called "Things to Be Careful Of." The cover of the booklet depicted a man-eating shark, but also a smiling crab and fish and, Wyatt's favorite, a redheaded Ariel-like mermaid perched on an underwater rock. Inside, each page had a drawing and a reminder of what should be avoided, including strangers in cars who offer you candy, getting stuck in a tree when you climb too high, slipping on ice, ink-squirting squids, avalanches, vampires, stampedes, and the abominable snowman. Playing with matches and swimming when you're not a good swimmer were also cited as dangerous activities. But the first words in the book were the most personal—and the most realistic:

You can have a bully. You know, the boy or girl who bosses you. Bullies are mean to you so stay away from them.

CHAPTER 7

The Pink Aisle

ONE AFTERNOON IN EARLY MAY 2003, KELLY TURNED ON *THE Oprah Winfrey Show* to an interview with Jennifer Finney Boylan, an English professor at Colby College in Maine. Kelly had never heard of Boylan, and didn't know that she used to be James Boylan, but when Oprah introduced her, Kelly saw something unexpected: a pretty, very normal-seeming woman, who just happened to have once been a man. Everything she'd read on the Internet, all the images of cross-dressers, of men with bad wigs and worse makeup, melted away. Here was someone she could learn from.

Oprah had read Boylan's memoir *She's Not There: A Life in Two Genders* and said she couldn't put it down. Male at birth, Boylan knew from the time she was six years old that something was not right, that she didn't look the way she felt, which was female. She told Oprah, "My awareness of being transgendered is my earliest memory. But I also knew it was something that other people would find bizarre and hilarious. So I thought, I am going to make the best of things and be a boy, be a man."

In her imagination, she was female, she said. In her dreams she was female. And in private, when no one in the family was around, she dressed like a female, in her mother's and sister's clothes. "It was tremendously sad," she said. "Even I knew it was creepy, sneaking around, having a secret. You know that there is something very wrong; you know it intuitively. I think people know what their gender is based on what is in their hearts. If you have this condition, you know it."

For Kelly, this was the kind of affirmation she needed when she questioned whether what she was doing for Wyatt was right—that is, allowing him to wear his princess dress at home or to pull her down the "pink aisle" at Toys R Us. Yes, it was still very uncomfortable for Wayne, but it was perfectly natural for Wyatt, so how could Kelly doubt it?

"I did not want this other life," Boylan told Oprah. "I thought it was as strange as anyone. . . . You think you are the only person in the world that has this. In fact, we now know that there are tens and tens of thousands of people in this country alone who have this. One scholar says that it's as common as multiple sclerosis, it's as common as a cleft palate. It's something that many people in the country and across the world have, but these people are living in silence and shame because they are afraid to speak the truth."

When Oprah asked Boylan about the origin of her condition, she said, "No one really knows. I think there has to be a medical component. It's something you have from the age of two or three. Some people think that it has to do with the secretion of hormones in the mother's womb around the sixth week of pregnancy."

In her heart, Kelly believed this, too, that there was some medical explanation for Wyatt's behavior and feelings. They were so deep-seated, so seemingly rock solid, that even in her weakest moments, when she worried whether she might share some of the blame by indulging Wyatt in his choice of toys, she quickly dismissed those thoughts. Wyatt wasn't disturbed, he wasn't sick, he wasn't bizarre, and he wasn't a freak. He was unhappy as a boy—that was the bottom line, and so her job was to make sure he received the kind of help or assurances or whatever it was that he needed in order to be happy.

Listening to Boylan gave Kelly renewed confidence. Clearly she wasn't the only mother who'd ever had to figure out why her son wanted to be a daughter. Now Kelly was learning that there was also a protocol for perhaps fixing that cognitive dissonance. Boylan explained to Oprah that when patients transition from one gender to the other, doctors follow a process called the Standards of Care (SOC) for the Health of Transsexual, Transgender, and Gender Nonconforming People, originally developed by the Harry Benjamin International Gender Dysphoria Association more than thirty years ago. Basically, they are a set of medical protocols clinicians follow for patients seeking hormonal and surgical transition to the opposite gender of their birth. This was all fascinating and new for Kelly. Now if she could just find someone, some doctor, who could do all that for Wyatt. Kelly went out and picked up a copy of Jenny Boylan's book.

"She'd be a great role model for Wyatt," she said to Wayne one day.

"Uh-huh." Wayne had heard Kelly but didn't want to discuss it.

Kelly left Boylan's book on the coffee table for a few days, hoping Wayne might pick it up. He didn't. Then she moved the book to the bathroom. That seemed to do the trick. The book disappeared, but Wayne didn't say a thing. Clearly he wasn't ready to talk about it yet.

For the twins' seventh birthday, Kelly thought she'd finally found a toy both boys would enjoy. She'd noticed Wyatt engrossed by some action hero cartoon on TV one day and had made a mental note. In October, at the birthday party, Wyatt and Jonas both unwrapped a slew of action figures. Jonas loved them. Wyatt was disconsolate. Kelly couldn't figure it out. Finally, she asked him, didn't he like watching the action figure cartoon on television every day? Yes, he said, but what he really liked was the pretty house the action heroes lived in.

That was it for Kelly. Her last doubt about whether Wyatt might be transgender was gone. When she'd first come across the word in her research she'd put off talking about it too much with Wayne. She hadn't wanted to label Wyatt, to pigeonhole him, at least not at this stage in his life. How does a child this young know if he's really a girl? Up until Wyatt's seventh birthday she'd thought there was always the chance he might outgrow this. And in truth, she didn't care if he outgrew it. She just wanted to do right by her son. So she'd quickly become an expert in analyzing other parents' kids, looking for signs of passing phases in their behavior, such as the friend's child who painted his fingernails, or the one who liked to wear his sister's slip. But the behavior in those other boys was never really consistent, certainly not in the way it was with Wyatt. He wanted to wear dresses, be a princess, play Wendy in *Peter Pan* all the time, day and night. Sure, he also liked wrestling and was an athletic kid, but his sense of himself, the toys he played with the longest, the subjects of his fantasies, and the characters he playacted, were always female. Kelly didn't know any other boy who so consistently thought and acted like he was a girl.

Most of all, she was upset she'd failed Wyatt on his birthday of all days. Screw this, she said to herself, I will never again buy him something just because Wayne thinks that's what he should play with. It was all just too mean. The next day she went out and bought Wyatt the Ariel Playset he fervently wanted, and every Wendy, Cinderella, and Dorothy toy she could find.

CHAPTER 8

A Boy-Girl

Halfway through Jonas and Wyatt's first-grade year at Asa C. Adams Elementary School, the family was throttled by bad news. A lingering cold in January 2004 had finally pushed Kelly to make an appointment with her primary care doctor. During the physical examination the doctor felt a small lump or nodule on Kelly's thyroid. Typically these are tumor-shaped collections of benign cells, the doctor told her, but Kelly, who was forty-three, knew enough to be deeply frightened. At the time, she was helping a friend deal with a second bout of thyroid cancer. The woman had only just recovered from her first go-round the year before; now she faced deeply invasive surgery that would gouge out part of her neck.

The thyroid is a butterfly-shaped gland located in the lower front portion of the neck. Its job is to secrete hormones into the blood to help the body's brain, heart, muscles, and other organs stay warm and functioning. Between 85 and 90 percent of people who are found to have thyroid nodules do not have cancer, which is why Kelly's doctor had tried to reassure her. Tests needed to be done before there was any cause for worry. A chest X-ray, neck ultrasound, and thyroid function and blood tests followed. At last, a fine needle aspiration biopsy was performed. Then came the confirmation Kelly had feared all along: She had papillary thyroid cancer. Two surgeries in Boston followed, including a thyroidec-tomy, where doctors cut a three-inch-long incision in the front of Kelly's neck and pulled out the diseased gland. The cancer appeared to be con-tained, but just to be sure, doctors suggested radioactive iodine therapy, or radioiodine treatment, which they hoped would kill any remaining metastatic cells. The thyroid is the only tissue in the body that takes up and holds on to iodine. But radioactive iodine therapy is a punishing treatment, requiring patients to be isolated in a single room for several days, because after they ingest the iodine they remain slightly radioac-tive, evidenced in their sweat and urine. Patients undergoing the treat-ment are asked to flush the toilet twice after relieving themselves to rinse away as much of the leftover radioactive fluid as possible, and nursing staff change the sheets on patients' beds every day. A kind of medical Geiger counter is used to keep track of a person's radioactivity, and when it is finally low enough the patient is discharged.

After the iodine treatment, there were checkups and follow-up scans at the Dana Farber/Brigham and Women's Cancer Center in Boston. Sometimes Kelly's friend, the one fighting her own second battle with thyroid cancer, would drive her to the hospital—a 240-mile trek straight down I-95 from Orono to Boston. But often Kelly drove herself, once or twice in the middle of a snowstorm. When she did, her mantra was al-ways the same: "I need to live ten more years, just ten more years. If I can make it to ten years, Wyatt and Jonas will have a chance." It wasn't that she didn't think Wayne loved both boys, but if she died and he had to raise the kids alone, he would likely continue to struggle to understand Wyatt and not know what to do for him, and she dreaded the thought of Wyatt being alone, without his mother to tell him that everything would be okay.

Occasionally the whole family packed into the car for the trip to Bos-ton. Kelly had told the boys matter-of-factly that she was sick, but that

she was getting medicine in Boston to make it all better. She was petrified, of course, but there was no way she was going to frighten Wyatt and
Jonas. She had to stay calm for both boys.

When the family made the trip with her they stayed at a Holiday Inn,
where the kids could swim. Kelly and Wayne would sit and watch them,
all the while talking about how the twins were doing in school, or Wayne's
job—anything but cancer. They were having a hard time not feeling
sorry for themselves, when one day a young boy, not more than thirteen,
shuffled by them wearing a kind of housecoat. He had no hair, his face
was thin, and his eyes seemed lost. His parents walked alongside him,
and they were just as pale and worried looking as their son. Kelly and
Wayne watched the small family walk from the pool, down the hall, and
back into their room. Then they looked at each other and without saying
a word gave thanks for their own good fortune. No matter how much
they were being tested, they knew their children were safe and well.
When the months of treatment were finally over, doctors gave Kelly a
clean bill of health. Her cancer scare was over, and Kelly was more determined than ever to be there for her family.

ONE OF WYATT AND Jonas's favorite times of the day was when Kelly
read them a story before going to sleep. Between the boys' twin beds was
a wooden chair whose seat Kelly had painted yellow on the right side
(Wyatt's choice) and purple on the left (Jonas's). A red stripe down the
middle indicated where mom sat. Here she'd read to the boys, one son
squeezed in on each side. Wyatt's favorite story was Garrison Keillor's
"Cat, You Better Come Home," about a certain feline who felt underap-
preciated. The cat wanted to be special, to stand out, and so one day she
ran away from home in order to become rich and famous. Soon there
were parties and yachts and unending food, but it turned out to be an
empty life. After a while, all she wanted was to be normal again, to be
one of the crowd, and so the prodigal cat finally returned home, wel-
comed back by her owners without a question.

If other cats could only know
To hang their hats on the status quo,
And make the best of what they've got,
And be who you are and not what you're not.

Both boys were just beginning to figure out who and what they were. They each gravitated to the fictional characters they imagined they'd most like to be. For Wyatt, if it wasn't a princess, it was the Wicked Witch from *The Wizard of Oz* with long green hair and fingernails—and attitude—or Dorothy with braids and shiny ruby slippers. For Jonas it was the Tin Man—with an ax—or a pirate, like in the movie *Pirates of the Caribbean*. But for now, Wyatt was happy that his parents allowed him to skip off to the first grade dressed in pants and a shirt, but with pink sneakers, a pink backpack, and a pink *Kim Possible* lunchbox.

After school, the first thing Wyatt did when he got home was to throw off his pants and shirt and put on a skirt or dress—more hand-me-downs from Leah. The halfway dressing for school had been Kelly and Wayne's decision, a compromise that they weren't at all sure about. Somehow, they believed it was better to take a middle road for now, to set limits. Wyatt clearly wasn't happy with the decision, which made Kelly realize maybe it was finally time for him to see a therapist on a regular basis. She knew it wasn't going to be easy trying to hold Wyatt back, or even that she should hold him back, and knowing he was seeing a professional would make her feel more comfortable about whatever might come next.

Kelly combed through lists looking for doctors who treated kids for sexual issues. The first psychologist they visited in Bangor told them she worked with children who had been sexually abused, not children with sexual identity issues. Wyatt needed a gender specialist, she told them.

The next therapist asked Kelly and Wayne, "What kind of underwear does Wyatt use? Does he urinate standing up or sitting down?"

"Well, he pees standing up," Wayne answered.

"Well, then, he's not transgender," the shrink said.

Wayne and Kelly looked at each other and were glad Wyatt wasn't there. Wayne was nowhere near ready to accept that his son was really his daughter, but he thought the psychiatrist's questions and reasoning were simpleminded and ludicrous. He and Kelly stood up and thanked the therapist. On his way out the door, Wayne couldn't help himself.

"By the way, I pee sitting down, you know."

What Wyatt understood about himself, whether he felt different or odd or broken, neither Kelly nor Wayne really knew, until one day Wyatt looked up at his parents and said, "You know, I can have an operation that will fix me."

Wyatt didn't know the word "transgender" and he certainly didn't know anything about sex reassignment surgery. But somehow he did understand the concept of plastic surgery and that women were able to have their breasts enlarged and their faces made to look younger. If a doctor could give a woman bigger breasts than why couldn't a doctor give Wyatt little ones? Wyatt was an optimist, mainly because Kelly made a point to never instill doubt in him. She might have been holding him back, but she never discouraged or tried to dissuade him from becoming a girl if that's what he really wanted. From Wyatt's perspective, he just somehow knew it would all eventually work out. But an operation?

"Where did he learn that?" asked an incredulous Wayne.

Kelly said, "I have no idea."

CHAPTER 9

Wild in the Dark

UmmHappy, sad, mad, Unnspeakable blue red Unnsunshining
and hot and cool and red hot and ice cold.

                  —Wyatt Maines, diary, May 4, 2005

BEGINNING AROUND AGE SEVEN, WYATT'S MOODS SEEMED TO
fluctuate daily. On the cover of his second-grade "Secret Notebook," he
drew three suns, three clouds, and three smiling girls, all with long red
hair, standing on a green hill that sprouted pink and yellow flowers. On
the second page he drew a picture of himself with long hair standing
beside his brother. Neither was smiling:

> Dear Notebook,
>
> Sometimes when my brother does something bad to me, I
> punch him right in the guts!

Under a picture of Wyatt hitting Jonas, Wyatt wrote:

> Sometimes I punch my brother right in the center of his face
> with my fist.

The notebooks and diaries Wyatt and Jonas created at Asa C. Adams Elementary School usually included only sporadic entries, but in this one there were also drawings—of Wyatt throwing off his covers in the middle of the night, getting up, and going "wild in the dark," doing noisy gymnastics and pretending to be a vampire lady "and I bite my brother and scare his underpants right off!"

On page seven:

I mean this. I hit things. I kick things. I trip on things. And I throw things. This is how I practice my karate.

The final drawing in the notebook was actually a series of faces:

Sometimes I like to dress up as Daphany and Velma. My brother likes to dress up as Shaggy and his friends like to dress up as Scooby-Doo and Fred! I'd like to tell you more, but if I do, my brother might get mad and punch me!

The notebook was a second-grade assignment that Wyatt had to show not only his teacher but his parents. All of them then wrote comments on the back page:

Wyatt's teacher: "Wyatt, I used to do the same kinds of things
    with my three sisters!"
Kelly: "Wyatt, Your stories are getting so interesting. They're like
    reading store-bought books! Love, Mom."
Wayne: "Wyatt, What a great story! I am glad you like karate.
    I hope you continue to work on your black belt!!!
    Love, Dad."

In truth, Kelly and Wayne were both concerned. Because Jonas was the more passive of the twins, he was used to absorbing the blows, both physical and verbal. Fighting was to be expected between siblings, especially at that age, and identical twins were no different in that regard. But when they were physical, Wyatt sometimes seemed like he wanted to pummel his brother. Both parents gave them time-outs, tried to teach them they needed to talk instead of yelling and fighting, and told them that if they couldn't agree about something, they needed to come to them. Around this time Wyatt's anger also turned inward. The first sign of worry for Kelly were little tics she saw him develop. She noticed that when Wyatt was lying on the couch watching TV or doing his homework, he would absentmindedly pull at his eyelashes and eyebrows, trying to pluck them out.

"Wyatt, why are you doing that?" Kelly said one day.

"I have to."

"What do you mean you have to?"

"I mean I can't stop."

On April 13, 2006, nine-year-old Wyatt had his first appointment with child psychologist Virginia Holmes. Her office was in Ellsworth, about thirty-five miles southeast of Orono. Holmes had come highly recommended by the twins' pediatrician when Kelly told the doctor she thought Wyatt needed counseling. The weekly sessions were structured so that Kelly would talk to Holmes first and update the therapist about what was going on at home and at school. At first, Kelly and Wayne thought maybe Wyatt had attention-deficit/hyperactivity disorder, because he never seemed able to keep still. But his fidgeting, his constant restlessness, also seemed to point to a deeper anxiety, something perhaps even Wyatt couldn't explain.

Virginia Holmes wrote in her clinician's journal:

Met Wyatt for the first time. He is very feminine. He is wearing his hair long, and had a blue flowery barrette in it. . . . Wyatt displayed no anxiety or worries about wanting to be a girl. His eyes sparked with interest when I said my usual about knowing lots of boys who feel this way, but his main anxiety is not about that.

Wyatt's main concern is his overwhelming automatic desire to choke himself. . . . He does not feel able to stop himself from doing so, most of the time. He wanted to know did I know other kids who felt THIS? I talked a little about OCD, and he understood that: "Oh!" he said. "Like Tourette's Syndrome!" Right.

CHAPTER 10

Girls with Magical Powers

VIRGINIA HOLMES COUNSELED KELLY TO GO SLOW WITH WYATT, TO not necessarily give in every time Wyatt pushed her to allow him to be more like a girl. Holmes still thought Wyatt might be gay, not transgender, so until that could be determined, she thought it best to keep his feminine behaviors a bit more in check, at least in public, so Kelly insisted Wyatt continue to wear "boy" clothes to school.

When Wayne came home from work one night, Wyatt and Jonas were playing in the backyard with friends. They were sword fighting, and Wyatt was wearing a pink blouse and pants.

Wayne confronted Kelly, something he rarely did.

"Dr. Holmes said to go slow."

"She said to go slow with him in school," Kelly answered.

She was peeved. She knew Wayne was just using Dr. Holmes as an excuse for his own discomfort. Wayne was trying to adjust to the changes, but he was afraid the more feminine Wyatt was allowed to act, the harder it would be for him to go back to being a boy.

Wyatt compensated for the split life he was leading by escaping through a show called *Winx Club*, an Italian animated television series on Fox that highlighted a fantasy world of girls with magical powers.

Their love interests are called "the Specialists" and their enemies are three witches who call themselves "the Trix": Icy, Darcy, and Stormy. The witches, like most evil characters, get the lion's share of the drama, and they look the part with long hair, tall boots, and hourglass figures. The witches are powerful: capable of manipulating matter, specifically ice, darkness, and wind.

In his pink marble notebook for 2004 and 2005, Wyatt drew page after page of the Trix, the witches. The notebook begins with drawings of valentines, sunshine, and stars, and ends with sketches of a woman frowning and crying and a boy sticking his tongue out. Wyatt was first attracted to the characters because they were both feminine and powerful. Stormy, also known as the Storm Queen, has a cinched-in waist, purple eye makeup, and dramatic hair—a storm cloud of frizz and curls with long white bangs shaped like lightning bolts that frame her face. She is wild, even uncontrollable, and is capable of creating tornadoes, unleashing wind blasts, and stunning her enemies with shocks of electricity. As the youngest of the Trix sisters, however, Stormy is weaker than the other witches, but what she lacks in strength she makes up for in confidence and aggression. She's proud and quick to anger, and if someone crosses her, she will get her revenge, no matter how long it takes. Proud, outspoken, aggressive, and immature: That was Wyatt all over. Increasingly he was pushing limits, and sometimes even seemed to test his father. If they were in a department store, Wyatt would go straight to the girls' dresses, the ones he called "sassy" with their bold colors and glitter.

"Daddy, can I have this one?"

Wayne tried not to overreact. He didn't want to hurt Wyatt, but his job was to keep things neutral, which was what Kelly had suggested he do if he couldn't be more supportive.

"Maybe for Christmas, Wy-Pie, maybe for Christmas."

Usually Wayne didn't talk to Kelly about these incidents. But once, when they were discussing the possibility of Wyatt someday wearing a dress to school, he said they shouldn't do it, that once that happens, that's it, that's what he'll be forever known for—the boy who came to school dressed like a girl.

"Well, that's what he wants," Kelly answered.

WITH THE START OF the fourth grade, Wyatt's anxieties seemed to ratchet up. He pulled at his mouth, repeatedly touched his gums, pinched the skin under his tongue, and plucked out the hairs on his head one at a time. In his physical education progress report, his teacher noted: "Wyatt is very emotional and gets down or angry quickly. This behavior has emerged most dramatically in the past few months. Wyatt's self-confidence seems to have slipped."

These new stresses seemed to be more about how others saw Wyatt, and him wanting to fit in with the girls. He was desperate to wear a two-piece bathing suit, but Kelly had figured out a compromise several years earlier when the twins were first learning to swim at the YMCA. She'd convinced both boys to wear wet suits in order to avoid the whole issue of trunks versus bathing suit with Wyatt, although his wet suit was orange and pink.

Now Wyatt was pushing again, and it was getting harder to refuse him with his longer hair and his sense of himself as female growing stronger. Finally, Kelly gave in. Wyatt could wear a two-piece suit but with two conditions: no spaghetti-string top, and the bottom had to include a swim skirt. Agreed. At his swimming and diving lessons Kelly now sneaked Wyatt into the girls' dressing room. She hadn't told Wayne she was doing this, and when she told Virginia Holmes, the psychologist asked whether it was sensible to allow Wyatt to identify as a girl in such a public place. Kelly didn't often cry, but this time, in front of Holmes, she burst into tears. It was hard enough without Wayne's support, but now Holmes seemed to be questioning her parenting.

Wyatt had his own questions. He told Dr. Holmes that kids on the bus, especially one girl, often called him names that he didn't understand. Once, someone called him a "fruit basket," but he didn't know what that meant. Holmes mentioned the words "gay men."

"What are gay men?" Wyatt asked.

"Men who love other men instead of women."

"Oh! That's not me!"

Wyatt seemed perfectly confident of that, but Holmes said, well, they didn't know yet who he was going to love. But Wyatt did. Without question he did. He wasn't gay, he wasn't a boy attracted to other boys—that was as foreign to him as calling himself a boy. He was a girl. He was a girl who wanted to be pretty and feel loved and one day marry a boy—just like other girls did.

CHAPTER 11

A Son and a Daughter

As Wyatt continued to try to assert his femininity, his fights with Jonas became more frequent. At a session with his brother and Dr. Holmes in July 2006, Wyatt told the psychologist he worried that his brother wouldn't accept him as a girl the more he dressed and looked like one, especially in school. He also felt like Jonas wasn't as interested in playing with him, and maybe that was because he was embarrassed by Wyatt.

When Holmes turned to Jonas and asked him what he thought, Jonas was clear. He said he didn't mind at all that Wyatt dressed and acted like a girl. In fact, he felt protective of his brother and at times worried about how to defend him if other kids picked on him. But mainly he said he just wasn't that interested in playing with dolls anymore. He'd rather be outside with his friends.

"I'm growing out of those things," Jonas said.

In school Wyatt contributed seven poems to the class poetry anthology, including one titled "Alone with the Music."

You can breathe in
to be alone

So now
no one is with me

SO IF I WANNA RUN
OUTA HERE

But now I know
my heart

Because I've freed
my mind

SOME OF THE HARDEST times for Wyatt involved sports, especially swim-ming, because it required changing clothes and showering. Because sports were after-school activities, Wayne sometimes would oversee the boys' locker room, where Wyatt had to change. It was a locker room with an open shower and twelve shower heads. No walls, no privacy, just a lot of high-pressure water and steam. The boys would come in slipping and sliding around, shouting, and slapping each other with towels. Jonas and Wyatt were often the last to get dressed since their father was mostly cor-ralling the other kids. One time Wyatt was still in the shower area when one of the older boys said something to him. Wyatt didn't hesitate. He got up close to the kid's face.

"You got a problem with me?" he asked.

The other boy was at least a foot and a half taller than Wyatt and looked ready to push him to the ground when he saw Wayne headed their way.

"Hey!" Wayne yelled at the kid, who turned and walked away.

Wayne motioned to Wyatt.

"What the heck is going on?"

"Nothing," Wyatt replied.

"Are you nuts, Wy? If I hadn't been here he could have really hurt you."

"I can handle it," Wyatt said.

"No, you can't. Next time someone says something to you, you need to walk away and tell me or Mom what's going on, okay?"

Wyatt had never lacked chutzpah. He stood up for himself when he needed to. This was one thing Wayne admired about his son. He remembered when the twins were in second grade, for one of the class's frequent writing assignments, Wyatt, who had drawn himself with long curly hair, had made up a story about a girl pirate who beats up the bad boy pirates. At least Wyatt portrayed himself as a strong leader, Wayne thought.

Sometimes, though, the insults weren't even meant to be insults. That became clear when Wayne and Kelly signed the boys up for Cub Scouts. Wayne had a dream of his twins someday reaching the rank of Eagle Scout, the organization's highest honor. Duty to country, to others, to oneself; respect, honor, leadership—Wayne fervently believed in Scouting's core principles. But at the Cub Scout level, in a room full of unruly boys, Scouting's principles were not always in evidence. At Cub Scout events, older kids sometimes targeted Wyatt, commenting on his feminine behavior. Most of the parents weren't paying attention, but those who were did nothing to discipline their children, which deeply troubled Wayne. He and Kelly had thought Scouting was a good way to integrate into the community and a good opportunity for their kids to make friends, but how long could they expose their twins to words that might wound them and tear down their self-esteem?

During one den meeting, a mother asked Wayne and Kelly, in front of everyone, "Is Wyatt a boy or a girl?" Kelly quickly pulled the woman aside to explain that Wyatt was a girl in a boy's body and that if she wanted to know more, all she had to do was ask and she'd be happy to tell her about being transgender. Wayne still wasn't there yet, mentally. He wasn't convinced Wyatt was transgender, or maybe he just wasn't ready to accept it. In either case, Kelly knew she had to be the one to explain to others, to be the go-between for Wyatt and those who didn't, or couldn't, understand what he was all about.

The Scouting experiment was over before it barely began, and it was one more reminder to Wayne that his family was different from everyone else's. Unfortunately, his way of dealing with it all—or not dealing with it—was just to shut down, or, lately, to go swimming in a nearby lake.

After dinner and helping the kids with their homework, Wayne often didn't have much time left for exercising, but one night he was determined to go for a long swim. When he departed for the lake it was nearly ten o'clock and pitch-black. It was a short drive, and there were plenty of parking spaces when he got there. The distance across the lake was a quarter mile, far enough for him to tie a life preserver around his foot and drag it behind him just in case he needed it.

Barely a whisper of wind ruffled the lake's surface. Wayne pushed off from the shore and began to swim, back and forth, at a slow but steady pace. He used the streetlights from a nearby bridge to guide him in one direction, and the illumination from a campsite to guide him in the other. He must have made eight crossings, close to two miles, when he finally walked out of the water an hour or two later. And when he did, he was startled to find two police officers waiting for him, wanting to know what he was doing in the lake at midnight.

"I'm training for a race," he told them. "A triathlon." It was true, but not the whole story, not by a long shot.

"Well, could you maybe train during the daylight?" one of the policemen asked.

Wayne explained that he actually couldn't, that this was the only free time of the day for him to work out. The officers told Wayne that if it was up to them, they didn't mind, since he wasn't breaking any laws, but they had responded to a call from an elderly woman, someone who lived by the lake, who swore she saw a man trying to commit suicide. Wayne laughed, perhaps a bit too strenuously, then assured the men he had no such intention. They shrugged and headed back to their patrol car.

Wayne knew the exercising, the triathlons, the huge pile of firewood that kept reaching higher, were all about not wanting to deal with Wyatt. Actually, that wasn't quite right. It was more about not wanting to deal with his feelings about Wyatt. He had handed everything over to Kelly in terms of decision making, and even when he objected to letting Wyatt dress more like a girl, he ultimately let Kelly be the arbiter. With two kids, of course, it was impossible for Wayne not to be involved in ferrying them to their various extracurricular activities or being shanghaied into chaperoning parties. He probably took the most pleasure in doing "boy" things with Jonas, such as Little League. Wayne spent hours teaching him the art of hitting. Standing with his back to the garage door, Jonas would wait for his father to reach into a bucket of twenty or thirty Wiffle balls at his feet and pitch them underhand. Jonas did not come by his baseball skills naturally, though. After watching Jonas struggle one day, Wyatt sauntered up wearing a sparkly dress and heels.

"Let me try it," he said.

Wyatt then proceeded to hit four solid line drives, one after the other. Wayne laughed. Jonas did not. Sports for Jonas were never easy. He wanted to play, he was competitive, but as he grew older he appreciated what sports would *not* do for him—they would never be the way he'd feel good about himself. In a school essay he later wrote, Jonas concluded he didn't have the temperament, or the physical acumen, to be a stand-out athlete:

> Athletics are not for everyone to enjoy, but there are obviously those who are avid followers of many different sports. . . . To care for something with such passion is not a trait everybody has.

Jonas's passion was his imagination. He reveled in acting out stories in which he sometimes played a knight, fighting off enemies with sword and shield. Wyatt liked the weapons, too, but rather than play a knight or a pirate or Robin Hood, he'd rather be a sword-wielding princess.

Still, it hurt Jonas that he could struggle with a game as simple as

Wiffle ball, while Wyatt, in high heels and a dress, could step up and whack the ball. For one thing, sports was a proven road to social success in school, and Jonas wanted to play a sport if for no other reason than to be part of a team.

Wyatt was never one to doubt his interests or himself. He knew what he liked, who he liked, and what he wanted to be. Jonas was so unlike him. He knew he was a boy, of course, but that was about it. He didn't seem to fit the mold of other boys his age, and the more he retreated into himself, the less confident he became. He was curious, a questioner, dissatisfied with simple explanations and therefore more comfortable being alone.

But one thing Jonas was sure about was Wyatt.

After one back-and-forth between Wayne and Wyatt regarding feminine clothing, Jonas came up to his father and said, "Face it, Dad, you have a son *and* a daughter."

CHAPTER 12

Transitions

T HROUGHOUT THE THIRD AND FOURTH GRADES OTHER STUDENTS IN his class referred to Wyatt using male pronouns. In their minds he was a "boy-girl" as he'd told them on more than one occasion. Older kids might occasionally tease Wyatt, but if there were parents who weren't quite sure what it all meant, they kept it to themselves. Anxiety about how others saw him sometimes caused Wyatt to act out and his tics to flare up, but there was also a growing sense of self-esteem. Increasingly he was looking more feminine, and while keeping in mind Virginia Holmes's guidance about going slow, Kelly was increasingly allowing Wyatt to wear more girlish clothes both at home and in public. He still begged his mother to let him wear skirts and dresses to school, but without success.

Early in the fourth grade, Wyatt's teacher, Mrs. Kreutz, gave the class an assignment to go home and draw a self-portrait that she would then hang in the school's hallway. A couple of days later, at about one o'clock in the afternoon, Sara Kreutz scurried into the office of the school counselor, Lisa Erhardt, and closed the door.

"Lisa, I need your help." Kreutz held up a piece of paper. It was a drawing of a girl with long curly hair, purple eye shadow, and jewelry—actually it was a drawing of a bombshell of a girl, Erhardt thought.

"I don't get it," Erhardt said to Kreutz.

"This is what Wyatt drew for the school's open house—his self-portrait—the drawings I told the class we'd use to decorate the hallways. It doesn't look anything like him, but I want to honor his vision and I don't know what to do."

"I think we should call Kelly," said Kreutz.

Asa C. Adams Elementary was small, with only about 260 students in pre-K through fifth grade, so Lisa Erhardt knew all the students and was comfortable and confident in her job. She had grown up in a small town in Maine. In high school she'd made money by babysitting and was everybody's go-to friend whenever advice was needed. More than that, though, she just liked listening to kids. They had interesting minds, she thought. So did she. In the course of four years at Bates College in Lewiston, Maine, she went from majoring in biology to art history to psychology. The skipping around wasn't so much a reflection of indecision as it was of her ever-widening interests.

In the spring of her junior year, Erhardt signed up for her first class in the psychology department. It was a course in educational psychology, and part of the requirements included spending time observing children at one of the local public schools. She was struck by how relaxed kids seemed around her, how easy it was for them to open up and tell her what was on their minds. Maybe it was because she always treated children like people, with their own ideas and their own points of view. At the school in Lewiston where she was an observer, however, it seemed as though the teachers were too busy managing students and had little time for conversations with them.

"Is there someone else the kids can talk to?" she asked one of the teachers one day.

"A lot of other schools have counselors, but we don't," the teacher told her.

That did it. Erhardt devoted her remaining time in college to learning as much as she could about educational psychology with the idea in mind of becoming a school counselor. After graduation, she picked up a master's degree in the subject through an accelerated program at the University of Maine in Orono.

Erhardt was twenty-six in 2003, when she took the counseling job at Asa Adams. She saw herself as someone whose role was to level the playing field, to make school accessible for all students no matter their background or academic standing. She saw herself chiefly as an advocate for kids, whose goal was to figure out how the school could "grow" the whole child, how to help students identify their feelings and how to cope with whatever troubled them. "Conflict resolution specialist," was how she described it, but she was also fine with the simple title of school counselor.

ERHARDT HADN'T NOTICED WYATT right away when he and Jonas enrolled at Asa Adams. After all, he wasn't the first boy she'd seen who liked to wear pink sneakers and carry a pink backpack. At that age, a boy can be just as easily attracted to typically feminine things as masculine things and still be "all boy." Orono was a fairly liberal college town, where children were encouraged to be independent.

Not until Kelly had stopped by Erhardt's office about a month after Jonas and Wyatt began first grade in 2003 had the name "Wyatt Maines" come to her attention. Like any other concerned parent, Kelly had wanted to share her child's story with Erhardt—fill her in on her son's idiosyncrasies, so that maybe she could keep an eye on him.

"I don't know if you've met my kids yet," Kelly began. "They're twins and one of them, Wyatt, he really likes sparkly stuff. My husband isn't really happy with that, but I'm just trying to do the right things for him. So I was wondering, do you know anything about this?"

"I don't, not really, but I think I've heard of it."

Erhardt got up from her desk, pulled the *Diagnostic and Statistical Manual of Mental Disorders* down from her bookshelf, and combed through the index. There it was: "Gender Identity Disorder." Kelly already had read about this in her research online and from Virginia Holmes, but she'd never seen the whole description in the DSM, the bible of psychiatrists, psychologists, and counselors. Erhardt read out loud:

> There are two components of Gender Identity Disorder, both of which must be present to make the diagnosis. There must be evidence of a strong and persistent cross-gender identification. . . . There must also be evidence of persistent discomfort about one's assigned sex or a sense of inappropriateness in the gender role of that sex. . . . In boys, the cross-gender identification is manifested by a marked preoccupation with traditionally feminine activities. They may have a preference for dressing in girls' or women's clothes or may improvise such items from available materials when genuine articles are unavailable. Towels, aprons and scarves are often used to represent long hair or skirts. . . . They may express a wish to be a girl and assert that they will grow up to be a woman. . . . More rarely, boys with Gender Identity Disorder may state that they find their penis or testes disgusting. . . .

Kelly listened carefully. It all sounded a great deal like Wyatt. She and Erhardt talked a bit more, and by the time Kelly left twenty minutes later she felt she'd made an important connection. For her part, Erhardt knew she had a lot of catching up to do. Wyatt was going to be at Asa Adams through the fifth grade, and as the school counselor Erhardt knew she'd have to learn much, much more about gender identity disorder. She also knew she'd done the wrong thing by grabbing the DSM in front of Kelly instead of first talking to her about Wyatt. It was like she'd pathologized the child right off the bat, suggesting there was something wrong with him. That wasn't it at all, actually. The instinct to grab a book was simply because Erhardt didn't have the vocabulary yet to talk to Kelly about Wyatt. She needed to put a name to what the two of them were discussing, and almost as soon as Kelly closed the door to the office, Erhardt hoped the child's mother hadn't taken offense.

Erhardt told her clinical supervisor, who was not associated with the school, about the incident with Kelly and reading to her from the DSM and how mortified she'd felt.

"What do you think you should have done?" the supervisor asked.

"Well, I need to learn more about it."

Erhardt said she'd scoured the Internet but that she couldn't find much, certainly nothing of substance related to transgender children.

"Well, you know, you have this whole university here in Orono. Why don't you start by contacting its LGBT center?"

On a snowy February day, Erhardt walked over to the university, which was practically in her backyard, made her way up to the second floor of Memorial Union, the center of the university community, and stepped into the Rainbow Resource Center. It was just a single room, with a smattering of students mostly just hanging out, and they immediately jumped in to help her, pulling books off the shelves of the resource center's library and fielding all of Erhardt's questions. Forty-five minutes later, she left laden with information, suggestions, and contact numbers. She also couldn't quite believe the generosity and friendliness shown her by these students; it was a feeling she would never forget.

ERHARDT AND KELLY HAD spoken many times in the three years since their first meeting. Often Kelly called Erhardt to ask a question, and sometimes Erhardt came across information or an outside resource she thought might help Kelly. It was all about making sure Wyatt was comfortable at school, and it was a mission both women shared.

During the twins' third-grade year, Erhardt's office had been adjacent to the classroom, so after escorting the kids to school, Kelly often stopped by to chat, and it was something the two women continued to do when Wyatt and Jonas were in the fourth grade. The two women talked about what they were reading and exchanged things they'd recently learned. Other times they tried to anticipate what problems might arise for Wyatt in the coming weeks and months. Erhardt liked Kelly's commonsense approach to parenting. She never asked for special treatment for Wyatt. She was a problem solver, like Erhardt, and the two women, though fifteen years apart in age, shared a mutual understanding and respect.

When Kelly picked up the phone that afternoon in September 2006, Erhardt explained Mrs. Kreutz's dilemma about Wyatt's self-portrait. She told Kelly the portrait was quite beautiful, but the teacher wasn't sure how to handle the situation. Should she post the picture in the hallway or not? She didn't want to hurt Wyatt, but she didn't think he understood that it might cause problems for him. Kelly laughed.

"I've seen a lot of those pictures."

"What do you want us to do?" Erhardt asked.

"Well, what was the actual assignment?"

Erhardt put her hand over the receiver and asked Kreutz the same thing.

"It was 'What do you see when you look in the mirror?'" Kreutz said.

Erhardt repeated the teacher's answer to Kelly.

"Well, he didn't follow the directions. Tell him to bring it home and that he has to do another picture."

Erhardt did, and the drawing that was finally hung in the hallway looked much more like Wyatt on the outside than the previous picture. That person, the person he felt himself to be, wasn't quite ready yet for public display.

Did Wyatt really, truly see a woman with eye shadow and long hair and a sexy figure in the mirror when he looked at himself? If there is no one place in the brain that provides a sense of self, then perhaps there's no one place in the brain that provides us with a picture of that sense of self. After all, the feeling we have of being a body arises from several disparate places in the brain. There are a hundred million cells in the eye responsible for picking up visual information from the world, but they are connected to just a million neurons, the cells responsible for signaling the brain about what is being seen. In other words, the brain discards more visual information than it lets in. Which means the message from perception is constantly being massaged. There is no simple act of perception. What there is, is expectation. Coins appear larger to poor children than to those who are well off. Food-related words are clearer and appear brighter on the page to people who are hungry. Everything in our environment influences who we are and how we see ourselves—even our own bodies. Scientists have conducted experiments that show that people who deliberately take on classic poses of dominance and stand, for instance, with their legs apart and hands on their hips, even for just a few minutes, substantially increase their self-confidence. Ask someone to hunch over or curl up, and they will lose that confidence.

What is the mirror image seen by children who believe themselves to be the other gender? The body tells a story, but the story can change what a body sees. And a body can change a person's mind.

On another day, when the twins were still in the fourth grade, Kelly picked up the phone again. It was Kreutz.

"Wyatt is telling everyone to use female pronouns. Is that right?"

Kelly was surprised, but not shocked. Wyatt had never wavered in identifying as a girl, or at the very least as a boy-girl. It was so deeply embedded in his sense of himself that it made perfect sense to Kelly that he would want his classmates to treat him as such.

"If the kids are comfortable, I don't think it's a problem," Kelly said.

For Wyatt's classmates it made sense. The only thing still "boyish" about him was his name. If other kids at school who didn't know him well referred to him as "he," that was okay by Wyatt, too. Kelly's ability to accept Wyatt for who he was had helped instill a kind of confidence in him so that anything he said about himself to others seemed, in his mind, perfectly normal and ordinary.

But Kelly certainly knew how far society, not to mention her husband, still needed to go. Transgender issues were rarely raised in public at the time. Gay marriage was still being argued—and defeated—in courts around the country. On Election Day, November 7, 2006, eight states voted on amendments to ban same-sex marriage. All but one (Arizona) passed those measures. Inroads in transgender rights were few and far between. On January 1, 2006, however, the state of California became the most protective state in America for transgender people when gender identity was included in the state's nondiscrimination laws with respect to education, employment, housing, foster care, and health insurance. At the time, only three other states (Minnesota, New Mexico, and Rhode Island) had any laws on the books preventing gender identity discrimination in employment and housing. Those states also outlawed discrimination when it came to public accommodation—that is, restrooms. As liberal minded as California was, it wouldn't add public accommodation to its nondiscrimination laws until 2011.

Around the same time California passed its first gender identity law, twenty-seven-year-old Eric Buffong began to endure what would turn out to be months of mocking asides, insults, and outright harassment as a line cook at upscale Equus restaurant in Tarrytown, New York. A kitchen co-worker had discovered a 1998 White Plains High School yearbook with a senior-year portrait of Buffong—when he was Erica, not Eric. A trans man, Buffong was born female but for nearly a decade had lived as a man, worked as a man, and presented himself as a man. As soon as he was "outed" by a nine-year-old photograph, Buffong became the object of ridicule. His name was changed to Erica on the work schedule, his work hours were reduced, and four months later he was fired.

Buffong filed a $3 million lawsuit claiming his dismissal was based not on job performance but gender identity discrimination. The restaurant asked the court to throw out the case. "We are good people and we wouldn't do anything that is unscrupulous like that," the executive chef told the New York *Daily News* in August 2006 after the restaurant lost its bid to have the lawsuit dismissed. Although at the time the New York State Human Rights Law banned discrimination on the basis of sex and sexual orientation, it made no mention of gender identity. Nonetheless, a Westchester County judge hearing the case ruled "transgendered persons" were protected from workplace discrimination by the sex discrimination provision in the law.

The judge's decision was not universally praised. A New York law blogger, writing about the case, wondered if the decision might be overturned on appeal: "Is the alleged discrimination that occurred in this case based upon the plaintiff's gender or the fact that the plaintiff chose to dress in a way that was not consistent with her gender? How different is the alleged harassment in this case from that one would encounter if one chose to wear a clown suit at all times?"

In the middle of the first decade of the twenty-first century, the national debate on transgender rights was still mostly sotto voce, and advocacy centered on legal documents. At the time, the U.S. Department of State requested proof of sex reassignment surgery for passports issued to transgender people, and forty-seven states made evidence of sex reassignment a requirement for new birth certificates. Three states (Idaho, Ohio, and Tennessee) barred all changes to birth certificates even with proof of sex reassignment. No one really knew how many people in the United States identified as transgender. Research was plentiful on lesbian, gay, and bisexual people, but not on those identifying as transgender. In fact, getting someone to admit to being transgender, even anonymously, was extremely difficult, which made research nearly impossible.

To a child such as Wyatt, however, saying he was really a girl was as natural as saying he was right-handed. Wayne was still ceding nearly all the decisions about clothing and pronouns to Kelly, but the degree to which Wyatt's own schoolmates and teachers accepted his feminine nature was slowly making Wayne realize not only that his son's beliefs and behavior were not going away, but that most everyone else in Wyatt's orbit accepted him for who he was. It still frustrated Kelly, of course, that Wayne never seemed quite able to accept her opinion about Wyatt until it was validated by someone else. What was clear was that Wyatt's transition, if that's what it was, needed to be nurtured.

A chance to help that transition presented itself in December 2006. The fourth graders were giving a Christmas concert and Wyatt very much wanted to be a part of it. But onstage, the girls wore black skirts and white blouses and stood on one side, and the boys, in black pants, white shirt, and tie, stood on the other. He pleaded with his parents to be allowed to wear a skirt. Wayne wanted no part of the discussion. Kelly enlisted the help of Lisa Erhardt.

She suggested a solution, a true compromise: Wyatt could wear culottes, the baggy shorts that looked more like a skirt than pants. On the night of the concert, Wayne, in a rare moment of wanting to please Wyatt, presented him with a bouquet of roses. Wyatt stood in the girls' section, in his black culottes and white blouse, but whether by design or accident, he also stood right on the seam where the girls' and boys' sides met. Wyatt was beside himself, beaming with pride and joy throughout the concert. A transition had begun and no one even seemed to notice.

CHAPTER 13

Getting the Anger Out

Before starting the fifth grade, all fourth graders, including the twins, were asked to fill out a questionnaire about their thoughts, feelings, and goals for the upcoming school year.

Q: *"What do you hope to learn in the fifth grade?"*

Wyatt: "I hope to learn more about history during the History Fair. I want to be Abbie Burgess [an heroic nineteenth-century lighthouse keeper from Maine]. 5th grade will be so cool! I can't whate I'm gonna rock the 5th grade!"

Jonas: "I don't really know. I guess I'm looking forward to everything really. But if I really had to choose one thing I have to say it would probably be the rockets. I mean, I've wanted to do it since 3rd grade. And I cannot wait for the history fair. I've decided to do my project on president Teddy Roosevelt."

Q: *"What can you do to help yourself achieve your goals?"*

Wyatt: "I will learn more about Abbie Burgess. I will be nicer, I will wear sweet clothes, and again BE MYSELF!"

Jonas: "I can always study hard, it's like the #1 way to ace school. I think working is great for the mind. And it's really going to come in handy when it's time for the history fair. But I just don't know where to find clothes that look like Teddy's!"

Q: *"If you wrote a book, what kind would it be (mystery, comedy, etc.)? What would the main character be like?"*

Wyatt: "My book would be a mystery, comedy and fantasy. Comedy because I'm a little funny, mystery to expand the comedy and fantasy to open up more doors literally. My main character would be sassy and never afraid. But the co-star would be the exact opposite—except 10 times the sassy."

Late in April 2007, Wayne and Kelly sat down with Wyatt one night to watch a Barbara Walters *20/20* special on transgender children. Jonas was in the playroom, occupied with his action figures. Walters profiled a child named "Jazz," about the same age as Wyatt and Jonas, who was male at birth, but identified as female from a very early age. The Walters special documented all the struggles Jazz's family was going through, much like the Maineses. Jazz, like Wyatt, wanted to be open and "out" as a girl, but was being held back by his parents' fears. Jazz's parents, just like Wayne and Kelly, encouraged a gender-neutral look, especially in preschool: He was allowed to wear a feminine top, but only with pants. And just like Wyatt, this was an arrangement that only frustrated and angered Jazz.

According to the parents, who were not identified by their real names, their turning point came with a dance recital. They didn't allow Jazz to wear a tutu, like the rest of the girls in the ballet class. Afterward, it was acutely clear how devastated and out of place Jazz had felt.

"She just kind of stood there and snapped her fingers and did the tapping thing with the toe, and just looked so sad," Jazz's mother recalled. "It was heartbreaking to watch. Really heartbreaking."

So on Jazz's fifth birthday, there was a kind of public coming out at a pool party for friends and family. Jazz wore a girl's one-piece bathing suit, and "he" was now "she."

Wyatt was flooded with relief, knowing there was someone out there just like him. Wayne couldn't believe it. Wyatt, he realized, had all the same anger issues, and he and Kelly all the same anxieties, but Jazz's parents were openly discussing them on national TV. Wayne fought back tears for the rest of the hour.

"It's like looking in a mirror," he said to Kelly.

WYATT HAD BEEN SEEING his therapist, Dr. Holmes, for a little more than a year when he reported to her that he was feeling like sticking his fingers down his throat. Not to throw up, he said. He didn't really know why, and he said he didn't know if this idea of his was physical or just in his head. He admitted to Holmes that he'd gotten really angry at his parents about something the week before and that he'd slammed his bedroom door so hard his parents took it off its hinges so he couldn't do it again.

"I need to get my anger out," he told Holmes.

"It doesn't always work to slam things, though," she said gently.

Wyatt didn't seem to agree. Later in the session Holmes engaged him in play therapy. Wyatt identified several dolls as girlfriends of his at school, but they said mostly mean, backbiting things about him. One by one he walked each girl doll up to the grandmother-type doll, played by Holmes, to ask for advice about working things out instead of fighting with Wyatt. At the end of the session, Wyatt said, "Well, I didn't expect them to say *those* nice things!"

Wyatt and Jonas were becoming much more independent of each other, but it was Wyatt who was more vulnerable to feeling misunderstood. After one particular fight with his brother, interrupted by their mother, Wyatt felt so aggrieved he wrote her a letter:

My anger doesn't help. And I know that. It's just that I feel like you favor Jonas over me and I'm not saying that just so you should favor me over him, but when something bad happens you kind of assume that I did something. And you always treat me like I'm a bad guy. I'm not! And whenever your mad at me Jonas boosts his good boy act up a notch and makes himself look better and nicer than me. And I feel like you think that he's the perfect child and I'm just the "other" one. And when you do this stuff (all of the above) it makes me feel crappy. And when I sprayed Jonas you thought that I did it out of anger. I didn't. He was just spraying me a lot and I just wanted to spray him back! And that's the kind of stuff I'm talking about when I say you treat me like a bad guy. Mom, keep in mind that there are always two sides to every story. So don't jump to any conclusions. And before you punish me for future incidents, let me speak, your always cutting me off and punishing me before I'm done talking.

In order for Wyatt's doctors to truly plumb Wyatt's identification as female, he underwent his first full psychological evaluation in May 2007. The clinical psychologist at Eastern Maine Counseling and Testing Services, Tim Rogers, interviewed Kelly first, then Wyatt. Later, he observed Wyatt in the classroom. Rogers noticed he became especially nervous around people when he wore a new, feminine outfit. He loved his clothes, but he was increasingly conscious of what others thought of him and for this reason was suddenly finding it difficult to cultivate friends. When Rogers asked him about this, Wyatt told him, "Because I'm a boy who wants to be a girl and sometimes people don't understand." Rogers also noted Wyatt's fondness for shotguns, bazookas, and explosions.

"I like violent things," he told the psychologist. "I want to be a girl but

I also like violent things. It's fun to think about people I don't like and destroying them."

His greatest fear: "Going to high school looking like a guy."

There were no real surprises in the results of the psych tests. The family already knew the depth of Wyatt's identification with the female gender and certainly his fears and frustrations about possibly growing up male were likely fodder for some of his more violent fantasies. Kelly worried that the closer he got to puberty, the more anxious and upset he was going to get. Wyatt, she knew, really was transgender, and if he was beginning to make himself sick over the fear of facial hair and other masculine features, then it was time to find a doctor to take him the rest of the way.

| |

The Sexual Brain

There is no nature, only the effects of nature.

—JACQUES DERRIDA

CHAPTER 14

The Xs and Ys of Sex

HUMANS HAVE LONG THOUGHT THEY COULD CONTROL THE SEX of a newborn or, at the very least, influence whether a baby would be born male or female. Ancient Romans believed if a pregnant woman carried the egg of a chicken close to her breast, she would give birth to a boy. Aristotle contended that conception on the day of a strong north wind would result in a male child, on the day of a strong south wind, a female. In the first century, Pliny the Elder listed a host of recipes to increase the odds of a woman bearing a male child: Either the man or the woman should drink three cups of water containing lakeweed seeds before the evening meal for forty consecutive nights prior to conception, or drink the juice from the male part of the parthenon plant mixed with raisin wine. Last, but certainly not least, the one sure method of giving birth to a boy: eating a rooster's testicles.

Not to be outdone, Greek physician Galen, in the second century, offered up the following suggestions: A woman could ensure the birth of a male child if, before sexual intercourse, she bound her right foot with a child's white ribbon. A man could ensure the same if he engaged in intercourse while lying on his right side. Even a prank could influence the sex of a child if, unbeknownst to the pregnant woman, someone placed parsley on her head. Her baby's sex would then be determined by the sex of whomever she next addressed.

Hippocrates's solution, perhaps, was simplest, if also the most painful: binding of the right testicle for the birth of a girl; binding of the left testicle for a boy.

There is no shortage of only slightly more sophisticated theories today. For example, because X-chromosome-carrying sperm, which will produce a girl, swim slower and live longer than Y-carrying sperm, the odds of having a daughter are thought to increase if intercourse takes place several days before ovulation, giving male sperm more time to die off.

What we know for sure is that we all begin life essentially genderless, at least in terms of sexual anatomy. The last of our twenty-three pairs of chromosomes makes us either genetic males (XY) or genetic females (XX), but there are at least fifty genes that play a part in sexual identity development and are expressed at different levels early on.

Sexual anatomy, however, is determined in large part by hormones. All of us begin, in utero, with an opening next to the anus and a kind of genital "bud." The addition of testosterone drives the fetus in the male direction, with the "bud" developing into a penis and the tissue around the hole fusing and forming the scrotum. (This accounts for the "seam" over the scrotum and up the penis.) An inhibiting hormone prevents males from developing internal female reproductive organs.

Without testosterone, the embryo develops in the female direction: The opening becomes the vagina and the labia, the bud the clitoris.

Sexual differentiation of the genitals happens at about six weeks, but the sexual differentiation of the brain, including gender identity and the setting of our gender behavior, is, at least partly, a distinct process. Again, hormones play the crucial role, with surges of testosterone indirectly "masculinizing" the brains of some fetuses, causing subtle but distinct differences in brain structure and functional activity. For instance, the straight gyrus, a narrow strip that runs along the midline on the undersurface of the frontal lobe, is about 10 percent larger in women than men. The straight gyrus, scientists have found, is highly correlated with social cognition—that is, interpersonal awareness. These same scientists, however, caution that differences in biological sex are not necessarily hardwired or absolute. In adults, they found that regardless of biological sex, the larger the straight gyrus the more "feminine" the behavior. For most males, the action of male hormones on the brain is crucial to the development of male gender identity. A mutation of an androgen receptor on the X chromosome can cause androgen insensitivity syndrome, in which virilization of the brain fails, and when it does, a baby will be born chromosomally male (XY) and have testes rather than ovaries, but also a short vagina, and the child's outward appearance will be female. Its gender identity is nearly always female as well.

In other words, our genitals and our gender identity are not the same. Sexual anatomy and gender identity are the products of two different processes, occurring at distinctly different times and along different neural pathways before we are even born. Both are functions of genes as well as hormones, and while sexual anatomy and gender identity usually match, there are dozens of biological events that can affect the outcome of the latter and cause an incongruence between the two.

In some ways, the brain and the body are two very different aspects of what it means to be human, especially when it comes to sex and gender. Who we are, male or female, is a brain process, but what we look like at birth, what we develop into at puberty, who we are attracted to and how we act—male, female, or something in between—are all embedded in different groups of brain cells with different patterns of growth and activity. Ultimately gender identity is the result of biological processes and is a function of the interplay between sex hormones and the developing brain, and because it is a process that takes place over time, in utero, it can be influenced by any number of environmental effects.

Studying gender identity in the laboratory with animal models is virtually impossible. There is no way to know whether a male monkey feels like a male monkey. There is no experimental model of the transgender person; there is no lab protocol; no double-blind, placebo-controlled, randomized trials. There are just human beings, each of us understanding, often without thinking about it, who we are, male, female, or something in between.

The permutations are myriad. Some individuals have the chromosomes of one gender but the sex organs of the opposite gender. Others are born with male genitals and testes, but internally have a womb and fallopian tubes. Still others have male genitals, small testes, and ovaries. Then there are cases like the pregnant woman in Australia who in 2010 discovered that though she was about to give birth to her third child, a large number of cells in her body identified her as chromosomally male. How could that be? The woman was herself likely the result of twin embryos—a boy and a girl—that merged in her mother's womb. She was female according to her sex organs, but genetically she was female *and* male, a condition called chimerism. Some people have atypical chromosomal configurations, such as XXX or XXY or XYY, and still others may have different chromosomal arrangements in different tissues, a condition called mosaicism.

Beyond chromosomes, any kind of mutation, or change, in the balance of hormones will tip the sexual development of the fetus toward one side or the other independently of what the chromosomes "say." Scientists have identified more than twenty-five genes that are involved in creating differences in sexual development. With the advancements in DNA sequencing, they are uncovering an enormous range of variation in these genes as well. For more than forty years, researchers were aware of widespread microchimerism, in which stem cells from a male fetus cross the placenta into the mother's body and maternal stem cells cross over into the male fetus. But only recently have scientists discovered that those crossover cells can last a lifetime.

No one thing determines sex; rather, it's a system, and as with any system, small changes or interruptions can lead to nonbinary results, neither wholly male nor wholly female. As many as one in one hundred infants are born with sexual anatomy that differs in some way from standard male and female anatomy, according to Brown University gender researcher Anne Fausto-Sterling. In the past, those born with this condition were called hermaphrodites. Today, scientists estimate that about one in every two thousand infants is born with genitalia so noticeably atypical that an expert in sex differentiation is consulted.

Historically, how doctors decided at birth which sex to assign to intersex infants was based less on biology than on cultural expectations and stereotypes. The most common instances of ambiguous genitalia are an enlarged clitoris for female babies and a microphallus for male babies. At some hospitals in the 1970s, the medical standard for assigning male gender was based chiefly on the length of the penis. A baby born with a penis smaller than 2.5 centimeters, the size generally required for a male to urinate standing up, was assigned female. Medical professionals, in these cases, felt uncomfortable about leaving an infant with ambiguous genitalia. Most therefore urged parents to decide on a sex for these babies immediately after birth, then hand the infants over to the surgeons to "correct" the confusion.

That was the situation one Catholic mother in New Jersey faced on August 14, 1956, when she gave birth to a baby who had either a very small penis or an enlarged clitoris. At the time, no one could say for sure which it was, and the situation so confounded the doctors they kept the mother under sedation for three days while they tried to figure it out. Finally, they suggested the parents assign the infant a male identity, so the parents took baby Brian home. Eighteen months later, however, doctors performed exploratory surgery on Brian and discovered a uterus and ovotestes—that is, gonads containing both ovarian and testicular tissue. Because of the presence of the uterus, the physicians told the parents they had been wrong. Brian was really a girl, and so her microphallus (or enlarged clitoris) was removed and the baby was renamed Bonnie. The doctors also suggested to the parents that for the sake of the whole family they should move out of state and throw away any photographs of the infant dressed as a little boy. The parents, believing the doctors knew best, obliged.

When Bonnie turned eight she underwent yet another surgical procedure, this time to remove the testicular part of her gonads. Her parents told her the operation would help her stomachaches go away. Finally, when Bonnie was ten, her parents told her the truth. Although deeply disturbed, the child kept the secret, focused on her schoolwork, and eschewed intimate relationships. Eventually she graduated from the Massachusetts Institute of Technology with a math degree and founded a tech company. In her late thirties she corresponded with gender experts and wrote an open letter published by the journal *Sciences*, asking people with similar intersex conditions to join the Intersex Society of North America, though the society didn't actually exist at the time. She signed the letter with an alias: Cheryl Chase. Because of the wealth of responses, the organization soon came into being, and Cheryl Chase became a spokesperson for the intersex movement, advocating that doctors not do surgery on intersex babies but let them make that decision themselves when they reach an appropriate age.

The plea to hold off on surgery is based on the belief that sex assignment is a cultural pressure, not a biological one. Being intersex, Chase said, shouldn't be likened to being malformed or abnormal or freakish, and so surgical remedy shouldn't be the first thing doctors recommend.

Chase and the Intersex Society were standing in opposition to behaviorism, an approach that had a stranglehold on psychology, psychiatry, and sexual politics in the 1960s and '70s. One of behaviorism's most ardent proponents was Dr. John Money of Johns Hopkins University, who believed that gender identity was a social construct. In cases of ambiguous genitalia or abnormalities, he said, parents should simply choose the gender in which they wanted to raise their child, and, given appropriate clothing and encouragement to act in a certain way, the child would naturally adopt that gender.

Money's "showpiece" was a child born in August 1965: a healthy baby boy—an identical twin, in fact—named Bruce. A cauterization to correct an obstruction accidentally burned off Bruce's penis at the age of eight months. Money convinced the parents that it would be best to raise Bruce as "Brenda," and so his testicles were eventually removed, and he was given a girl's name, dressed and treated as a girl, and, unbeknownst to the child, administered female hormones during puberty, at which time he developed breasts. Brenda's childhood was marked by incessant bullying and teasing, because despite feminine dresses and female hormones she neither felt nor acted female. As a suicidally depressed teenager, she was finally told the truth by her parents, and at the age of fourteen began the transition to being male. By his thirties, Brenda, who now called himself David Reimer, had gone through a mastectomy, testosterone injections, and two phalloplasty surgeries to rebuild a penis. Eventually he married and adopted children, but he remained tortured by what Dr. Money and his parents had allowed to happen. His twin brother, who was mentally ill for much of his life, died from an overdose of antidepressants in 2002. Two years later, at the age of thirty-eight, David committed suicide as well.

While his patient was alive, however, Money continued to update the public about his "test" case of sex reassignment. In 1972 and again in 1977, he published articles extolling the success of the experiment. Not until the 1990s, when Dr. Milton Diamond tracked down the psychiatrist who treated David when he was a teenage Brenda, did the truth spill out. Money's overwhelming success story was, in fact, an unmitigated disaster. Brenda had grown up tearing her dresses off, stomping on dolls, and being relentlessly harassed, referred to as a "gorilla" and called a "cavewoman." The true story of David Reimer's tortured life was revealed in an academic paper in 1997 and in a book in 2000 and did much to turn the focus on the nature versus nurture debate, at least as regards gender, back to the brain.

The more acceptable view became that gender was innate and determined before birth, but Reimer's case did nothing to explain how there could be a disconnect between sexual anatomy and gender identity. In fact, Reimer's situation might have made it harder to understand. In 1953, when former GI George Jorgensen returned from Europe—and the first widely known sex reassignment surgery of an American—as Christine Jorgensen, the idea that someone born a male would want to be female was considered not a medical problem, but a psychiatric one.

Such people were referred to in sensational-sounding language as "sexual inverts," "pseudo-hermaphrodites," and "sex changelings." By the 1970s, British author Jan Morris and tennis player Renee Richards made mainstream headlines and bestseller lists with their male-to-female sex changes, but transsexuals, as they were now called, were still outliers, aberrations of nature and scientifically inexplicable.

Only gradually, but especially in the past decade, has gender come to be regarded as a spectrum, and people as not wholly masculine or wholly female, but often a mixture of the two: tomboyish girls, for instance, and feminine boys. Recently, Facebook and the dating website OkCupid have added a third "custom" tab beside the boxes for male and female, with a drop-down menu containing dozens of options, including "agender," "bigender," "pangender," "genderqueer," and "androgyne."

The first institutions to adopt nonbinary gender classifications have been mostly academic. Scores of universities across the country have added gender-neutral options to their in-house information systems, and when they distribute class lists to professors they include the personal pronouns a student prefers, including "he," "she," "they," and the third-person, gender-neutral pronouns of "xe" (pronounced "zee"), "xyr," and "xem."

But for those whose sexual anatomy is truly discordant with their mental identity, there is no such thing as psychosexual neutrality. They may agree that gender is a spectrum, but they also know exactly where they fall on it. A study out of Stony Brook University in New York confirmed as much in 2015. Researchers questioned thirty-two children, ages five to twelve, who were all transgender and all came from supportive families. None had yet entered puberty. After asking the children a series of questions widely regarded as being accurate measures of gender identity—the implicit association test measures the speed with which subjects associate male and female genders with concepts of "me" and "not me"—the scientists found there was no difference in the responses of the transgender group, which included males to females as well as females to males, from the control group of cisgender children—that is, those whose sexual anatomy matches their gender identity.

It is that incongruity between body and mind that is the source of a tortuous physical alienation. As much as cisgender persons may like or dislike their bodies, and engage in altering or enhancing them, they don't deny their bodies are their own. It's a knowledge so intimate that it remains largely subconscious. When it comes to that physical self, for a transgender person every waking moment, every conscious breath, is a denial of who they truly are. For these people their bodies are at odds with their ideas of themselves, or their ideas of who they should be. They are estranged from the very thing that sustains them in the world, and there is no way to reconcile this conflict through psychological counseling or behavioral conditioning. There is only one way out of the alienation, and that's to make the body congruent with the mind.

In Germany in 2008, Kim Petras was just sixteen when she underwent sex reassignment surgery. Just like Wyatt, she'd been male at birth, but preferred playing with Barbie dolls and wearing dresses as early as two years of age. Over time both parents realized their son was right when he insisted he was a girl. The father seemed to echo something Kelly thought about Wyatt right from the beginning: "We saw Kim as a girl, but not as a problem."

Much of the rest of the world, including parents and many in the medical profession, have long disagreed with that last part. In the past (and often still), parents would take their female-identified male child to doctor after doctor, only to be told the child needed intensive therapy or should be delivered to a psychiatric hospital. Others, however, realized that forcing their children to go through puberty in a body they had essentially disowned would be deeply damaging.

It was with this in mind that Kim Petras's parents finally found a doctor who said he could help. Bernd Meyenburg, the head of the Psychiatric Special Outpatient Clinic for Children and Adolescents with Identity Disorders at the University of Frankfurt Hospital, told them few pediatricians understand gender dysphoria. He also asked them to imagine what it must be like for a girl to grow facial hair and have her voice deepen or a boy to suddenly grow breasts and menstruate. Kim Petras began female hormone therapy at the age of twelve. In Germany, sex reassignment surgery can't take place until a person is eighteen, but Kim was given special dispensation, and at sixteen successfully underwent the procedure. Later, her father told the press, "I suppose it took me longer than my wife to accept it, but Kim is a very persuasive girl, she knows what she wants and how to get it. I am very proud of what she has achieved, how she has managed to get there and how she sticks to her dreams no matter how hard and painful they are to follow."

Prior to the beginning of the twenty-first century, transgender children could not forestall puberty, could not push it off to gain a few precious months or years before their bodies fully settled into being male or female. And prior to the twenty-first century, all sex reassignment surgeries were performed on fully developed men and women. The deep-seated desire to look on the outside the way a person feels on the inside impels many transgender people to undergo sex reassignment surgery, but the psychological consequences of trying to transform a fully developed male into a female or vice versa can be devastating if the results do not meet a person's expectations. And often they don't.

On April 26, 2007, fifty-year-old Mike Penner, a veteran sports journalist at the *Los Angeles Times*, published his usual Thursday column under a most unusual headline: "Old Mike, New Christine." The first four paragraphs were startling, even unprecedented:

> During my 23 years with The Times' sports department, I have held a wide variety of roles and titles. Tennis writer. Angels beat reporter. Olympics writer. Essayist. Sports media critic. NFL columnist. Recent keeper of the Morning Briefing flame.
>
> Today I leave for a few weeks' vacation, and when I return, I will come back in yet another incarnation.
>
> As Christine.
>
> I am a transsexual sportswriter. It has taken more than

40 years, a million tears and hundreds of hours of soul-wrenching therapy for me to work up the courage to type those words. I realize many readers and colleagues and friends will be shocked to read them.

They were, but Penner was resolute. He had chosen the name "Christine Daniels" as his new byline. "Christine" was in honor of trans-gender pioneer Christine Jorgensen. "Daniel" had been Penner's middle name. What followed was thirty-one months of euphoria, public acclaim, private challenges, depression, and ultimately a second transition back to being male. At six feet three inches tall, the broad-shouldered, deep-voiced Penner had hidden his gender dysphoria from nearly everyone in his life, including his wife. Although his public self-declaration was psychologically liberating, the loss of his marriage and the adoption of a life lived fully as a woman were difficult. One of the first signs came just weeks after his announcement, at a press conference in Los Angeles for British soccer star David Beckham. For Penner, who was now writing as Daniels, this was her first professional appearance at a sporting event in her new identity. Later, she wrote about the experience on her personal blog:

> [Beckham] arrived wearing a silver-gray Burberry suit, surrounded by a phalanx of assistants and yes-people. I arrived wearing a golden-hued top from Ross and a multicolored paisley skirt from Ames and a pair of open-toed tan heels from Aerosoles, sur-rounded by nobody.

One other journalist at the press conference decided to mention Christine in his own blog:

> I hate to be judgmental about these things, but Christine is not an attractive woman. She looks like a guy in a dress, pretty much. Except anyone paying any attention isn't going to be

fooled—as some people are by veteran transvestites. Maybe this is cruel, but there were women in that room who were born women in body, as well as soul. And the difference between them and Christine was, in my mind, fairly stark. It seemed almost as if we're all going along with someone's dress-up role-playing.

It was cruel and it was devastating to Daniels, who was taking female hormones and wearing makeup, feminine wigs, and clothes, but who in many ways still looked, unfortunately, too much like Mike Penner. Daniels agreed to be interviewed for a story about her transition by *Vanity Fair* magazine and a photo shoot was set up. Later, the photographer tried to explain the disaster the shoot turned into. He said he'd been trying to say the right things during the photo session, but that it hadn't been easy. "How do you tell someone who looks like a man, 'You're a beautiful woman'?" he told *The New York Times*. The reporter for the story backed up the photographer's account and said that because he feared Daniels was suicidal after the photo shoot debacle, he pulled the plug on the story.

Daniels's wife filed for divorce, a number of friends disappeared, and, though she gained new friends and untold admirers as Christine Daniels, when the publicity died down she found herself alone, in a small apartment, without the companionship of the one person with whom she'd spent most of her adult life.

Mired in depression, Daniels stopped taking female hormones and distanced herself from both old and new friends. She felt a failure as a woman and so, tortured by loneliness, decided to revert to being male, including using the old Penner byline on his L.A. *Times* column. So it was as Mike, dressed in a blue shirt, black jeans, and black-and-white Adidas sneakers, that Penner took his life on November 27, 2009, dead of carbon monoxide poisoning inside his 1997 Toyota Camry in the underground parking garage of his apartment complex.

CHAPTER 15

Perpetrating Gender

THE NEED TO DEFINE OURSELVES AS INDIVIDUALS IS A PECULIARLY modern obsession, but the importance of personhood to self-definition had its beginnings in the Enlightenment. The British empiricists declared experience, not reason, to be the central constituent of being human, which meant individuals had certain legal rights but also moral responsibilities. By the nineteenth century, urbanization, mechanization, and population growth meant the state needed to keep better track of all these individuals. Categorization and classification weren't intellectual tools. They served the social, economic, and political status quo. Individuals have identities, but identities can be arranged systematically any way we want, by religion, by class, by trade, by sex, making it easier for the government to control its citizens.

"We know that it matters crucially to be able to say who we are, why we are here, and where we are going," writes Peter Brooks in his book *Enigmas of Identity*. "And it seems to be the case that the individual search to know the self is matched by society's concern to know, to classify, and to order the range of selves that are out there." Those divisions aren't just racial or religious or economic. They can also be sexual.

Brooks claims the trial of author, intellectual, and general bon vivant

Oscar Wilde on charges of homosexuality at the end of the nineteenth century illustrates "the increasingly rigid classifications of sexual identity," where one was either heterosexual or homosexual. For most of human history, gender classifications were just as rigid. They were integral to the creation of economies that depended on a division of labor, inheritance laws, even religious rites.

Gender boundaries were maintained by various rituals and practices, even at the highest levels of the Catholic Church. Cardinal Rodrigo Borgia, who was elected pope in 1492, was said to have been required to sit on a portable throne with an area cut out on the seat so that Vatican officials, in full view of the college of cardinals, could grope the genitals of the future Pope Alexander VI. When everything appeared to be in order, Vatican officials announced to the cardinals, *Habet duos testiculos et bene pendentes*, "He has two well-hung testicles."

There are various theories for why this strange ritual was supposedly performed—and some Vatican insiders protest that it was not—but chief among them was reassurance that the man who was about to become the next leader of the Catholic Church was not, in fact, a woman. This particular theory rests on accepting the disputed claim that in the ninth century, upon Pope Leo IV's death, a monk he'd made a cardinal became the next pope, and this monk was actually an Englishwoman. The reign of this papacy (John VIII or "Pope Joan") lasted just two years and four months, allegedly ending the day she collapsed during a church procession and gave birth. For her act of papal impersonation she was summarily stoned to death, according to popular legend.

Gender "frauds" have more frequently been perpetrated in the world of sports. In the 1936 Olympics in Berlin, Nazi officials forced high jumper Hermann Ratjen to compete as Dora Ratjen in order to ensure the Third Reich would garner more gold medals. Unfortunately, even as Dora, Hermann couldn't make the podium, finishing out of the medals in fourth place. The impersonation went undetected until two years later when a sports fan happened to notice an unusual five o'clock shadow on the face of a particular German female athlete at a track event. When medical personnel confirmed Dora was really a man, Ratjen was barred from international competition.

At those same Berlin Olympics, Helen Stephens, a female sprinter from St. Louis, was accused by a Polish journalist of being male. The reason was likely the journalist's support for the Polish runner Stella Walsh. Stephens blew away the competition as well as the previous world record—held by Walsh—with a gold-medal-winning performance in the one-hundred-yard dash. Accusations were made, protests filed, and finally after Olympic officials performed a visual sex test, Stephens was exonerated.

Oddly, though, the same couldn't be said of Walsh. In 1980 she was accidentally shot to death in the parking lot of a discount store in Cleveland, the victim of a stray bullet fired during a robbery attempt. When Walsh's body was autopsied, the coroner discovered she had a nonfunctioning micropenis and mostly, but not entirely, male chromosomes. She likely never knew of her mosaicism, since her competition days had ended long before genetic testing.

The International Olympic Committee instituted genetic testing in 1968, but officials were faced with difficult decisions when, at the 1996 Olympics, seven of the eight women who tested positive for the presence of male chromosomes were determined to have androgen insensitivity syndrome. The syndrome causes babies to be born with normal-looking female genitals but with undescended or partially descended testes, a short vagina (or none at all), and sometimes no cervix. The gender test confusion was enough to force the IOC to stop gender testing three years later. The bottom line: No one test could confirm that someone was 100 percent male or 100 percent female. In 2004 the IOC did take a radical step in revising its rules to allow transgender athletes to compete as long as they'd already undergone sex reassignment surgery and completed a minimum of two years of postoperative hormone replacement therapy. In 2011, the National Collegiate Athletic Association amended its bylaws to accommodate transgender student-athletes, obligating the male-to-female transgender person to undergo a year of male hormone suppression to qualify to compete.

In 2014, a transgender woman named Chloie Jönsson sued the fitness company CrossFit after it rejected her application to compete in the women's division of CrossFit's annual strength competition. A personal trainer from Los Gatos, California, Jönsson had undergone sex reassignment surgery eight years earlier and had been taking female hormones since then. Nonetheless, the letter explaining the decision, written by the company's lawyer, spared no insult.

> The fundamental, ineluctable fact is that a male competitor who has a sex reassignment procedure still has a genetic makeup that confers a physical and physiological advantage over women. . . . Our decision has nothing to do with "ignorance" or being bigots—it has to do with a very real understanding of the human genome, of fundamental biology, that you are either intentionally ignoring or missed in high school.

Amanda Eller, at the time the marketing manager for the performance underwear start-up called Dear Kate, summed up CrossFit's ignorance in an article she wrote for the online fitness newsletter *Tabata Times*: "I can see the horizon, so the world must be flat." Even the NCAA handbook *Inclusion of Transgender Student-Athletes* made it clear that CrossFit's argument was wildly off base:

> According to medical experts on this issue, the assumption that a transgender woman competing on a women's team would have a competitive advantage outside the range of performance and competitive advantage or disadvantage that already exists among female athletes is not supported by evidence.

Doctors and scientists agree that after a year either on female hormones or male hormone suppressants, any competitive advantage a transgender athlete might have had initially is gone. In fact, because a woman's ovaries also produce a small amount of testosterone, transgen-

der females (who typically do not have ovaries) may have even less testosterone in their bodies than the average woman born with female
reproductive organs.

In a show of support, Dear Kate invited Jönsson to take part in the
company's Hazel Sport Collection photo shoot in 2014. "This shoot was
a celebration of the different forms of fitness and the different shapes of
female athletes," Eller wrote. "And we are so proud to feature her as a
face of Dear Kate. Not to mention the fact that she couldn't be a nicer
or cooler person."

THE EXPANDING PRESENCE OF transgender athletes in all sports has
helped to drive the demand for more medical professionals who understand the special biological, physiological, and psychological needs of
the transgender person. In 2007, however, there was basically only one
endocrinologist in the United States who specialized in the medical care
and treatment of transgender children, and he'd just opened the Gender
Management Service, or GeMS, at Boston Children's Hospital—sixty
miles from the southern border of Maine.

CHAPTER 16

Nature's Anomalies

D R. NORMAN SPACK'S OFFICE IS LOCATED IN A SLEEK BUILDING with an atrium and wide windows, as open and relaxed as Spack himself. A balding man in his sixties, Spack began his career as a pediatric endocrinologist and helped run an endocrine clinic in the 1970s and '80s. Because of this work, he had seen a variety of children and adults with disorders of sex development. But it was his volunteer work at the time with a nonprofit group called Bridge Over Troubled Waters that drew him to what would become his life's work.

Bridge Over Troubled Waters still serves homeless youth in the Boston area. In the 1970s, Spack and another doctor, usually another pediatrician, would take the agency's van out once a month and make stops all around Boston Common, down by what was called the Combat Zone, and in the Bay Village area of Boston, where they were most likely to see homeless kids. Most of them were runaways, kids fifteen to seventeen years old, and mostly white. Usually they'd walk up to the van in a haze of marijuana smoke. One night, Spack's co-worker turned to him and asked him a question.

"You've been coming out for three or four months now. Don't you wonder why you see the same kids?"

Spack hadn't thought about it, but yes, it was true, they did keep seeing the same kids, even after the police tried to take some of them back
to their parents. The ones who said they were gay or the ones who were
boys but dressed like girls, or girls dressed like boys—those were the kids
they'd see again and again.

"They're not runaways," the other doctor said. "They're throwaways."

Spack had never been particularly judgmental about the people he
saw. He was a physician, after all, and he was treating medical conditions. The idea of kids being transgender wasn't something foreign or
uncomfortable. In fact, Spack was unusually familiar with nature's
anomalies. As a student at Williams College in western Massachusetts,
Spack majored in history, even though he dreamed of becoming a doctor. He loaded up on pre-med courses in his junior and senior years, and
in one of them the professor asked him if he wanted to continue the research project of a student who was about to graduate. That seemed easy
enough, Spack thought. The research involved newts and their life span
from larvae to adults, showing how an amphibian metamorphosis takes
place as they begin life in the water, like tadpoles, then come ashore,
then return to the water to lay eggs. The experiment Spack took over was
meant to show how the administration of hormones alone could initiate
this metamorphosis in the newts.

As early as college, then, Spack began to understand that who we
are—creatures of land or sea, male or female—is malleable. The transgender teens he met during his volunteer work or the intersex individuals he met in his endocrinology practice were as much a part of nature
as the lowly newt, and therefore not aberrations or mistakes. But it took
his first transgender patient to drive that home for Spack. The patient
was a student at Harvard, someone assigned female at birth but living
and dressing as a man. His college roommates knew and accepted him,
even the Harvard registrar listed him under a male name, but he'd been
rejected by his upper-class family in the Midwest. The Harvard under-
graduate wanted Spack to give him testosterone, but Spack was a pediatric endocrinologist, used to dealing with children. He'd have to step

outside his comfort zone if he took on this patient. Spack agreed, on one condition: "I'll treat you if you teach me."

Lesson number one: "Sexual orientation is who you go to bed with," he told Spack. "Gender identity is who you go to bed *as*."

Spack was surprised to find support among his colleagues for treating the transgender college student. They were all beginning to see children with gender issues, and, by treating an adult, Spack could gain valuable knowledge for his pediatric practice—and theirs.

His colleagues were right. Soon Spack was traveling overseas, especially to the Netherlands, where medical treatment for transgender people, including children, was years ahead of the United States. Leading the pack was Louis Gooren, a Dutch endocrinologist known worldwide for his work with transgender people. He was also one of the first to treat transgender youth. Gooren opened Spack's eyes to the possibility of treating transgender kids before they go through puberty, thus sparing them both the trauma and, later in life, the challenges, of sex reassignment surgery. Gooren had found a safe, effective way to suppress puberty long enough for transgender kids to undergo intense psychological testing to find out how deep-seated their gender dysphoria was. Then, by giving them the appropriate hormones, they could develop in the direction of the gender their brains were telling them.

When Spack got the go-ahead, and the money, to open his gender clinic in Boston at Children's Hospital, his first patient was a prepubescent British boy who identified as a girl. Jackie Green had tried to kill herself four times and was destined, if she went through male puberty, to be about six feet four inches tall. Spack gave her puberty-suppressing drugs, then estrogen to close her growth plates and develop natural breasts. Great Britain didn't allow sex reassignment surgery if you were under eighteen years old and there were few people willing to do it at that age in the United States, so Jackie completed sex reassignment surgery in Thailand when she was sixteen. Two years later she was competing in the Miss England beauty pageant, a strikingly beautiful five-foot-eleven-inch-tall woman. Her only complaint, she half-joked to Spack, was that she was going to be a model and would have preferred a couple of extra inches in height.

In 2006, while under the care of psychologist Virginia Holmes, nine-year-old Wyatt Maines became one of Spack's first American transgender pediatric patients. The entire family showed up for the initial appointment, all a bit tongue-tied. Spack put them at ease by making one thing perfectly clear: Gender identity is in the brain, not the anatomy, and there are many, many things that can happen to a developing brain to change or alter how a child will develop, including a child's gender identity. But he also told them that just because some children prefer to act and dress like the opposite gender doesn't mean they all are truly transgender. Only about a quarter of those who express themselves as the opposite gender early in life still feel that way as they approach puberty. But for that 25 percent who remain convinced they were born into the wrong body, the idea of going through puberty in that wrong body is anathema to them.

It was something Wyatt certainly feared deeply, and it was incredibly reassuring when Spack told him that by taking puberty-blocking drugs he would never have a visible Adam's apple, no deepened voice, no accelerated height, thicker bones, or facial hair. But first, Wyatt would have to undergo psychological tests. If he passed them, then he would officially begin what was sometimes called the "12-16-18" program. At age twelve, or earlier if need be, Wyatt would take puberty suppressants: injections to stop him from becoming an adult male. Then at about sixteen, Wyatt could begin taking female hormones, and breasts would soon develop. All the while, his identical twin, Jonas, would be going through his own puberty naturally, growing taller, his voice deepening, a faint mustache appearing on his upper lip—exactly what Wyatt would have looked like and become, were he not to take puberty suppressants. By the age of sixteen, Jonas would be several inches taller than his brother and his face would be squarer than Wyatt's. Finally, at about age eighteen, Wyatt could have sex reassignment surgery.

"I can make you as tall as you want to be and give you whatever kind of voice you want to have," Spack kidded with Wyatt during that first visit.

"Why can't I just start the hormones now?" he asked.

"If you do, it will stunt your growth, and we can't have that, but as soon as it looks like Jonas is beginning puberty, that's when we'll begin."

Jonas, in other words, would be the guinea pig. The timing of puberty varies greatly from one person to the next and is highly hereditary. Because Jonas and Wyatt were adopted and their biological mother, Sarah, knew little to nothing about their father, no one could predict when the twins would begin puberty. So while Wyatt was taking puberty-suppressing drugs, it was all-important to watch Jonas. Jonas didn't mind. In fact, he felt good to be able to contribute somehow.

For Wayne, once again it was about hearing from someone outside his family, an expert, that this was the right thing to do that helped push him that much further down the road to realizing Wyatt's transition was going to happen with or without him, and if he wasn't entirely convinced yet that Wyatt was transgender, he was not holding Kelly back from moving ahead. The sense of relief that enveloped Kelly, especially after meeting Dr. Spack, seemed almost miraculous. Years of tension, of worry, of having to figure things out on her own—suddenly it all melted away. Finally, here was someone who could make it all better. Someone who understood. Someone to whom she could entrust her child.

CHAPTER 17

Being Different

WITHIN A FEW MONTHS WYATT AND HIS PARENTS WOULD HAVE to face another watershed moment: the fifth grade. Asa Adams had so far been a positive experience for both children, mainly because the overwhelming majority of students appeared to be accepting of Wyatt. But in a town like Orono, things could change quickly. While it was a college town, it was also a very old town with families that had lived there for generations and whose views on life tended toward circumscribed and conservative. Parents of one student might be mill workers while the parents of the kid sitting next to him might be professors at the university. The other problem with moving into the fifth grade was that the classroom was in a different part of Asa Adams than the third and fourth grades had been. In this other section of the school, the girls' and boys' bathrooms were multi-stall. That minor architectural alteration represented a psychosocial leap of enormous proportions for Wyatt.

The use of public bathrooms is fraught with controversy and anxiety when it comes to transgender people who prefer to use the restroom of the gender with which they identify. It hadn't ever been a concern for Wyatt, or anyone else for that matter, because all the bathrooms up to that point had been unisex and single stall. Kelly worried what the change would mean not so much for Wyatt, but for other kids or, more particularly, the parents of other kids. She'd learned that children were far more accepting of differences, including gender-fluid behavior. When it came to their parents, however, Kelly was never sure who might voice an objection.

On January 7, 2007, Lisa Erhardt, in her capacity as school counselor, submitted a Section 504 form to the Special Services Office of the board of education in Orono: "Parental Notice of Initial Referral to Pupil Evaluation Team." The 504 is put in place to prevent discrimination against any student with a disability, which is defined as anyone who:

> has a mental or physical impairment which substantially limits
> one or more major life activities;
> has a record of such impairment; or
> is regarded as having an impairment that affects activities such
> as caring for one's self, performing manual tasks, walking,
> seeing, hearing, speaking, breathing, learning and working.

Kelly had been talking to Erhardt about how to make sure Wyatt would be protected going into the fifth grade, and the 504, which usually pertains to kids with physical disabilities, learning disorders or mental or behavioral issues, was Erhardt's idea. At first Kelly didn't think it would work, or that it was even appropriate. There was nothing wrong with Wyatt. But it was also true that he had been diagnosed with a disorder that manifested itself when other people misperceived or mistreated him. Erhardt convinced Kelly a 504 would protect Wyatt. And besides, his gender dysphoria diagnosis qualified him for it. Bottom line: Kelly and Wayne would be allowed to take part in meetings with teachers and school staff when it came to evaluating Wyatt's needs.

On March 28, 2007, Kelly, Erhardt, Wyatt's future fifth-grade teacher, the principal of the middle school who was filling in at Asa Adams while its regular principal was on sick leave, and the head of special services all met to discuss a range of issues related to upcoming changes in Wyatt's life, including the likelihood of a legal name change. Wyatt's friends at Asa Adams already treated him as a girl; they talked about clothes and makeup together, they giggled, and they poked fun at the boys. Wyatt was comfortable and he was popular, but in the fifth grade he'd have a new teacher and a few new peers, and both the family and the school wanted to make sure there were "safe" people Wyatt could turn to if he needed them. Wayne was still not fully committed to believing his son was transgender, but he was certainly committed to seeing that he was safe and his needs at school were met.

Wyatt's hair was long, and he wore nail polish and girls' blouses, but beneath all the surface accessories, he knew his body was a boy's. He still had a penis, and one of his greatest fears was that other students would see it and know it, too. That may have been why he was having trouble concentrating at school. He was more fidgety, nervous, and even argumentative with his friends if he did not get his own way. Under the most recent "Behavioral Difficulties" section of the 504 form, Lisa Erhardt had filled in: "Does not complete assignments," "easily frustrated," "cries easily," and "anxious." The most important result of the meeting between Kelly and the school was that they all agreed Wyatt should use the girls' bathroom.

Sometimes there were unforeseen consequences of the accommodations made for Wyatt. Both he and Jonas participated in sports, but as he got older, Wyatt's pleasure in them was more about the social rituals than the athletic ones. At age nine, the twins began to play on single-sex teams. When it came to Little League, there was no question Wyatt wanted to play softball with the other girls, not baseball. Wayne supported Wyatt's decision, but once again left it to Kelly to make it happen. She contacted the Maine Principals Association, which included a number of standing committees that regulate team sports. Then she called around to different school systems in Maine. Virtually all of them had nondiscrimination policies, but none that specifically addressed gender identity.

It was another frontier, and Kelly did what she always did: She forged ahead, first by writing to officials at the local softball organization, educating them on the issues, and introducing them to Wyatt. They replied that they would review the rule that "regular season, special games and tournaments teams in all divisions of softball must be composed of either all females or all males." Kelly wasn't going to wait, though. She consulted with an EqualityMaine attorney, then wrote to Orono-Veazie Little League to say that she and Wayne were willing to answer any questions they might have about "this unique situation." Attached to the email was a letter from the EqualityMaine lawyer explaining that Wyatt's rights to participate in girls' softball were protected by the state of Maine. Again, Kelly didn't wait for a response, and sent off another email, this time, just to be sure, to the regional Little League office in Bristol, Connecticut. It was the first time Kelly referred to Wyatt using feminine nouns and pronouns in any kind of official correspondence:

> Our daughter will be joining her team, with her welcoming
> friends, when the season begins. It is our sincere hope that we
> can count on you and your organization to support her right to
> be there, and her right to privacy.

Two weeks and a flurry of letters later, the regional office approved a waiver request from the Orono-Veazie Little League softball team on which Wyatt wished to play. He was officially eligible. But being part of the team meant he had to abide by regulations regarding the wearing of certain equipment. Wyatt shared his concern with his therapist after several games had been played. When Dr. Holmes asked him why he seemed so anxious and upset, he explained he felt bad about his softball uniform.

"Why?" Holmes asked.

Wyatt wanted to play softball with his girlfriends because that was more natural to him than playing baseball with boys. But no matter how female he felt, under his uniform he had to wear what no other girl did: a cup and an athletic supporter.

"Because it's different than the others. Because *I'm* different," Wyatt said.

"Different in what way?"

"I really *am* a boy, not a girl."

"Yes, you *are* different."

Wyatt did a double take. Usually Dr. Holmes went along with him, agreeing he was a girl if that's what he said he was. But now she was confirming something he never had really talked about with anyone— deep down he knew he still looked like a boy under his clothes. There was no disputing he had a penis and testicles. And he hated it.

After the session, Holmes wrote in her notes: "Then I talked about how much I appreciate the way in which he is different: how special it is that he knows who he is in spite of all the evidence. I don't think he took that in, but we will work more on that. *Really dealing with the true pain: not harassment, REALITY. Great.*"

Holmes had escorted Wyatt out to the parking lot after the session. Wyatt had almost gotten to Kelly, waiting in the car, when he told his mother "Just a minute." He ran back to Holmes and gave her a big hug.

CHAPTER 18

Becoming Nicole

KELLY HAD GUIDED WYATT THROUGH SO MANY TRANSITIONS, ALWAYS trying to balance his desires with her sense of caution. They'd navigated clothes, sports, and what pronouns to use at school, and it hadn't been easy. For so long it had made Kelly heartsick in stores when she passed by the racks of girls' dresses looking for things for Wyatt to wear that were more gender neutral: She knew she was denying her child the thing he most coveted. Kelly and Wayne had made him live with compromises until, one by one, each had fallen by the wayside. With the start of the fifth grade, and the boys' and girls' bathrooms no longer single stall, they decided Wyatt should be allowed to wear all the feminine clothes he wanted—within reason. The problem was, everyone still called him Wyatt. The idea of a name change had been hanging over the family for quite some time. If they were going to let Wyatt look like a girl and dress like a girl, then surely he deserved a girl's name.

When they asked Wyatt what name he'd like, he said "Raven," a character on one of his favorite television shows.

"That's a not a real name," Wayne complained. "That's a TV name."

But TV names were the ones with which Wyatt was most familiar. He considered Quinn, a character on the Nickelodeon teen comedy/

drama *Zoey 101*, but he kept stumbling over the spelling. Finally, he settled on Nicole, or Nikki for short, one of Zoey's sidekicks.

Whether "Nicole," or "Nikki," it was difficult for Wayne to get the name out, so he tried to avoid using either. Once again, still feeling ambivalent, he left it to Kelly to sort out the details. When she called the family lawyer she quickly discovered legally changing a name wasn't nearly as simple as filling out a form. In Maine, by law, name changes are announced in the newspaper. If the Maineses wanted to keep this out of the public eye, they'd have to petition the court to make an exception. The last thing Kelly and Wayne wanted was to make some public announcement, no matter how small, that their son was now their daughter.

It wasn't simply a matter of strangers knowing their personal business; it was about keeping their child out of the crosshairs of the right-wing religious community. Both of them knew that the Christian Civic League of Maine was not only vehemently anti-gay and anti-transgender, they were politically active and media savvy. The organization frequently published articles on its website decrying the "gay agenda" and wrote letters to the editor of the *Bangor Daily News*. The Christian Civic League had recently created controversy when it publicly objected to Maine intellectual and author Jennifer Finney Boylan playing the role of a transgender therapist on the ABC soap opera *All My Children*. The league warned parents about the program in an article titled "All My Tranny Children," using a common slur to refer to transgender people. A few months later, the league again took to its online news site to disparage the production of a play called *Hidden: A Gender*, written by a trans woman, and performed at the First Universalist Church of Auburn, Maine. Kelly and Wayne had every right to feel like their family would be targeted next if word of Wyatt's name change was made public.

Before any petition would be granted, however, the parents had to appear in person at the county courthouse. The family's attorney reassured Kelly and Wayne it was just a formality. They'd stand before a judge, with counsel, and it would take only a few minutes.

The day of the court appearance, the lawyer's office called to say he wasn't able to attend, but his wife, a real estate attorney, would fill in for him. Seated in the small courtroom on a hot summer day, Kelly and Wayne fidgeted nervously waiting for the judge. When he finally entered, their hearts sank just a bit—he was an elderly gentleman, probably over seventy, with white hair, and a pair of sneakers peeking out from under his black robe. Uh-oh, here we go, they both thought. The judge sat down without so much as glancing at the couple in the front row, read through the file a clerk placed in front of him, then finally looked up.

"Why are you changing your son's name to a girl's name?" he asked.

Kelly's back arched slightly. Their lawyer, or rather the real estate attorney filling in for their lawyer, answered, "Their daughter is a transgender child, your honor, and has been presenting as a girl for a number of years. The parents, doctors, and counselors agree this is the right thing to do at this time."

"Why are you petitioning to keep this out of the paper?"

"Due to the recent protests . . . by the Christian Civic League, they are requesting this be kept private," the attorney answered.

"Maybe the Christian Civic League should appear in court to have their say," the judge said.

What the hell is going on? Wayne thought. Kelly's eyes welled and Wayne shifted uncomfortably in his seat. Neither could believe they were being put through this, and not even for the name change, just to keep the name change out of the newspaper. Thank God Wyatt wasn't there. Wayne knew he needed to do something. He raised his hand and asked if he could say something. The judge looked down at him for a moment.

"Who are you?"

"I am the father of this child."

"Step forward."

Wayne approached the judge and began to speak, but the judge motioned for him to stop.

"Take the stand."

The judge wanted Wayne to testify under oath. Then he asked him his profession and his level of education.

"I'm a safety director at the University of Maine and I have a master's degree and doctorate in safety management with a minor in adult education."

Wayne explained that his son Wyatt had been expressing feelings he was a girl from the age of two, and that his insistence he was born in the wrong body had made it difficult for him in school. They were convinced, and Wyatt's doctors agreed, that he should be allowed to transition to being a girl.

Wayne had finally said, out loud, in a courtroom no less, that he agreed with Kelly, that Wyatt should be allowed to make a full transition and in as safe a place as they could make it.

The judge asked Kelly if she wanted to say something and she was sworn in, too. It wasn't in her nature, but she'd be damned if she was going to sit there silently and not defend her child. Afterward, neither Wayne nor Kelly could remember what she said, but the judge appeared mollified and a lot less hostile. Perhaps it had to do with hearing that Wayne and Kelly weren't some screwed-up parents who really wanted a girl and so were pressuring one of their twins into being transgender. They weren't. They were a white-collar middle-class couple. Upstanding citizens. Regular Maine folks.

The judge told Kelly she could step down, then stared at the papers in front of him for what seemed like several minutes. Finally he looked up.

"I see no reason to deny your request," he said. "You are obviously very concerned about your child's safety."

Kelly and Wayne breathed a huge sigh of relief. They'd been wrong about the judge. When he walked in all they'd seen was his white hair and his age, and they did what most people do and what they themselves wished others wouldn't do with Nicole: They made an assumption based on appearances. How could an elderly man, who was surely set in his ways, understand, or be sympathetic to, their transgender child? But he was.

For Wayne, this was the first time he'd shown any kind of public support for Wyatt being transgender. His instincts as a father had been tested without his even realizing it, and he'd responded to the challenge. The petition was granted, and in a matter of days Wyatt Benjamin Maines would officially and legally become Nicole Amber Maines. The middle name was Kelly's idea. She just liked the sound of it.

CHAPTER 19

A New Adversary

JONAS WAS UNRUFFLED BY THE NAME CHANGE. WHEN A NEIGHBOR'S son, Logan, came over to hang out with the twins, Jonas asked him if he wanted to play ninjas, then said. "Oh, and Wyatt's new name is Nikki."

"Okay," Logan answered. "Nikki, can I have that sword?"

Listening to this back-and-forth between Jonas and his friend, Wayne laughed to himself, but he knew he now needed to explain the situation to Logan's parents, something he didn't exactly relish. The parents were conservative Republicans and the father former military, just like Wayne, only a bit younger. To Wayne's complete relief, Logan's parents said they weren't surprised. No judgments. No rejections. Wayne almost cried.

Just before the start of the fifth grade, Kelly and Wayne and the kids visited Wayne's parents in upstate New York. Bill and Betty Maines had been supportive all along; they'd seen how Wyatt behaved, practically from birth, so they knew this wasn't some passing impulse on the child's part or something Wayne and Kelly had encouraged. Still, it was going to be strange, calling Wyatt Nicole after all this time. Eventually, what everyone was dreading finally happened. There was a slipup.

"Wyatt, do you want some ice cream?" Grandpa Bill said.

Before Nicole had a chance to even answer, Bill realized what he'd just done.

"I'm so sorry. I meant Nicole. I'm so sorry."

Nicole walked right over to her grandfather and gave him a hug.

"It's okay, Grandpa. I know it's hard. I love you."

Nicole and Jonas adored their grandfather. He gave them "whisker kisses" when he pecked them on their cheeks, and reveled in holding them in his lap. Once, when the kids were about four years old, Grandpa and Grandma came back from a trip to Hawaii with tiny grass skirts and shell necklaces for the boys. Their grandparents' house was only five minutes away when they lived in Northville. The twins had spent the earliest part of their childhoods romping around the little house on the lake where their grandfather had built a wooden raft and where he'd often take them swimming or canoeing. After they moved, the twins always looked forward to get-togethers at their grandparents' place every Fourth of July. Aunts and uncles played Yahtzee at the picnic tables while a swarm of cousins cannonballed into the water.

For the rest of the family vacation, the kids played and swam, the adults went fishing, and they all had cookouts. But Wayne couldn't stop thinking about his mother and his father and his brother and what they were thinking. Finally, on one of their last days together, Wayne, his brother, Billy, and their father visited the family's deer-hunting cabin just up the road. It was a typical Adirondack hunting camp, a place where the guys could play cards, drink beer, and tell stories about the big bucks they'd bagged or the ones that got away. Mostly it was a place for the men to relax and be themselves.

The three men rode up in the truck together. Wayne rehearsed in his head what he wanted to say, and how to bring it up. Finally he just blurted it out.

"You know, this thing with Wyatt, with Nicole—Kelly and I didn't make it happen, you know."

He talked about the Barbara Walters special on Jazz, the transgender child. He talked about just wanting to make sure Nicole was healthy, happy, and safe. And he explained how Nicole had become jealous of Jonas—that he got to be who he was, that his body was perfect, and hers wasn't.

Wayne's father and brother were mostly quiet, listening, nodding occasionally.

"We want what's best for Nicole, too," said Billy. "If anyone ever lays a hand on her, they'll have to go through me."

Without saying anything, Wayne's father hugged him. Then Billy chimed in again: "Let's go get a beer."

BACK IN MAINE, WITH the approach of the new school year, Nicole suddenly began to lose weight and complained of stomachaches. Kelly was alarmed and took her to the doctor. She told her pediatrician she sometimes felt like she was going to throw up. Other times, it was pain, she said, but always it was like someone had turned her insides upside down.

"When I try to talk, my stomach feels weird," she said.

"She just lies around moaning," Kelly told the doctor.

He suggested an antidepressant, Prozac, which Nicole began taking in August. The medication seemed to help, until one week before school opened, Nicole was again saying her stomach hurt. When she finally began the fifth grade on September 11, 2007, her anxiety seemed to immediately abate. Why had she been so worried? She wore her first skirt on the third day of classes. It had a denim waistband and was long, green, and billowy. Her girlfriends thought it was pretty, and in short order she was elected class vice president, signed up for choir and viola lessons, and joined a team of girls pursuing "Destination Imagination," a program from a nonprofit national educational organization that encourages students to develop their math, science, and arts skills.

Everything, miraculously, seemed to be going smoothly. At one point, the mother of another fifth-grade girl phoned Lisa Erhardt, wanting her to know that the idea of Nicole using the girls' bathroom hadn't bothered her until she thought about the fact that Nicole was anatomically a boy and her daughter was on the verge of puberty. Erhardt reassured the woman that for a transgender child such as Nicole, the last thing she wanted was anyone to see her "birth genitals."

"Oh, I just didn't know," the mother responded. "That seems fine then."

But it wasn't fine for someone else. Paul Melanson, the grandfather and guardian of another fifth-grade student named Jacob, had heard talk at the residential facility where he worked that there was a transgender child at his grandson's school, a boy who said she was a girl and was using the girls' restroom. If it was true, Melanson, in his late forties, wanted to know about it. For more than a decade he had advocated against extending rights to gays and lesbians, signing petitions and speaking up at public meetings. He was a strict believer in rules, in all the tried-and-true verities with which he'd been raised in rural Maine. Call them laws, call them biblical mandates, Melanson believed men and women were not interchangeable. If people, including children, were allowed to "choose" their own gender, he argued, then why couldn't he "choose" to rob a bank? It seemed crazy to him. Where was all this talk of rights and privileges going to end?

A few days later, Jacob reported back to his grandfather. Yes, it was true. There was a student who looked like a girl and dressed like a girl and had a girl's name, but she was really a boy—and he was using the girls' restroom. Outraged, Melanson visited the acting principal at Asa Adams, Bob Lucy (who was also the principal of Orono Middle School, next door), then the school administrator Kelly R. Clenchy. Neither man appeared to want to hear Melanson's complaint. Clenchy's assistant blocked Melanson from entering the administrator's office, though he could see him sitting behind his desk. Unable to talk to the man face-to-face, Melanson said in a voice loud enough to be heard by Clenchy and everyone else in the office exactly what he thought. It was wrong, he said, to have a boy using a girls' restroom and the school needed to stop it, and if it didn't he would find a lawyer who would. Melanson knew the law, and after fifteen years in the navy he took pride in never backing down from a fight. At home he sat his grandson down.

"You have female cousins," Melanson said to Jacob. "How would you like to have them forced to share a bathroom with a boy?"

Jacob had come to live with his grandparents two years earlier when tensions with his mother, who lived 145 miles west of Orono, grew too much for both of them. He listened intently to his grandfather. No, he wouldn't like that, he said.

Melanson answered: "Then there's only one thing to do about it."

CHAPTER 20

Freak

"FAGGOT."

It was a word Nicole had never heard before, but she knew it wasn't good. Just a few weeks into the new school year, she and her friend Emily left class to use the girls' bathroom. Walking down the hall they heard another friend, Ana Eliza, yell, "Watch out!"

As the two girls walked into the bathroom, Jacob brushed past them. "I didn't know there was a faggot in my class," he said.

He continued walking right into one of the stalls in the girls' restroom. Nicole and Emily just stood there, frozen, not knowing what to do. They could hear Jacob urinating, then zipping his pants. When he came out of the stall, he walked to the sink to wash his hands. A moment later, Mrs. Elisabeth Molloy, their teacher, rushed in, beet faced and furious.

What on earth are you doing in here? she demanded, as she pulled Jacob out of the bathroom.

"This is not acceptable," she told him.

"I'm just a boy using the girls' bathroom," he singsonged back to the teacher. "If Nicole can go in then I can go in."

Melanson had told his grandson that if a boy who said he was a girl was using the girls' bathroom, then he had every right to use it, too. Melanson wanted his grandson to make a point, and to make it forcefully: It was absurd the school was allowing an anatomically correct male to use a female bathroom.

Mrs. Molloy marched Jacob into Lisa Erhardt's office and explained the situation, at which point Erhardt called acting principal Bob Lucy. In his forties and with receding gray hair, Lucy was still the trim, solidly built athlete who had starred in three sports at Orono High School thirty years earlier. He was a local legend. In 1977 he was an all-state middle linebacker and captain of the undefeated state championship football team. After graduating from the University of Maine in Orono, where he was again a varsity athlete, he took a job coaching football at his high school alma mater, and quickly accumulated a record of eighty wins against seventeen losses. "Intense" and "intimidating" were words often used to describe Lucy. He'd been the principal at the middle school for about six years when he was asked to also take on the same duty at the elementary school while its own principal dealt with a serious health issue.

After Bob Lucy and Lisa Erhardt spoke, Nicole and her two friends were told to see the school counselor. Erhardt's office was filled with stress toys and coloring books. The three girls sat at a table and Erhardt asked them to tell her exactly what had happened. Then she wanted to know if anything else had been going on with this boy before the bathroom incident. Emily and Ana Eliza shyly offered that Jacob had been calling Nicole a faggot behind her back. Nicole was used to some kids calling her "it" or "girly boy" but she'd never heard the word "faggot." Just the way her two friends said it, their voices low and embarrassed, she knew it was an ugly word.

Twenty minutes later, the three girls were back in their classroom, but there was no sign of Jacob. Jonas, who had heard the earlier ruckus in the hallway, was confused about what had happened. He'd seen Mrs. Molloy practically pulling Jacob from the girls' bathroom and he'd heard Nicole's girlfriends screaming, but he didn't really know what it all meant.

Nicole zoned out for most of the rest of the afternoon. Only later at home, when she told her mother what had happened, did she begin to cry. She'd never been so humiliated. For the most part, she'd always been able to handle her differences, and as for those who couldn't handle them in return, she mostly dismissed them from her life, with few repercussions. But this felt worse. She'd done nothing wrong, and yet she'd been embarrassed in front of her friends. When a teacher got involved she knew it was only a matter of time before the whole school would find out about the incident. For the first time she felt ashamed, and "freakish."

Kelly called Wayne at work. It was about five thirty in the afternoon and Wayne drove straight home. Kelly and Nicole were upset. Wayne simmered, not sure what to do, and Jonas was still trying to process everything that had happened. The next day, after dropping the kids off at school, Kelly tried several times to call Lisa Erhardt, who didn't respond to her messages. Eventually Kelly learned that Erhardt had been instructed by acting principal Bob Lucy not to talk to either her or Wayne about the incident. She couldn't believe it. Lucy had ordered his school counselor not to talk to a student's parents? Lucy had a reputation for being stern; he was a law-and-order man, and he wanted as few complications as possible. This would be handled in-house, the way a team handled a problem player. That's the way a former football coach and ex-athlete thought. He was strict and he was direct and you did what he told you to do, no questions asked.

Kelly knew Erhardt was on her side but being muzzled. For what purpose? She called the school administrator, Kelly Clenchy, and insisted on meeting with staff to discuss the incident. Kelly and Wayne wanted Jacob moved into a different fifth-grade classroom. They also wanted Nicole back using the girls' bathroom, from which she'd been temporarily barred.

"We can't do that," Clenchy said. "Anyway, it's best to keep your friends close and your enemies closer."

Kelly was appalled. This wasn't politics. This was the fifth grade! So it was Nicole's job to keep an eye on the kid who appeared to stalk her in the hallways? Over the next few days Nicole could indeed tell that Jacob was watching her. He stared at her during recess and followed her whenever she was in the hallway. Once, when he was serving detention in the hallway, he'd been allowed to place his chair next to the girls' bathroom where he looked like some kind of grade school bouncer.

Since leaving his mother's home in western Maine a few years earlier, Jacob had developed few friendships. Both his grandparents worked. In fact, his grandmother worked two jobs, so he was often alone in the house, content to either watch TV or fool around on the computer. Otherwise, it was a fairly lonely life. Jacob's grandfather was obviously a strong influence. He'd told his grandson that when he came of age he could make his own decisions about right and wrong, but until then he'd tell him what to do and how to act. Jacob had gotten into periodic fights with other students, but there had never been any real problems between him and Nicole.

Then, in early October, Jacob did it again. He followed Nicole into the girls' bathroom. That afternoon, when she got off the bus, she collapsed, crying, in her mother's arms. It was Kelly's birthday.

After hearing the details of Jacob's latest intimidation, Kelly dialed special services director Sharon Brady. Brady agreed that Jacob had violated his agreement with the school that he not follow Nicole into the girls' bathroom. Even so, she said, the school couldn't guarantee Nicole's safety in the student bathroom. She would have to use the staff restroom. That was crazy, Kelly said. It was also unfair. Hours later, she sat down and wrote a letter to school administrator Clenchy. She was mostly upset that no senior staff person from the school had called her to discuss what had happened and, more important, to talk over what precautions the school would be taking to prevent it from happening again:

> We are requesting a meeting immediately to develop a plan to ensure the safety of our daughter, her twin brother, and other children in the school that utilize the 5th grade restroom facilities.

The next day, at about eight in the evening, Kelly and Wayne called the Orono police department to make an official complaint. The chief and another officer followed up on October 5, contacting Lisa Erhardt and then visting Wayne at work. When they arrived, Wayne said, "I don't give a shit about your politics. This is my baby."

The chief looked him in the eye.

"I got this, Wayne. I promise, we'll go out there and see what's going on."

A short time later, two officers from the Orono Police Department visited Paul Melanson at his home and told him his grandson had caused considerable trouble at school. If the officers' presence was meant to be intimidating, it sorely missed its mark. Melanson told them he wanted his grandson to have the same rights as "that boy," meaning Nicole. If a male-gendered student was allowed to use the girls' bathroom, then his grandson should be allowed the same privilege. It was the principle that mattered, he said. The officers asked Melanson not to use his grandson as a pawn, but Melanson believed the school was pandering to the parents of a "disturbed" student.

"You stop what you're doing and I will stop what I'm doing," Melanson said.

The policemen asked him if it would settle the issue for him if they could get assurances from the school that the transgender student would no longer use the girls' restroom.

"I'll stop my game right here," he said, if they could assure him of that.

He had nothing against Nicole or the school, he said. He was just trying to point out, through his grandson, that people can't go around and make up their own rules as to who gets to use what restroom. And by the way, he added, as the officers walked out the door, "Don't come back again, because if you do you'll have to talk to my lawyer. I know my rights."

CHAPTER 21

The Christian Civic League of Maine

DURING LUNCH AT SCHOOL ONE DAY, JACOB SAT DOWN RIGHT NEXT to Jonas in the cafeteria, practically daring him to say something. Jonas didn't, but within twenty-four hours Kelly and Wayne had shot off more emails: to the staff at the elementary school, to Sheila Pierce of the Maine legislature, and to attorney Bruce Bell at the Gay and Lesbian Advocates and Defenders organization, known as GLAD.

> As you know, when our children are at school, we are entrusting their education and safety to the hands of your staff and senior management team.

Kelly and Wayne wanted them all to know that Asa C. Adams Elementary School had, to this point, provided a wonderful and safe learning environment. They believed they could work through this with the school and help school officials determine how best to protect Nicole while not interfering with her rights. They also wanted everyone to know that Nicole was suffering, that she was experiencing feelings of real depression, and because of her "freak-ness," a word she recently used to describe herself, she was now questioning her self-worth. Most of all,

Kelly and Wayne believed, there now needed to be specific plans for Nicole's safety.

On Friday, October 12, 2007, Orono's Special Services Office, which had provided the 504 plan, issued its "planned next steps," none of which had been conveyed to Kelly and Wayne. First on the list: "The unisex bathroom in the classroom wing will be assigned for Nicole's use." Lisa Erhardt would take responsibility for making sure staff monitored Nicole and Jacob when they were on the playground before school and during recess at lunchtime. Sharon Brady was to meet with staff to ensure that Jacob's bathroom use was appropriate and that there would be no "unplanned encounters" between him and Nicole. Officer Andy Whitehouse said he would visit Asa Adams school whenever possible just to establish a presence, and acting principal Bob Lucy would consult with the fifth-grade team about using a bathroom sign-in/sign-out procedure with all students. Later, when asked by a lawyer whether he could recall ever resolving a bullying situation in part by telling the target of the bullying that he or she could not be present in a specific part of the school, Bob Lucy answered, "No."

This plan was not at all what Kelly and Wayne were hoping for or expecting. When Kelly called Lucy about the new 504 she was particularly mystified by one item.

"How are you going to prevent 'unplanned encounters,'" she asked him, "when Jacob and Nicole are in the same class?"

Lucy had no good answer. Although the school acknowledged that what Jacob had done was clearly wrong, Lucy seemed to regard the incident as less about bullying than poor decision making, or simply bad behavior. There was no commitment to addressing with Jacob, or the fifth graders in general, why that behavior was intolerable.

The school seemed to be closing ranks around itself; instead of protecting Nicole it was protecting itself from Melanson's threat of a lawsuit, which he later repeated in an article in the *Bangor Daily News* under a front-page headline that read "Grandfather Plans Rights Suit over Boy Using Girls' Bathroom." Neither Nicole nor the Maines family were identified by name in the story, but they now felt targeted by people beyond the boundaries of the school, including the Christian Civic League of Maine.

More than one hundred years old, the league, an educational and research nonprofit, promoted itself as trying to bring a biblical perspective to public policy, especially where it concerned traditional family values. One of those values, according to the organization, was that gender was inviolate; it was assigned at birth by God, evidenced in a baby's sexual anatomy, and was part of the "God-ordained pattern of human creation." From 1994 to 2009, Michael Heath was the executive director of the Christian Civic League, and his avowed mission, he said many times, was to defeat "the gay agenda." Any politicians who supported rights for homosexuals, he wrote, were "publicly and boldly devoted to training [children] through their 'public' schools in the ways of fornication and transgendering. Jesus went further than Paul in speaking out for children. He said that children of the devil who violate the innocence of our little ones should be cast into the sea with a millstone hung about their neck."

Originally from Maryland, Heath had spent the last two years of high school in Augusta, Maine, where he graduated in 1979. He then attended a series of Christian colleges, including Central Bible College in Missouri as well as Elim Bible Institute and Roberts Wesleyan College, both in upstate New York. Heath was a close friend of Peter LaBarbera, who at the time was the head of the Illinois Family Institute and later Americans for Truth About Homosexuality. Both are included in a list of eighteen anti-gay organizations the Southern Poverty Law Center has designated "hate" groups. Like LaBarbera, Heath has called gay people "the enemy" and "pure evil" and anyone who advocates for gay rights "a child of the devil." When Heath caught wind of the story about the bathroom controversy at Asa Adams, he pounced, writing a guest editorial in the *Bangor Daily News*:

Profound matters that concern all Maine people rest at the root of this controversy. For example, does God and nature determine gender, or do individuals decide that? . . . Should little girls be going to the bathroom next to little boys in elementary school? Is there any difference at all between girls and boys? Should adults be allowed to decide the gender of biological males who are in their care? We thank God for one courageous grandfather.

Wayne and Kelly were relieved that the majority of comments on the website were supportive of the family. Two dozen of the town's residents even wrote an open letter to the editor:

We are dismayed that members of an Orono family, including their child, have been subjected to public criticism by the Christian Civic League and another Orono resident for a matter going to the core of personal rights that are the bedrock of our society and our decency. The issues may be difficult, but no family—and certainly no child—deserves to be publicly harassed about them. We wish to express our support for the family at the center of this painful public controversy. We want you to know your neighbors are with you.

Kelly and Wayne did their best to protect Nicole from the controversy and discussed the Christian Civic League's apparent vendetta only when she was not in the same room. Her humiliation, though, was hardly unique. Several weeks later, on October 25, 2007, and 120 miles southwest of Orono, Brianna Freeman was having lunch with friends, as she did two or three times a week, in a Denny's Restaurant in Auburn, Maine. And just as she had dozens of times before, she got up from her table after her meal to use the women's restroom, only this time she was stopped by a restaurant manager and told that because her sex at birth was male, she could only use the men's restroom. The forty-five-year-old former software developer was in the process of transitioning from male to female. She had long red hair, wore makeup and feminine clothes, and was taking female hormones. Although she hadn't yet had sex reassignment surgery, she was

in every other way obviously female. Six months later, she sued Realty
Resources Hospitality, the owner of the Denny's franchise in Auburn, for
unlawful public accommodation discrimination in violation of Maine
state law. "I live and breathe as a female every day," she told a local public
radio station at the time of the lawsuit. "I dress it, I portray it. I exhibit
it. . . . I see a counselor about three times a month. And I see a doctor
regularly and get hormone treatments every day." Using the men's room
would not only be inappropriate, she claimed in the lawsuit, it would be
unsafe. "I would feel too vulnerable and very much at physical risk of
being attacked by any of the male patrons. . . . There are some men around
here that think this is wrong and people like this don't deserve to live. I'm
not willing to take that chance."

By December, the antagonism in Orono had only increased. Heath
of the Christian Civic League was writing editorials on the organization's website excoriating the Maineses (though not by name) and claiming the school, the media, doctors, even the residents of Orono, were
looking the other way:

> Ten year old boys should not even be thinking about whether
> they are a boy or a girl. This entire issue is totally absurd. If the
> medical profession can't figure this out then the medical profession
> needs it's head examined . . . I promise you this, the League is a
> friend to common sense. . . . Like John the Baptist everyday we
> come to work and speak truth to power. Some choose to repent
> and change course while others (King Herod) take another path.

Heath closed his editorial asking for financial contributions to the
Christian Civic League and its evangelical work for the people of Maine:

> Click on the paypal button above. Don't wait.

Kelly and Wayne were afraid, for good reason, that Heath and his
allies had only just begun to fight.

CHAPTER 22

Defending Nicole

KELLY AND WAYNE WERE CONSUMED WITH ENSURING NICOLE'S rights, but it was Jonas who was there every day at school—not in the same classroom, but close enough to know and see and hear the sorts of things being said about, and to, Nicole.

During recess one day, Jonas and several other boys were heatedly engaged in the playground game of four square. Drawn onto the pavement, each square is occupied by one player, and each player must bounce the ball to the others, in turn, while also trying to get them to misplay it. In one version of the game players are not allowed to move beyond the lines of their own box. Several boys waited to get into the game with Jonas when a new competitor took up his position in the lowest square. It was Jacob. Jonas looked away, a slow anger building inside him. He didn't like Jacob, and he didn't like what Jacob was doing to his sister, and, frankly, to him.

Ever since Wyatt had publicly transitioned to Nicole, Wayne had been careful to explain to Jonas that he needed to protect his sister at all times. That was *his* job, his father said, and as long as he was at school, on the bus, or somewhere out in public with her, it was his duty to keep her safe. When he'd been younger, Jonas had never thought of his sister as someone needing protection. First of all, she was more aggressive than he was, and second, why would someone threaten her for how she felt about herself? Lacking credible answers to his questions, Jonas had to be on the alert, and when people were too afraid to ask Nicole questions about her gender identity, they came to Jonas, the quiet, more approachable twin brother. It was a heavy burden for a youngster—making sure his sister was always safe—and it had sometimes made Jonas a bit paranoid, unsure whom to trust. He'd never forgive himself if something happened to Nicole. And when something did—not physically, but psychologically—he hadn't been there. Perhaps that's why he now felt incensed whenever he saw Jacob, and why, when Jacob joined the four square game, Jonas felt sure it wasn't going to end well. It didn't take long before the two boys clashed. After one volley, Jonas accused Jacob of stepping on the line of his box, a violation.

"You're out," he said, then added: "You think you and your grandpa can push my sister and me around. Well, you can't."

"We're right, and you're wrong," Jacob answered. "We don't have to have fags in our school."

Jacob turned to walk away, but before he'd taken a few steps Jonas had bounded across the four square board and jumped on Jacob's back. That's when he realized he wasn't sure what to do next. He'd never been in a schoolyard fight before, had never thrown a real punch in anger, and now he was on Jacob's back as Jacob, several inches taller, turned, and in one swift movement flung Jonas to the ground. Both boys were collared by a nearby teacher and taken to the principal's office. The punishment—the loss of recess for the next two weeks—was as severe as Jonas had ever been handed at school. Kelly and Wayne didn't hear about the incident for a couple of days, and when they did, they sat Jonas down, telling him they understood his frustration, but he just couldn't get into physical fights. Jonas nodded in agreement. He knew his parents were right, and he knew the moment he jumped on Jacob that he shouldn't have, but he also knew, deep inside, given a second chance, he'd probably do it again.

———

ON THE EVENING OF Tuesday, December 18, 2007, a middle-aged gentleman stood at the microphone in front of the Orono school board. It
was the end of a long meeting, the time when parents, students, and
concerned citizens get to make statements or ask questions.

"My name is Paul Melanson. The story I'm about to tell happened in
the past few months. On or about the twenty-seventh of September, I
was told we had a young boy—"

"I'm going to ask you not to discuss individual students," the chairman of the school committee interrupted.

Melanson didn't look up.

"At this kid's request, this little boy is being treated as a little girl. I
asked my grandson 'What restroom is this kid using?' I called the superintendent and was told this wasn't happening. I gave my grandson permission to use the little girls' restroom. On October fourth he did, when
this little boy was there. He was taken to the principal's office and given
the riot act. The next day I was visited by the Orono Police Department
and was told if the behavior didn't stop we'd have a bad year. . . . On or
about the fifth of December I was informed by my grandson it was still
going on—"

"I'm told the individual is not using the bathroom in question, but
the appropriate bathroom," a board member interjected. "The Orono
School Department is complying with all the laws. The situation is not
occurring at this time."

"Which restroom is the student using now?" Melanson wanted to
know.

The committee chairman said he would not discuss the matter further.

"The individual is using the appropriate bathroom. Thank you for
your comments."

Melanson wasn't quite through.

"My attorney will follow up."

The incident made the local news that night and the papers the next day. The *Bangor Daily News* had been alerted to Melanson's appearance before the board and interviewed him after he gave his three-minute presentation.

"I'm going to keep fighting it," he told the paper. "It's going to continue. I want the law straightened out."

Melanson, who had previously lobbied to repeal the 2003 Maine law creating domestic partnerships for same-sex couples, said he was being supported by the Maine Christian Civic League. Michael Heath, the league's director, had been unable to attend the meeting, but his written comments were entered into the committee's minutes by someone else: "Support for the privacy of the student and the family is leading public officials, including the police, to make some profound errors. The reign of tyrannical political correctness is making us mad."

None of the news outlets mentioned Nicole, her parents, or Jonas by name, but the story was being discussed everywhere in the state. Wayne scoured the online forums and blogs, wanting to know what people were saying. Some of the things they wrote were downright vile. Others were simply crude. Most were just ignorant.

> The fifth grade boy needs counseling. Anyone who helps him persist in the mental illness . . . should be arrested for child abuse.

> Who are the people encouraging this kid? Probably mom and dad.

> Mom wanted a little girl instead of a boy?

A letter addressed to the office of the principal arrived at Asa Adams the second week of February 2008. It was from the Portland attorney representing Paul Melanson.

> Mr. Melanson tells me that you are letting another boy use the girls' bathroom because he thinks he is a girl. However, you are

not allowing Jacob to use the girls' bathroom because he thinks he is a boy.

Under the circumstances, you are discriminating against Jacob because of his "sexual orientation," which is a violation of the Maine Human Rights Act.

It is my considered legal opinion that Jacob has an absolute right to use the girls' bathroom too, and any attempt to stop him or punish him will result in legal action.

Melanson was a student of the law, especially of an individual's rights, having sworn to protect those rights as a member of the military. He'd served overseas as a second-class machinist's mate in the navy and had been involved in the fringes of several conflicts, from the Iran hostage crisis to Bosnia to Desert Storm. In 1984 his ship, the USS *Hector*, steamed across thirty-five thousand miles of ocean to rescue more than two dozen Vietnamese refugees from rickety wooden boats. He was also aboard the *Hector* when it delivered disaster aid to storm-battered residents of Madagascar, including a leper colony, where volunteers from the ship did everything from pulling teeth to amputating limbs. Melanson had certainly gotten to see the world, and the world, he often said, was not a nice place. He'd visited countries where homosexuals were executed. Things were too soft in America, too easy, he said, and political correctness was a slippery slope. For whatever reason, this fight over the use of a bathroom by a nine-year-old girl felt personal. It was as if *his* rights were being infringed upon every time his country invented new ones for special interest groups.

Melanson also didn't feel any sympathy for the hardships of gays or transgender people, he told his friends, so he certainly didn't think his country should go out of its way to give them special privileges. He'd seen, up close, the terror of people who had no privileges at all. "I'm off fighting for the rights of other people," he'd say about his time in the military, "and people over here are trying to take mine away."

CHAPTER 23

May I Have This Dance?

E VERY SCHOOL DAY NOW THREATENED DRAMA, NOT JUST FOR NI-cole, but for the school—indeed, the community. The funny thing was, Nicole wasn't really bothered at first about having to use the teachers' restroom. It was a nice single-stall bathroom and it was very private, which she liked. One thing she didn't like: The mirror over the sink was too high for her to fix her hair or adjust her outfit. It was clearly hung at the height of an adult.

At home, though, Nicole would overhear her parents talking about how unjust it was that the school was making her use a different bathroom than the one that matched her gender identity. She kept hearing the words "separate but equal," and she was beginning to understand what those words meant. She was also beginning to notice that having to use the staff bathroom felt more and more like a kind of punishment. Why should she have to change because of something Jacob did? By the beginning of the second half of the school year, and without official permission, Nicole simply started using the girls' restroom again. Her friends didn't say anything, and she wasn't sure if any of the teachers noticed, but she soon realized that one student had.

One day, as Nicole walked into the girls' bathroom, she glanced across the hall into another classroom. There was Jacob, staring her down. She knew exactly what was about to happen. The moment the door of the girls' restroom closed behind her, it opened again and there he was. Later, in the principal's office, Nicole was told she shouldn't have been using the girls' bathroom in the first place, which only made her feel like the school was pointing out: Here are all the normal kids, and here are you.

Kelly still believed she and Wayne could turn the school administrators around, that maybe it was just a matter of educating them about transgender issues. Kelly, after all, had been doing it on her own for years, on the playground, at school, in the supermarket. She hadn't shied away from the task; she'd embraced it.

"There's nothing wrong with him," she would tell someone, often a stranger. "He just likes girl things more than boy things."

Eventually, Kelly acquired the vocabulary to fill out the story and became better equipped to tell others what it meant to be transgender, but she felt she'd run out of words. When she volunteered to head up a diversity club, Bob Lucy nixed the idea. "What can we do to help you understand?" she often asked the staff. She had brainstormed many times with Lisa Erhardt, who was always supportive. It was during one of those meetings that Kelly suggested inviting an outside expert to the school. Erhardt thought it was a great idea. So in February 2008, Jean Vermette, founder of the Maine Gender Resource and Support Service, held a workshop on transgender issues for the teachers and staff at Orono Middle School. Most of the educators actively participated, but some of the administrators, including Bob Lucy, seemed reluctant to do more than just politely listen.

It was slowly becoming evident to Kelly and Wayne that perhaps it wasn't simply ignorance about the issues that accounted for Lucy's intransigence. Part of it could have been fear—of the subject, of lawsuits. But no matter when or where one of the Maineses brought up the issue of harassment or bullying, Lucy's response was always the same: "We have a fair, safe, and responsive school."

Young couple: Wayne and Kelly at a family wedding, circa 1995, before the twins were born.

The twins as infants, with Nicole on the left. The parents could tell them apart because Nicole's face was slightly rounder than Jonas's. Nicole went by the name Wyatt, and was referred to as "he" or "him," until about the fifth grade. These captions reflect that.

The twins at one year old, with the Chicago Bulls caps Wayne gave them. Wyatt is on the left.

Wayne acting silly with two-year-old Wyatt at the farmhouse in Northville, 2000.

Illustrations by Kelly depicting Wayne in his many outdoor activities, date unknown.

Wyatt at age four, with Barbie dolls, May 2002.

Wyatt's Secret Notebook, in which he depicted himself as a redheaded, long-haired girl on the About the Author page. Wyatt was seven at the time.

A drawing of a prince and princess by Wyatt, circa 2002.

Wyatt and Jonas on a camping trip, 2007.

Wyatt, age eight, with the family cat, Erma. This photograph was used to show the Maine Supreme Court justices that Wyatt was indeed a girl.

Jonas, age ten, poses in his football uniform in the front yard of the Maineses' home in Orono, 2008. The following year, because of continued harassment at school, he and Nicole would move with their mother to Portland.

Jonas, Wayne, Nicole, and Kelly, sightseeing in Washington, D.C., in front of the U.S. Supreme Court building, June 2012.

Jonas and Nicole at a victory party at the Wilson Center on the campus of the University of Maine, several weeks after the family won its civil lawsuit in Maine's highest court, 2014.

Wayne and Nicole at an April 2015 gala in Boston honoring Norman Spack, who co-founded America's first clinic to treat transgender children. Nicole introduced Dr. Spack.

The family at Crescent Beach State Park, Cape Elizabeth, Maine, summer 2015.

In March, Jacob followed Nicole into the girls' bathroom for a third time. And again, both students were punished. Enough was enough. Kelly told Wayne she wanted to file a lawsuit.

"I don't think we should do it," he said.

He said Nicole was too young for all this, and maybe they should just wait and see how it all played out. If it was made public, it could be devastating.

Kelly wondered if by "devastating" Wayne meant devastating to Nicole or him. She hoped Wayne would support her, but if it came down to it, she'd go it alone and for one reason only.

"I have to, Wayne. For her protection."

On April 10, 2008, Kelly filed a complaint with the Maine Human Rights Commission alleging that Orono School Department administrator Kelly Clenchy, as the senior official in the school district, and others, had violated the Maine Human Rights Act by excluding Nicole from the girls' restroom based on her gender identity. The legal wheels were set in motion, and without Wayne.

The following month, at the community pool, Nicole suffered yet another humiliation when she was teased about her feminine swimsuit by girls who were friends of Jacob.

"You look so *pretty*," they said, in a mocking tone.

Kelly quickly walked over to them.

"Is there something going on here?" she asked. "Just move along."

Nicole was embarrassed, not the least because she was increasingly self-conscious about her body. She told Dr. Spack in March that she was worried about a bit of fuzz on her upper lip. She was petrified of growing a mustache, she said. When could she begin taking puberty suppressants?

"Nothing needs to be done at this point," Spack said.

He explained her genitals hadn't enlarged and her testicular volume hadn't increased. Only when it doubled would it be appropriate for her to start the puberty-suppressing drugs. There was plenty of time. He did urge Nicole to try to gain some weight—she was four feet eight inches tall and just 69 pounds—and said she should also try to stop pulling at her eyelashes. Spack was open and frank with Nicole and talked to her sometimes more like a father than a physician, so she usually felt relieved after her visits. If he wasn't worried about her beginning male puberty, then she'd try not to worry, either.

A FEW MONTHS EARLIER, as the family was cooking dinner one night, Nicole made an announcement: There was going to be a father-daughter Valentine's Day dance on Saturday at the Orono recreation hall. Wayne's head jerked up from whatever he was doing. He couldn't believe it. He'd just been told about the dance at work that day, and he'd been mulling it over ever since.

"That's great!" he blurted out.

Nicole smiled and hugged her father.

The dance was a family affair. Nicole and her mother wore new dresses along with wrist corsages, courtesy of Wayne. Jonas wore a shirt and tie and Wayne his one good suit. He was more nervous than anyone, and it surprised him that the nervousness had less to do with dancing in public with his daughter, than just dancing. He was no good at it, he told people, and had avoided it his whole life. But this was important. Maybe even more important than his own wedding, where it had taken everything he had inside him to fulfill his promise to dance at least once with his new wife.

Wayne had been on a longer journey than anyone else in the family. He knew it had been Kelly, not he, who had been there for Nicole since day one. Even Jonas had always accepted Nicole as his sister, never mourning the loss of a brother the way Wayne mourned the loss of a son. When Wayne looked in the mirror at himself he saw a man, a husband, a hunter, a fisherman. He saw a father. All of them were just names. They were categories. Wasn't *he* more than a name or a category, just like Nicole? He was the sum of all the elements of his life. He wasn't a category. He wasn't even just Wayne. He was the story of Wayne. He was who he felt himself to be. It had taken him years, but he'd slowly come to realize the problem wasn't Nicole, and it certainly wasn't Kelly. He had been the problem all along.

The rec hall smelled faintly of sweat and pine tar. A disc jockey played both old and contemporary tunes, and a disco ball spilled colored lights across the makeshift dance floor. Wayne was nervous, of course, about whether he might trip over his own feet, but he also worried that others might mistake his nervousness for embarrassment about his being there with his transgender daughter. Actually, it felt surprisingly natural to him, which is why, when the DJ announced the father-daughter dance, Wayne knew exactly what to do.

He turned to Nicole, bowed from the waist, and smiled.

"May I have this dance?"

"Yes, you may."

Nicole floated across the floor, oblivious to her father's many glances down at his feet. (Wayne had to keep telling himself to breathe.) They glided and twirled, Nicole's head close to Wayne's chest, her right hand in his left. Out of the corner of his eye, Wayne saw Kelly watching them. She was smiling. He breathed more easily, finding his rhythm. Nicole felt beautiful.

"Thank you, Daddy," she said, looking up at her father.

Wayne answered, "I love you, Nicole."

CHAPTER 24

She's All Girl

IN EARLY JUNE 2008, WAYNE RECEIVED A CALL FROM A FRIEND TIP-
ping him off that Paul Melanson was going to hold a press conference
with the Christian Civic League in front of the Orono Town Hall that
night. Wayne showed up, but hung back, not wanting to be identified by
the press or recognized by anyone he knew. Melanson, his grandson
Jacob, and a couple of other students were there. It was all Wayne could
do to keep his mouth shut. One of the girls, a seventh grader, said she'd
seen the transgender fifth grader, meaning Nicole, use the girls' bathroom at the middle school after normal school hours, and that it was "an
invasion of privacy."

It was clear to Wayne that the girl had been coached. She was being
used by Melanson or the Christian Civic League or both.

"If a person has to be eighteen to undergo a sex change," Melanson
told the crowd, "then that person should have to be eighteen to use a
bathroom for the opposite sex."

The following day there was local voting all across Maine for a variety of referendums. As Wayne and Kelly walked up to the township office building to vote, they were forced to pass the petition table of the

Christian Civic League. Wayne grit his teeth; Kelly looked the other way.

Melanson didn't exactly have an easy time of it, either. After checking off his ballot inside city hall he came out of the voting booth only to have a woman tell him, "Mr. Melanson, do you know the heartache you've put on the school and the community?"

The navy veteran was quick to answer. "You know, if me exercising my freedom of speech causes you heartburn, I have no problem with that. I have no problem with people hating me. The last thing you're going to do is stop me from speaking my mind."

For their part, Kelly and Wayne had already reached out to a few liberal-minded state legislators who were supportive of their efforts. One of them was Representative Emily Ann Cain, who told the Maineses she'd shared some harsh words and debate with Paul Melanson outside the polling station where he was asking residents to sign his petition. She noted that many other citizens did as well.

The following day, the *Bangor Daily News* released the results of its Election Day poll question: Should a twelve-year-old boy who identifies as a girl be allowed to use the girls' bathroom at school? An appallingly high number of people seemed to agree with Melanson.

Yes: 17.2 percent
    No: 82.8 percent

Although he'd received a few death threats and his wife experienced some harassment at her healthcare job—colleagues said her husband was nasty and that she should make him shut up—Melanson received many messages of goodwill from those who agreed with him. Probably 80 percent of the phone calls were positive. They called not only from Maine, but from South Carolina and Texas and California. Some calls came from individuals, others from religious organizations, many of them extolling Melanson for his guts.

"No," he'd say to callers. "It's just standing up for what's right and wrong."

The Maineses, too, received many messages, including dozens by way of the LISTSERV Friends of Orono Schools. The majority of theirs were, likewise, sympathetic, such as the one from Susanne and Jonathan White, dated June 11, 2008:

> As a family, we have sat quietly furious for some time now about the absolutely disgusting show of ignorance, intolerance and bullying that has been taking place in Orono. . . . In trying to look for the silver lining here, the only positive thing all the protesting, harassment, and bullying have accomplished is to serve as the most PERFECT example for our children, and in fact all children, of how NOT to conduct themselves. It has spurred many discussions in our home about basic human kindness, how to treat others, that all people have value, and what to say to bullies. We have talked frankly with our children about diversity and tolerance, and standing up for others who are being mistreated instead of looking the other way. Our children have learned a lot—but not the message Mr. Melanson and the C.C.L are looking to spread.

Best of all, though, were the responses from young people, including those who knew Nicole from afar.

> I think the entire thing is ridiculous. . . . When my friends and I were still at Asa, we used to think that it was wrong for that little boy to be like he is, but we've learned. There's nothing wrong with it, and if he thinks that inside he is a girl, then he is and no grandfather should make a big fuss over a GIRL using the GIRLS BATHROOM. Just because he has "non girly parts" doesn't mean anything. Gender has nothing to do with "privates," it's more a state of mind, and I've realized that as I've gotten older.

There was no turning back from the media attention now. The family's story had made the newspapers, the morning newscasts, and the evening newscasts. It was fodder for the Left as well as the Right. On the ultraconservative website WorldNetDaily, one headline crowed "District Allows Boy in Girls' Restrooms."

Reading some of the negative articles emboldened Wayne. It had been a long, slow process, learning that Nicole would need him to fight for her rights. He'd spent too much time dwelling on the loss of a son and had never really considered the special rewards of a daughter. One day, he took the twins to Walmart to shop for a present for Kelly. As Jonas jumped out of the car and was about to cross the street, Wayne instinctively reached out for his hand. Jonas, just as instinctively, pulled his hand away, embarrassed by his father's protectiveness. Nicole, though, bounced out of the car and immediately reached for her father's hand. The two swung arms all the way across the street and into the store. Wayne smiled, thinking to himself that maybe having a daughter was something he could take pleasure in, because girls were more willing to hug and kiss and hold hands with their fathers.

CHAPTER 25

Eyes On

Our goal is to provide a school environment that enables students to:

Believe in themselves as successful people;
Feel liked and respected;
Learn things that are meaningful and worthwhile;
Have physical exercise and freedom to move;
Feel school is safe and fair.

—from the handbook for incoming students
to Orono Middle School

BY THE END OF NICOLE'S FIFTH-GRADE YEAR, A STAFF PERSON WAS following her everywhere she went on the school grounds. It was called an "eyes-on" policy and it was meant to protect Nicole. It was also supposed to be temporary. Instead, it was unrelenting. An adult was always waiting for her, standing across from her locker when she arrived at school in the morning, sitting in the back of her classroom all day, and if she got up to go the bathroom, following about six to ten feet behind her down the hallway.

The twins would attend sixth grade at Orono Middle School. Not much would change except the building, which was adjacent to Asa Adams. Nicole and Jonas would pretty much have the same classmates and the same administrators. Two weeks before the start of sixth grade, Kelly was up early, writing an email to Sharon Brady, the special services director for Orono public schools, checking to make sure that Jacob wasn't in Nicole's or Jonas's class and that their lockers weren't anywhere near his.

A few weeks after the start of the sixth grade, a troupe from the Young Americans, a nonprofit performance and music education organization, arrived in Orono. The players and performers spent the day and evening in the high school gym, on the same campus as Asa C. Adams Elementary and Orono Middle School, performing and holding workshops. During a break for dinner, Nicole followed a group of several older students on their way into the girls' restroom. There was no gender-neutral bathroom in the high school. She'd have had to go next door, to an empty elementary school, and walk to the other side of the building, to use the unisex bathroom. As Nicole approached the restroom, one of the older students attempted to bar the way.

"You're not allowed in here," she said. "It's against the rules."

"That's only during the school day," Nicole retorted.

"You're still not allowed. It's on school property. No girls' bathroom."

The others chimed in: "You can't be in here."

"Get out."

"You're a boy in a girls' bathroom."

Nicole lashed back, calling the girls "bitch" and "asshole." More words were exchanged. The next day Kelly phoned the school to complain her daughter had been bullied. An investigation was launched, and then, more than three weeks later, the school finally wrote an official response to the Maineses. It was essentially Nicole's fault, wrote assistant principal Robert Sinclair. She was supposed to be using the gender-neutral bathroom. His conclusion: "[Mrs. Maines's] daughter was not harassed during this incident."

What little trust Wayne and Kelly had in the Orono school system to protect Nicole and do the right thing was completely gone. For her part, Nicole began to loathe using the unisex bathroom, feeling she was being singled out. It was now a source of deep embarrassment, even shame, every time she had to use the restroom, which is why she sometimes excused herself before a class was over so she could escape down the hallway and into the bathroom without being seen. Depressed, Nicole isolated herself from friends. Once, when she heard another student describing her mental "happy place"—Nicole said, under her breath, "That must be where there are no Nikkis around."

If Kelly had a safe place it was probably work. She'd landed a part-time administrative position in the University of Maine Police Department where her job was to help steer the department through a voluntary accreditation program in public safety communications. That meant keeping track of whether officers were meeting written directives and standards for everything from how to make good management decisions to preparedness for natural disasters. Work was not a place Kelly typically shared her personal or family concerns; it was a place to distract her from them, if that was possible.

Kelly's problem was that she was always trying to figure things out— bad things, complicated things—before they happened, and that kind of anticipatory stress wore at her. She liked to joke that sixth grade was when she got that deep wrinkle on her forehead and the gray in her hair, and it wasn't too far off. Because she worked part-time, she was always outside the twins' school before the final bell rang. When the twins were in the fifth grade, Kelly would actually position herself in the hallway outside Nicole's classroom when the school day came to an end. It was a lonely time for Kelly, especially with Wayne working full-time and not helping much with day-to-day problems. Even in the evenings he wasn't around much, off biking, running, or chopping down trees. He had been stirred to protect his daughter and stand up for her rights when other people said or wrote hateful things, but it still wasn't easy for him even to say the name "Nicole."

In the winter months, when it snowed, Wayne relished shoveling the three-hundred-foot-long driveway because it ate up so many hours, hours he'd spend trying not to think about his family. When she could, Kelly would retreat to the basement, where she painted in a makeshift art studio. But most of the time she was making sure she was doing everything she could to keep Nicole and Jonas happy and on track. The eyes-on policy, though, was beginning to wear Nicole down. If there was an eyes-on policy that should have been in place, she felt, it should have been eyes on Jacob.

In the spring of the sixth-grade year, one of the school's annual events was an overnight whitewater rafting trip. Nicole was told by the administration she needed to make special arrangements. She would not be allowed to sleep in the girls' tent. Instead, her parents would have to accompany her and sleep with her in a separate tent. Kelly flipped. She marched into Bob Lucy's office the next day and asked him probably the most ridiculous question she'd ever uttered: "Are you saying Nicole is a predator? Is that why she's not allowed to sleep with the other girls and instead have her parents monitor her?"

Lucy had no response.

"Where are the gay kids sleeping? Or don't they get to go on the trip, either?"

Again, no answer.

Kelly called Wayne at work and told him what had happened.

"We're out of here," she said at the end of the conversation.

Kelly knew now there was nothing more they could do as parents or as community members to help the school do right by their kids. They were going to have to move.

Nicole vacillated between anxiety and anger. That was obvious to

Christine Talbott, her new mental health counselor after Dr. Holmes retired. She practiced cognitive behavioral therapy and often engaged Nicole in art assignments during their sessions. In one early meeting she asked Nicole to draw a picture of herself. The pencil sketch was in the style of her favorite comic book characters from the *Winx Club* TV series. Like Darcy and Icy and Stormy, Nicole's figure had a tiny waist. She wore a blouse and bell bottoms, smiled, and had her right hand on her hip and the other hand held aloft, giving a big thumbs-up sign. Talbott wrote down in her notebook: "Self drawing was very strong, client has flair for imitating comic book art. She has identified with comic art style of large hands in proportion to the rest of the body, suggesting that client must defend herself."

In the second session, Talbott asked Nicole to pick a card from a stack that contained simple line drawings of people and animals, then to imagine something happening to the person or animal and drawing that scene on a piece of paper. The test was, in part, to assess for depression and any tendencies toward violence. Nicole asked if she could pick multiple cards and do several drawings. Of course, Talbott said. Scoring was on a scale of one to seven, with one being the most negative—suicidal or homicidal—and seven being the most positive. Later, Talbott scored Nicole's drawings:

> The first drawing of an Indian trying to be found "worthy and the best archer" suggests a 6-point score: "effective, strong and fortunate." The second drawing about an evil man climbing an evil volcano to get a golden pistol that shoots the queen who banished him suggests a circular struggle that client has with her GI [gender identity] and social pressures she is receiving. The golden gun suggests a magic solution to her pain.

Talbott's score for this drawing: two.

The challenge for the therapist was to help Nicole find better ways to soothe herself than plucking at her eyebrows or touching her gums. One of the ways she suggested was called the Emotional Freedom Technique, a counseling intervention developed in the 1990s. It was modeled on the principles of alternative medicine, especially acupuncture, and one of the techniques involves tapping the body's "energy meridians," which are located all over the body, most of them between the head and the collarbone and under the arms. The patient first identifies an issue to target, figures out the intensity level of the problem, then chooses a self-affirming phrase to repeat as he or she taps their energy endpoints. For Nicole, whose own self-soothing activities exploited her OCD tendencies, the physical repetitions appeared to help.

In another session with Talbott, Nicole seemed ecstatic.

"I just had an epiphany!" the ten year old told her therapist. "I've been on a treadmill, a treadmill of negativity!"

Talbott asked Nicole to visualize getting off the treadmill, which she did, imagining herself actually crumpling the treadmill and throwing it away. The session ended with Talbott guiding Nicole through two rounds of the tapping technique. Over the next few months Talbott noted that Nicole was less and less the flighty, theatrical speed talker she'd been in earlier sessions. Instead, she appeared much more grounded. At the end of one session, the psychotherapist asked Nicole to do the tapping technique because she said she felt her "throat was clogged with swear words."

Afterward, Nicole told the therapist she felt better.

"Client beginning to understand basic [cognitive behavioral therapy] skills," Talbott wrote in her notes.

In May, with the end of sixth grade fast approaching, both Kelly and Nicole felt exhausted and anxious. Talbott, on talking to Kelly before one session, suggested maybe *she* needed to see her for a few sessions. Kelly agreed. She needed the emotional support and help with coping skills, since Nicole was ending the school year on a low note. Jacob harassed her twice in May. The second time he mocked her about having a "mustache." She was furious and vented online, which caused her mother to take the computer away from her for two weeks. The social pressures at school were unrelenting, and Nicole clearly was not handling them well. She resented the popular girls and fantasized about hurting them; she was angry at Jacob and a girl who often teased her, and sometimes she imagined killing them both.

Talbott suggested that when faced with harassment or bullying, Nicole just stare blankly back at the person instead of being provoked into swearing or hitting. "Client admitted she can provoke, too," Talbott wrote in her notes. "Hates current school."

In April, Nicole came home one evening from an after-school activity particularly downcast. Kelly and Wayne tried to get her to talk. Finally she admitted she had been with her girlfriends and they were all about to go into the restroom so they could touch up their makeup, when principal Lucy whistled loudly at the group, pointed at Nicole, then gestured toward the staff restroom.

"We're using the other bathroom," he said, using "we" to refer only to Nicole.

She was mortified.

"I hate being transgendered," she said to her father on the way to bed that night.

Dear Universe,

Hi it's me, Nikki. I know that we haven't talked in awhile, but I thought that I would just bring up something that has been bothering me lately. Transgenderism. No, not transgenderism itself, more like, how we are treated, and why can't we do this or that, or why it's such a big deal to everybody.

For starters, why IS it such a big deal to everyone what somebody has in their pants? Now, I don't mean to get too philosophical here, but isn't this the same argument that we have been having for years now? First it was African Americans, then it was Jewish people, now it's the LGBTQ community. Really I think people just want something to complain about, so they target minorities. They make a big fuss that we are the bringers of doom, so they try to put us in separate bathrooms and invoke laws to put us at the bottom of the pile. . . . And here's another thing, if the medical world is going to call transgenderism "Gender Identity DISORDER," why don't they treat it like a disorder? Insurance companies have labeled Sex Reassignment Surgery as cosmetic, not necessary. It's ridiculous! It's like people will do anything to make this harder for us! The only surgery that insurance companies see as necessary is surgery that will keep you from dropping dead. And in a sense, SRS surgery is a matter of life and death, seeing as 41 percent of transgender people have attempted to commit suicide—this is more than 25 times the rate of suicide attempts by average citizens. It makes me wonder how much lower this percentile would be if every trans person's surgery was covered by medical insurance. And as much as I wish I could say that it would be 0 percent, I know that there are still factors that would cause suicide attempts, like bullying in school. . . . So if you wouldn't mind, universe, can you please change so that the LGBTQ community is safer? It would be greatly appreciated.

Gender Matters

Diversity is not disease.

—GEORGES CANGUILHEM

CHAPTER 26

The Transgender Brain

S CIENTISTS STUDYING GENDER HAVE RECENTLY BEEN ABLE TO build upon the burgeoning research into the genetic and neurophysiological underpinnings of homosexuality. Researchers have found, for instance, that a son born to a woman who undergoes stress early in her pregnancy is more likely to grow up being gay than a son born to a nonstressed mother. The reason: Stressed pregnant mothers release a hormone called androstenedione, which mimics testosterone but is, in fact, much weaker. This stress hormone disrupts the timing and amount of the release of testosterone into the fetal brain, which, in turn, interferes with the development of the part of the brain linked to sexual orientation.

But where is the physiological evidence for being transgender? Beginning in the mid-1990s, multiple studies looked at the brains of transgender individuals postmortem and when researchers compared brain anatomy between males and females they found a profound difference where the amygdala, the brain's emotional center, begins to send projections into the hypothalamus, the source of many of the body's essential hormones. This area, called the central region of the bed nucleus of the stria terminalis, or BNST, is responsible for, among other things, sex and anxiety responses. On average it is twice the size in males as in females. Likewise, the BNST in the brains of transgender females—individuals with male external anatomy, but who have lifelong female gender identification—look exactly like the BNST in the brains of those with female genitalia and reproductive organs, that is, smaller than a man's. Interestingly, these differences hold whether the transgender individual has undergone sex reassignment surgery, hormonal treatment, both, or neither. Likewise, when scientists autopsied the brains of patients whose testicular cancer was treated with heavy doses of the feminizing hormone estrogen, they found no shrinkage of these men's BNST.

In 2008, Australian researchers discovered a genetic variation in transgender women: Their receptor gene for the male sex hormone testosterone was longer than in gender-conforming males and appeared to be less efficient at signaling the uptake of male hormones in utero, resulting in a more "feminized" brain. The number and size of neurons in the hypothalamus of male-to-female transgender adults is similar to females, and the number and size of hypothalamic neurons in female-to-male transgender adults is similar to males. The size of the deep brain structure called the putamen, which forms part of the basal ganglia, is also different in transgender individuals, corresponding to a person's gender identity, not biological or sexual status.

If further evidence is needed that gender identity rests not in anatomy but in the brain, take the cases of men whose penile cancer forced them to have their genitals removed. In one study, 60 percent of these men experienced feelings of pain where their genitals used to be, similar to those who have lost a limb. In elective male-to-female sex reassignment surgery, however, where the genitals are removed and refashioned into a vagina and clitoris, there have been no reported cases of "phantom penis" syndrome.

What never felt like it belonged is never missed. "I'm a girl," Nicole would say growing up. "I don't think I *could* be a boy." She didn't think she could be a boy because she'd never known what that felt like. Similarly, Jonas didn't know what it was like to have a brother because he claimed he always knew Wyatt, now Nicole, was his sister. Sometimes it all made Kelly and Wayne's heads spin. But just because they didn't understand it all didn't make it any less true. What remained such a puzzle to them both was how identical twin boys, who developed out of the same egg and with the same DNA, could be so very different. Why wasn't Jonas also telling them he was really a girl?

The relatively new field of epigenetics looks at the external modifications to DNA that turn certain genes "on" or "off." Researchers in epigenetics seek to explain the no-man's-land between nature and nurture where environment influences a person's genetic makeup. This happens when changes in the environment trigger some genes to activate and others to deactivate. Identical twins may have the exact same DNA, but not the exact same molecular switches. Those switches often depend not only on environmental influences outside the womb—what the mother does, how she feels, what she eats, drinks, or smokes—but inside the womb as well. Identical twins, developing from a single egg, usually share the same placenta, but each fetus floats in its own amniotic sac and each has its own umbilical cord. Scientists have found that fetal position in the womb can cause differing amounts of hormones to reach each developing embryo. Every molecule affects every other molecule, and even in close proximity to each other, identical twins will be affected differently, which is why they also have unique fingerprints.

Even after birth, gender identity may not be completely set in stone. In March 2015, researchers at the University of Maryland School of Medicine reported they were able to change the gender behavior of newborn female rats simply by injecting a form of testosterone into the preoptic area of the hypothalamus. Despite being a week old, the female rat brains were masculinized by this testosterone derivative, and the females displayed sexual behavior typical of male rats. Physically the rats were female, but their reproductive behavior was male-like. The scientists believe that injections of the testosterone-like substance triggered a mechanism by which certain virilization genes in the brain that had been deactivated in utero were suddenly turned back on.

Unquestionably, there are multiple factors that affect gender identity, from the biological to the sociological, and while there are still many questions to be answered, what we know now is that the interaction of genes with prenatal exposure to hormones in the second half of pregnancy affects brain development in such a way that it significantly influences gender identification. Recognizing that the sexual differentiation of a fetus's brain happens later in pregnancy than genital differentiation and that both are complex biological processes, the fact that variations in gender identity exist should ultimately come as no surprise.

If anything, these variations have reinforced the idea that gender identity itself is not a fixed target. Rather, it is only one ingredient of a person's sense of self, and for some the sense of being male or female is simply not as central as it may be for others. Studies have shown that even those whose gender identity aligns with their birth sex vary in their levels of contentment with their gender identity. Gender variance, it seems, is the norm not the exception, and yet the binary view of male/female and the pathologizing of anything that doesn't conform to these expectations is stubbornly entrenched.

Epigenetics has also caused researchers to question the Darwinian principle of sexual selection—the rule that there are just two genders, male and female. The theory of evolution states that most characteristics of the human species, including gender, are adaptive insofar as they increase the chances of survival of the species. In this way certain physical and psychological traits evolved to create competition for the best mates and therefore the best chance of survival. Having two genders, Darwin believed, aided competition, increased survival, and hence was adaptive. Under Darwinian rules, sexual aberrations, such as homosexuality, are just that—outliers—decreasing survival because they are maladaptive for reproduction.

Nature itself, however, appears to contradict this. At the beginning of time, life was asexual. More than a billion years ago two cells simply got together, knocked against each other's nuclei, and swapped DNA. Single-cell blobs eventually gave rise to amphibians, then to reptiles, mammals, and humans. But why and when did male and female sexes originate? To the question of how two different organisms became necessary for reproduction, science has theories but no definitive answers. Darwinians believe the chromosomes of two organisms probably promoted better genetic diversity, and diversity, on the face of it, would seem to increase survivability. The problem with sexual selection theory, however, is that there are so many exceptions to the binary rule.

In nature, gender is fluid, dynamic, and even interchangeable. Sex change, in fact, is a normal process in many fish species, including moray eels, gobies, and clown fish. In the hierarchy of a school of clown fish, the female occupies the top rank. When she dies, the most dominant male switches genders to take her place. When the sole male in a school of reef fish dies, the largest female begins acting more aggressive and within ten days produces sperm. In Tanzania, in a species of hyena, all the females have distinctly male-like external genitalia. There are intersex deer and male kangaroos with pouches. In 2015 researchers discovered that the males of a species of Australian lizard, called the central bearded dragon, change sex when the temperature rises, at which time they become super-fecund females. Like humans, the lizards have two sex chromosomes, Z and W. A male carries the ZZ chromosome, a female the ZW. But when male eggs are exposed to temperatures above eighty-nine degrees Fahrenheit, the ZZ male embryos grow up female. It's important to remember that all this complexity of sexual reproduction among species is not an argument against sexual reproductive success, just further evidence of variation, which some scientists believe carries over to humans.

Some human societies do embrace the reality of multiple genders. In the Eastern Highlands of Papua New Guinea, a third gender is recognized. Some of these third-gender babies are born with a condition known as 5-alpha-reductase deficiency, in which an infant's ambiguous genitalia makes it appear mostly female at birth but at puberty, masculinization occurs: the testes descend, the voice deepens, and facial hair appears. These "third-gender" people are called *kwolu-aatmwol* by the

Papua New Guineans, meaning "changing from a female 'thing' to a male 'thing.'" In the Dominican Republic, children born with this same condition are called *guevedoche* (vulgar translation: "balls at twelve") or *machihembras* ("first woman, then man"). In India, Pakistan, Nepal, and Bangladesh, millions belong to a transgender group known as *hijra*, which dates back at least four thousand years. According to ancient Asian myths, the *hijra* were accorded special powers that could confer luck and fertility on others. In Indonesia, the Bugis people believe there aren't two or even three genders, but rather five: male, female, those who are physically male but take on the role of female, those who are physically female but take on the role of male, and those who take on the aspects of both male and female. Without all five genders represented in their culture, the Bugis believe the world would cease to exist. Gender is necessary, in other words, but not necessarily binary.

CHAPTER 27

Gender of the Heart

THE DEFINITIONS, THE DESCRIPTIVE BEHAVIORS, THE LOOK AND FEEL
and experience of gender have all changed over time. Certainly, how we
define a person's gender has become increasingly more difficult the
more science reveals gender's complexity. Recently, a few gender-
bending situations have ended up in court where judges are not only
trying to understand the biology of being transgender, but what constitutional protections apply to transgender individuals.

Sorting out legal rights in cases involving transgender people is made
that much more difficult when you consider that some of society's ideas
about gender and gender expression are still firmly rooted in antiquated
beliefs and stereotypes. In 2013, Timberlake Christian School in Lynch-
burg, Virginia, sent a letter home with student Sunnie Kahle, informing
her grandparents (her legal guardians) that she would no longer be wel-
come at Timberlake if she didn't start dressing more like a girl. Her short
hair, sneakers, and T-shirts made other students uncomfortable, according to the school official, because they weren't sure if Sunnie was a boy
or a girl. "We believe that unless Sunnie and her family clearly understand that God has made her female and that her dress and behavior

need to follow suit with her God-ordained identity, that TCS is not the best place for her future education," the letter read.

In the fall of 2013, a thirteen-year-old eighth-grade boy in Kansas was suspended from his public school for carrying a flowered purse on his shoulder. Although the school dress code did not address purses, school administrators nonetheless claimed they were not allowed in certain classes, so when the eighth grader refused to ditch the bag, the school ditched him. When the incident hit the news, it garnered so much attention the designer of the handbag offered to send more to the male student.

And in 2015, school administrators in North Carolina told a nine-year-old boy he needed to leave his My Little Pony lunch box at home because other students teased him. The school said the container was a "trigger for bullying." The student's mother said, "Saying a lunch box is a trigger for bullying is like saying a short skirt is a trigger for rape."

There are also, on occasion, unexpected positive stories. In March 2015, in Michigan, the owner of a Planet Fitness franchise rescinded the membership of a woman who repeatedly complained about a transgender woman using the female locker room and facilities. In terminating the woman's membership, Planet Fitness said her behavior had been "inappropriate and disruptive to other members." Days later, the woman filed suit against Planet Fitness arguing she'd been "wrongfully denied the benefits of her contract" as well as public accommodations at Planet Fitness, because of the gym's policy, which favored the rights of the transgender woman over hers. The suit is still being litigated.

Not all gender controversies end up in court, of course. Some are debated in the classrooms, dorm rooms, and administrative offices of this country's finest institutions of higher learning. There remain dozens of all-women's colleges in the United States, most of them founded in the late nineteenth and early twentieth centuries, when women were discouraged from pursuing higher education and were shut out of male colleges and universities. The feminist movement of the 1960s and '70s helped secure a future for many women's colleges, though many have subsequently decided to accept men. Of the traditional Seven Sisters colleges, five remain all-female entities: Smith, Mount Holyoke, Wellesley, Barnard, and Bryn Mawr. All are struggling with how to handle women who identify as men, especially those who transition to being trans men while at school. Most women's colleges still consider for admittance only those who identify themselves as female on their applications, although Mount Holyoke in Massachusetts and Mills College in California recently decided to admit those who described themselves as trans men. In April 2015, Smith joined Mount Holyoke and Wellesley in reversing its policy on trans women. Anyone who identifies herself as female, regardless of birth sex, is eligible for admission. Generally, the reason cited by trans men for attending women's colleges is that they feel both physically and psychologically safer there. Some women's colleges have changed their charters to include gender-neutral pronouns; others encourage use of the word "siblinghood," instead of "sisterhood."

If there is no one test for gender, if it rests somewhere in that illimitable space between nature and nurture, then gender truly is less about biology and more about what we tell ourselves—and others—about who we are.

"The only dependable test for gender is the truth of a person's life, the lives we live each day," Jennifer Finney Boylan once wrote. "Surely the best judge of a person's gender is not a degrading, questionable examination. The best judge of a person's gender is what lies within her, or his, heart. How do we test for the gender of the heart, then?"

CHAPTER 28

Separate and Unequal

On June 5, 2009, the Maine Human Rights Commission, where Kelly had filed a complaint against the Orono school system, issued the results of its investigative report as to whether there was a basis for the suit to move forward:

> There are reasonable grounds to believe respondents, School Union 87, Superintendent Clenchy and Orono School Department, unlawfully discriminated against Complainant in education and access to a place of public accommodation because of her sexual orientation when she was denied access to the common bathrooms that are consistent with her gender identity.

It was just an initial ruling, but it had gone in favor of Nicole. The commission recommended "conciliation," which was what the family had been hoping for all along. Kelly and Wayne just wanted the school to listen to them, to take their suggestions to heart, and to find a way for Nicole to be integrated back into the fabric of the school.

While they waited to hear from the Orono school administrator, the family was shaken with bad news. Wayne's father was seriously injured helping a neighbor burn an old stuffed chair in a fire pit. His clothes had caught fire and now he was in the intensive care unit in critical condi-tion. Considering his age and the state of his health, the doctors said, it was unlikely he'd pull through.

Wayne and Kelly decided not to tell the twins how bad it was. Gradu-ation from sixth grade was just a few weeks away, and maybe Grandpa would somehow recover. All they told them was that he'd been hurt in an accident and their father had gone to visit him in the hospital. The day after graduation, however, Kelly told the kids what had really hap-pened. And a short time later Grandpa Bill died.

Dozens of family members gathered for the funeral in upstate New York. At the wake, Wayne was pleased to catch up with cousins and un-cles he hadn't seen in years. But he also couldn't help noticing a few of the younger people—friends of nephews and nieces, mostly—whispering to one another and pointing at Nicole. For her part, Nicole didn't seem to see any of it. Instead, she revisited memories of the large family get-togethers at her grandparents' lake house, memories filled with the fra-grance of fir trees and summer flowers. They were such good memories and they had nothing to do with being transgender, nothing to do with Jacob or Paul Melanson or the Maine Christian Civic League. It was comforting to her to see how many people had come to pay their re-spects to her grandfather.

What she didn't like was that all her relatives and all of Grandpa Bill's friends were dressed in black. Nicole thought it was a mistake— a waste of a chance to colorfully celebrate someone's life. For her, every-thing was physical, palpable, and sensuous. That was how she experienced the world, and she realized now that what she was going to miss most about her grandfather was simply having him, physically, in her life. She'd never be able to hug him again, never feel the tenderness of his kiss or the tickle of his whiskers on her cheek. But most of all he would never get to see her in the body she was meant to have, and that broke her heart.

———

KELLY AND WAYNE HOPED they'd see some positive movement from the Orono school system after the unanimous decision of the Human Rights Commission, but they didn't. It was that silence, and the apparent un-willingness of the school to act on Nicole's behalf, which convinced the Maineses to file a civil lawsuit in Penobscot County Superior Court "as-serting claims for unlawful discrimination in education (Count I) and a place for public accommodation (Count II) on the basis of sexual orien-tation." The lawsuit also made a claim for intentional infliction of emo-tional distress and "failure of the school to remedy a hostile education environment resulting from peer harassment during Nicole's fifth and sixth grade years."

At the heart of the suit was a simple question: Was forcing someone such as Nicole to use a separate, staff-only restroom constitutional? In other words, was it "separate" but "equal"? More than a century ago, the U.S. Supreme Court had made a mess of its ruling in the first "sepa-rate but equal" case. In 1892, in New Orleans, a mixed-race shoemaker named Homer Plessy deliberately took a seat in a railroad car reserved for whites only. Four years later, when the Supreme Court released its opinion in *Plessy v. Ferguson*, all but one justice agreed that racially seg-regated public facilities did not violate the constitution because "social rights" were not guaranteed to all races. Justice John Harlan, the lone dissenter, wrote about the decision:

> The thin disguise of "equal" accommodations for passengers in railroad coaches will not mislead anyone, nor atone for the wrong this day done.

For more than half a century, Jim Crow segregation laws helped make "separate but equal" the law of the land until it was struck down in 1954 in *Brown v. Board of Education of Topeka*. Then, with the passing of the

Civil Rights Act of 1964, no one could be turned away from a public facility because of race, religion, or sex.

In the past ten years, laws against discrimination based on sexual orientation and gender identity have been gaining a foothold. In 2015, twenty-two states and the District of Columbia prohibited workplace discrimination against gay people. At least eighteen of those states and the District of Columbia also prohibited workplace discrimination against transgender people. Similarly, fair housing laws protected gay people in twenty-one states and the District of Columbia, and sixteen of those states, as well as the District, protected transgender people. In Maine, both employment and housing laws made it illegal to discriminate against someone based on either sexual orientation or gender identity.

It was clear that whatever the courts decided in the Maineses' lawsuit would set a precedent that other litigants in other states would likely look to for years to come. No one had been identified by name in the press or in the court documents, where Wayne and Kelly were cited as "John and Jane Doe" and Nicole as "Susan Doe." Many people in Orono, of course, knew who they were and what they were fighting. Beyond their own small New England community they were hardly public figures, but they all felt it was only a matter of time before the larger world knew them by name.

In June, Kelly had another face-to-face meeting with acting principal Bob Lucy, who was also the principal of Orono Middle School. She needed to know exactly what the arrangements were going to be for Nicole going into the seventh grade. Was the school going to continue the "eyes-on" policy, and would Nicole be forced to continue to use the staff bathroom? Neither was supposed to have been a permanent response to Jacob's harassment, but that's what seemed to have happened. The situation was so stressful, so toxic, Kelly believed something had to change, or the family couldn't continue to live in Orono. Certainly, the kids couldn't continue to go to school there and, frankly, without moving, there weren't many other options.

Lucy's response was unequivocal: Nothing was going to change, he said; the rules would remain the same.

"Well, I guess that means we're going to have to move," Kelly responded.

She looked Lucy straight in the eyes when she said it. He had nothing more to say, but for the first time since she'd met the man, a smile crossed his face. Here was the acting principal of an elementary school and the principal of a middle school, and he seemed pleased a family felt forced to uproot their lives because of an intolerable situation at his school—a situation he had all the power in the world to change but for whatever reason had decided not to.

Kelly talked to Wayne that night. She'd also heard from someone at the school that Jacob had asked a teacher where the staff bathroom was in the seventh grade. It looked like Jacob's behavior—which had felt at times like stalking to Nicole—was definitely going to continue. Wayne and Kelly knew it might come to this, and they'd made tentative plans that if they had to move they'd go to Portland, 140 miles south of Orono. Wayne and Kelly had met Barbara, the mother of a transgender son, when she owned a business in nearby Bangor. Barbara and her family had since moved to Portland, where her son, about the same age as Nicole and Jonas, was enrolled at Helen King Middle School. It was a diverse school in a diverse city. The administration and teachers at King, Barbara said, were very supportive, and frankly that was all Kelly and Wayne needed to know.

Neither Nicole nor Jonas was particularly happy with the news. They'd been protected from much of the back-and-forth between their parents and the school and had no idea how contentious the situation had become. Now it was clear to them, too, that no compromises on the rules would be made. Nicole couldn't take another year of looking over her shoulder for Jacob, of being trailed by a teacher through the school halls and being banished to the staff bathroom.

There was also no telling when the lawsuit would be decided. The

kids might be in high school by that time. The family had hoped graduating from Asa Adams and moving on to middle school would be enough
of a change, but since the elementary, middle, and high schools were all
located next to one another, it didn't help as much as they'd thought it
might. Kelly and Wayne realized the only way to protect their kids was
for them to start fresh. Wayne's job was again the sticking point. He was
making a good salary, and finding an equivalent position anywhere else
in the state—even with Portland's generally better wages—seemed
nearly impossible.

They decided to sell the house and find a smaller one in Portland,
perhaps even rent a place first, since it was clear Wayne would have to
stay in Orono for work. Kelly and the kids would move to Portland, and
Wayne would commute on weekends and holidays to be with them.
They'd always thought they were on an upward trajectory in their lives,
with success and promotions at work fueling an increasingly better life-
style, but Jacob and his grandfather Paul Melanson had bizarrely
changed all that. Suddenly, Wayne and Kelly were downsizing and their
lives were in reverse.

To make it all worse, they knew that even with a new school and a
more accepting administration, no one could know for sure what the
students and their parents might say or do if they found out there was a
transgender girl in their middle school. None of the Maineses had the
energy or the emotional strength to go through what they'd endured at
Asa Adams again, and so it was settled. Wayne would stay in Orono,
Kelly and the kids would move to Portland, and Nicole and Jonas would
have to go to school "stealth." No one, except the school principal and
teachers at Portland's King Middle School, would be told Nicole was
transgender.

Leaving Orono meant leaving the woodlands that backed up to their
property where Jonas and Nicole played manhunt for hours. Kelly would
lose the basement Wayne had converted into an art studio, and Nicole
the lavender-colored bedroom with its glow-in-the-dark stars stuck to the

ceiling. She'd even miss the stripe that ran around the top of the walls in her bedroom because it was painted in a color that had the wonderful name of "pucker-up green."

But the toughest part was that Nicole and Jonas would have to leave their small circle of overlapping friends. Those friends all understood the hardships of the past couple of years and they understood why the family had decided to move. What the twins had not yet come to terms with was that whoever their new friends in Portland were going to be, those new friends could know nothing about the past two years in Orono—nothing about Nicole being transgender, the harassment, the unyielding school policy at Asa Adams, the fights, and the lawsuit. The most painful two years of their lives, in other words, would have to be buried.

CHAPTER 29

Going Stealth

THE MAINESES WERE ABOUT TO ESSENTIALLY SHRED THE WORLD they'd lived in for the past decade and trade it for an unknown one. Time was not on their side. They had to put their house on the market, then find a home for Kelly and the kids in Portland. They had to register Jonas and Nicole at King Middle School, meet with the principal and teachers, pack up everything they owned and put some of it in storage — and they had two months to do it. The easiest part was registering the kids and meeting with more than two dozen of the staff and teachers at King. No one, except this group of adults at King Middle School, could know about Nicole. If anyone found out she was transgender the family would have to come up with a new game plan, perhaps even move again, and that seemed unimaginable. Could Kelly and Wayne trust the school to keep Nicole's secret? Yes, the administrators said. But there was one other worry: Kelly wasn't 100 percent sure Nicole could keep the secret.

THE TEMPERATURE HOVERED AROUND ninety degrees the day of the move, and the heat baked the blacktop on the roads out of Orono.

Wayne was getting over a bout with pneumonia, and when he finally slid behind the wheel of the rented U-Haul he was already exhausted. There was little joy and a lot of frayed nerves and the whole family couldn't help but feel as if they were somehow sneaking out of town. On the highway, the truck whined louder the faster Wayne drove.

"Dad, it sounds like it's going to blow up," Jonas said.

Wayne tried not to push the truck. It had clearly seen better days, and the last thing he needed was for the engine to break down. Nearly three hours later he finally pulled into the driveway of the Portland du-plex they'd rented, and the moment the truck came to a stop, the en-gine's manifold loudly disconnected from the exhaust system. On top of everything else, Wayne now had a useless U-Haul he had to get back to Orono.

The University of Southern Maine is located in Portland and its law school was just two blocks from the duplex. Generations of students liv-ing in off-campus housing gave the neighborhood a worn, dilapidated feel. There was more traffic on the street in front of the house, including police cars and ambulances at all hours, than either Kelly or Wayne had ever experienced, and it took them quite a while to learn how to sleep through the noise, especially with Wayne visiting only on weekends.

The entrance to the house had two doors, separated by a few feet, with the inner door secured by two locks. That was something Wayne had never seen before. Then again, he and Kelly had never felt the need to lock their house in Orono. Immediately inside was the living room, with just enough space for a couch and an armchair, wedged around a large cast-iron radiator. Layers of paint from one tenant after another coated the walls, and cracks in the plaster spidered across the ceiling. Three windows opened up one side of the living room to a bit of light, but the house sat so close to the one next door, occupied by six female college students, that Kelly and the kids could watch them ironing their clothes in the morning. The back door of the house was only thirty feet from the girls' porch, which was the scene of many raucous parties. Once, when Wayne was cooking dinner, a drunken young man stumbled through the back door and began talking to Wayne as if they were both at the party.

"You better turn around and walk away before you get shot," Wayne told him.

The young man quickly sobered up and scampered out.

WHEN THEY FINALLY FINISHED unloading that first day in Portland, Wayne took a moment to lean against the bumper of the truck. From the other side of the street he watched Jonas and Nicole lug their toys into the tired old apartment. The bright blue wallpaper was peeling, the attic bedroom had no heat, and the only emergency exit was a small window with no outside staircase. After more than a decade of marriage, he and Kelly weren't moving up in the world, they were moving down. They'd bought the house in Orono when real estate prices were sky-high and it was going to take a long time to sell. They were paying a mortgage on a house only Wayne was living in and rent on a new one where Wayne would only ever be a visitor.

Wayne found himself vacillating between panic and depression. They were breaking up the family. How was he going to leave them here and drive home alone to Orono? He didn't want to let the kids see him crying. They really didn't know how serious it all was, and now Kelly was going to have to shoulder everything alone. In truth, she was used to it. She'd pretty much steered the family through one crisis after another on her own. In a way, she thought, living apart might be good for both of them. Now she could focus all her attention on Nicole and Jonas without worrying about her husband's obstinacy.

Wayne shook off the mood. His self-pity wouldn't do anyone any good. Kelly was already trying to make the best of things. While his wife scrubbed the apartment from attic to basement, he went out and bought a small hot-oil heater, a thermometer to keep track of the temperature in Nicole's attic bedroom, and a fire escape ladder for her little window. He also tried to glue the wallpaper back into place—a losing battle.

Closing up the truck that first night in Portland, Wayne could hear the faint sounds of a sports announcer floating over the treetops from the high school football field a few blocks away. Taking the kids to University of Maine games was something he'd enjoyed when they all lived in Orono. So a few weeks after the move, on one of his weekend visits, he suggested to Jonas and Nicole they all walk over to the high school to watch the football game. At halftime Jonas said he was going to the snack bar for a hot dog. Nicole wanted to watch the cheerleaders closer to the field. During a break in the cheerleaders' routine, Nicole hiked back up into the stands and sat down next to her father. Jonas was still nowhere in sight.

Nicole looked up at her dad.

"Sometimes I hate being transgender," she said. "Transgender kids commit suicide or they're killed."

Wayne was caught by surprise. It had been a hard year, with all the harassment in school and the lawsuit, then this move to a new city. But this seemed different.

"Why do you say that?"

"It was in a movie I saw. They said most transgender kids commit suicide or are killed."

Nicole had seen a documentary called *Two Spirits: Sexuality, Gender, and the Murder of Fred Martinez*, about a transgender Native American teenager. It had been shown at a meeting of the Proud Rainbow Youth of Southern Maine, or PRYSM. Kelly had pressed hard to find a place in Portland where Nicole could be herself, and PRYSM was the only group that seemed like it might be a good fit. The PRYSM meetings were held at Portland's Community Counseling Center, in a neighborhood just north of shabby, and were mostly attended by older LGBT individuals.

As PRYSM members filtered into a room at the center to watch the film, the smell of stale cigarettes lingered in the air. When the room darkened and the movie started, interviews with experts on hate crimes were interspersed with pictures and videos of Fred and his mother, scenes from the reservation, including the place where Fred was killed, and a close-up of the bloody twenty-five-pound rock that was used to bash in his skull.

Nicole sunk lower in her chair. On screen an activist described other hate crimes against transgender people: a man who was repeatedly run over by the same car, another person who was set on fire. Nicole felt sick to her stomach. Fred Martinez, the murder victim, hadn't been a troubled teen; he was described by someone who knew him as having "a high degree of self-acceptance about who he was," just like Nicole. Fred's eighteen-year-old killer, who was eventually convicted of the crime, had bragged to his friends before his arrest that he'd "bug-smashed a fag."

Nicole didn't tell her parents or Jonas about the movie when she got home. She didn't want to talk about it, and not too long afterward she stopped going to PRYSM meetings, primarily because she had failed to meet any other transgender teens.

"Many of the trans kids mentioned in that movie didn't have parents who loved and accepted them and were supportive of their children," he told Nicole. "They didn't let them be who they needed to be."

Wayne wasn't sure if this was the right thing to say, because being who you are was, in many ways, more dangerous. It had proved fatal for Fred, and it was that danger that chiefly worried Kelly and Wayne.

"That doesn't mean there aren't mean, dangerous people out there who can hurt you," he said. "You have to be very careful about who you let into your circle of trust. You have to watch where you go and who you are with at all times. Never go anywhere alone."

ON NOVEMBER 25, 2009, JUST three months after the family moved to Portland, the Maineses' lawyers filed a civil lawsuit. Although the Maine Human Rights Commission had essentially ruled in their favor, its recommendations were not mandatory. Nothing had changed in Orono. So the legal advice given to Wayne and Kelly was to sue in civil court,

claiming the policy of the school had intentionally and negligently in-
flicted emotional distress on Nicole and the family, and that the lack of
change on the school's part had created a continuing hostile educational
environment. At the conclusion of the letter informing Kelly Clenchy,
Asa C. Adams Elementary, and the Orono school district of the civil
claims, the Maineses' attorney wrote:

> As of July 31, 2009 Mr. Clenchy has failed to take affirmative ac-
> tion to ensure that N.M. (Nicole Maines) was able to attend
> school in an educational environment free from prejudice, stig-
> matization and intolerance. As a direct and proximate results,
> N.M and her twin brother were forced to leave . . . the Orono
> School System.

CHAPTER 30

On the Outside Looking In

O<small>N THE FIRST DAY OF SEVENTH GRADE, THE TWINS WALKED THE</small> half mile to King Middle School under a chilly, overcast sky, saying little to each other. The school, a sprawling two-story brick and concrete building, sat at the bottom of a hill in a working-class neighborhood. Two years earlier King had made the news when it became the first middle school in Maine (and one of the first in the nation) to offer birth control to students as young as eleven years old. The decision was made after Portland's three middle schools reported seventeen pregnancies over a four-year span.

When Nicole and Jonas arrived at King that September morning, they were told they had to wait in the parking lot with about five hundred other students before the first bell signaling the start of the school day. This would be a daily ritual. To Jonas, the other students looked much older and, for some reason, unhappy. Many were children of recent immigrants—Africans, East Asians, Muslims, and Sikhs. In fact, there were more minorities in their middle school than Jonas and Nicole had ever seen in Orono. It was hard not to feel both intimidated and terrified, and all the twins wanted to do was blend into the background.

The seventh graders were split into two sections and assembled on opposite sides of the parking lot. They also ate lunch and had recess at different times. So from the second day of school, Jonas and Nicole actually saw very little of each other.

Nothing about King Middle School felt right. It was large and unfriendly, especially if you didn't belong to one of the many cliques. Having to hide who they were, and why they were there, only added to the twins' sense of not belonging.

Nicole was always acutely aware of leading a kind of double life, never more so than the time, only two months into the seventh grade, when a boy in one of her classes asked her out on a date as they stood talking in the hallway. The boy was lean and lanky with short hair and braces. And he was the first boy to ever ask her out on a real date, to go to a concert. It took her aback. She knew she couldn't say yes, and yet she also didn't want to hurt the boy.

"I'm sorry, I can't," she said as gently and politely as she could.

No explanations were asked for. "Can't" was better—or at least easier—to say than "won't," and it had the added benefit of being true. There was no way she could go out on any dates for the next two years, a source of both sadness and frustration. But it was more than that. It hurt deeply because it confirmed for Nicole the reason she'd never been asked out on a date in Orono, where all her schoolmates knew who she was: It was because she was transgender. The word, the identity—she had already fought long and hard for them. And yet, it was precisely that identity that seemed to prevent any boy who really knew her from getting too close. It was that distance she dreaded she'd never overcome, and, ironically, this boy had just reminded her of it.

There was an edginess to the school that made it hard for the twins to let their guard down. Several times during the seventh grade, brawls broke out. Neither Jonas nor Nicole had ever seen someone their age in a fistfight, much less partaken in one, but that soon changed. Jonas had developed a crush on a girl and, trying to fit in, had made it known to some of the other boys in his class that he was interested in her. Unfortunately, one of the other boys decided he liked this girl, too, and asked her out. Jonas felt betrayed and quietly seethed. Not long afterward, when his class was playing a vigorous game of floor hockey, Jonas singled out the student he was angry at, and was a bit more physical with him than he should have been. Arms and elbows flew, shoulders crunched. Finally Jonas called the other boy a "bitch" and the other boy retaliated. Before he knew what he was doing, Jonas turned around and punched the kid in the face. Immediately he realized he'd done something very wrong. Fighting was something he generally didn't do, but his anger had gotten the best of him.

Maybe that's why Jonas withdrew into music and playing the guitar—things he could do on his own. At Asa Adams he'd played the drums in the school band and orchestra. Maybe he'd try that again. He signed up for band class, but on the first day, when he walked into the room, he immediately felt out of place, as if everyone was looking at him. When Jonas began drumming, another student mocked him loudly. Wounded, Jonas simply stood up and walked out.

As attuned as they were to what was happening with Nicole on a day-to-day basis, Kelly and Wayne both knew they needed to be more aware of what was going on with Jonas. He had a tendency to be passive, to step aside and let the world—or Nicole—not only rush by him, but overwhelm him. Their whole lives, Kelly had made sure each child had the same opportunities. What one received the other received, and most of the time the twins were in sync, not only sharing toys and games but most of their friends as well. But where Nicole was impulsive, explosive, and domineering, Jonas was reflective and intellectual. Sometimes indolent, he let others make decisions for him. What worries he had, he usually buried, but every now and then they came surging to the fore, sometimes with disastrous results.

Toward the end of April 2010, almost eight months after Wayne and Kelly and the kids started living apart, Wayne lingered on the phone with his son a bit longer than usual. That's when Jonas admitted to his father that some kids at school had punched him.

"Why didn't you say something earlier to your mother?" Wayne asked.

"Because Mom would have gotten upset and she would want to do something."

"Do something" meant calling the school or the parents of the boy who punched Jonas, and that was the last thing he wanted. What he did want, just like Nicole, was to fit in, to be a normal kid, not the brother of a transgender sister, and especially not the identical twin of a transgender sister. Jonas understood that at King Middle School you didn't tell anyone anything or you'd be labeled for life. But Jonas's sense of justice was acute. He told his father that when he heard another student refer to someone as a fag, he couldn't just stand there, even if it wasn't directed at his sister. So he'd confronted the kid and the kid threw a punch.

Wayne told him he understood, but he still needed to deal with things differently.

"I don't want you to fight. You need to look the kid in the eye and tell him not to do it again and if he does, then walk away and tell someone. There are better ways to deal with things."

Nicole knew this, too. And while she never wanted to respond physically to someone, there were many times she wanted to say exactly how she felt but couldn't for fear that it would inevitably lead to being outed. Being true to her beliefs, and not just about being transgender, had never felt this dangerous. The hardest times were keeping her mouth shut when she'd hear someone say "Oh, that's so gay," which kids often did. She knew if she tried to object, the other person would only say, "Why do you care? Are *you* gay?" And then she'd be stuck. She had good reason to challenge others' prejudices, but she couldn't because they hit too close to home. So she kept her mouth shut, buttoned down her anger, and sealed off her sense of self-righteousness.

Jonas, like Nicole, walked to school every day, and nearly every day walked home right afterward and watched TV or played video games. He had a couple of friends, who were also Nicole's, but neither twin hung out with them much after the school day was over. No one could get too close for fear they'd find out too much. It was strange and stressful, trying to be "half friends" with certain classmates. As for classwork, Jonas found it hard to motivate himself. He was extraordinarily bright, but being around so many other disinterested kids sapped him of his normal curiosity and love of knowledge. King was an expeditionary learning school, modeled on the reforms of Kurt Hahn, the German educator who also founded Outward Bound. The central idea was project-based learning, which involved multidiscipline group activities. The theme that year was invasive species, but as far as Jonas could tell, neither the students nor the teachers seemed all that excited about the project. There was very little joy in learning, on either side of the desk, Jonas thought. By the end of the year he'd sunk into a deep depression and admitted to his mother he felt like cutting himself. Kelly immediately called Wayne. What could he do two hundred miles away? He would talk to Jonas on the phone, but Kelly would have to handle it with the school. She sat down and sent an email to school officials:

> Yesterday, Jonas came home and said he felt like cutting himself. My husband and I have decided to pursue counseling for him and I will arrange that today. Meanwhile, we would appreciate all of you keeping a close eye on him while he is in school. I will be giving him a ride to school and walking with him after school until we are sure he is not truly going to hurt himself. Thanks for your help, and any insight you may have would be greatly appreciated.

Wayne and Kelly both realized that hormones were likely playing a big part in Jonas's life at that moment. Jonas was also a thinker, and sometimes he was just too far inside his head for his own good. Kelly set

him up with a therapist, and he appeared to benefit from having someone to talk to outside the family. But Jonas also liked figuring things out
for himself, turning them over in his mind until he'd explored every
nook and cranny and felt satisfied he understood the issue. It was a tool
he had to use frequently at King Middle School because nearly every
day something got under his skin. He couldn't abide meanness in others, or stupidity, but he also knew it was pointless and self-defeating to
expend the energy to lash out every time something bothered him.

Jonas knew this acutely because he had that same strange ability his
mother had, the capacity to look at himself as if he were floating outside
his own body, and when he did, he came to the conclusion that it was
unreasonable to respond to every single thing that irritated him. Instead,
he needed to keep things at a low simmer, to suppress his frustrations
and let them out slowly. It was all about self-control, and Jonas saw himself as immensely self-controlled. So he examined the slights as they
came his way, first figuring out why others felt the need to act the way
they did. Next he examined how those acts or words made him feel.
Then he put them away. Puzzles solved, frustrations defused. It was all
very neat and clean—until it wasn't.

Nicole isolated herself in her own thoughts as well. She read, played
video games, and talked online with former classmates in Orono. But
the house in Portland was almost too quiet when the kids were home.

Jonas stayed in his room, Nicole in hers. Concentrating on homework was hard for both of them. Jonas, an excellent science and math
student, had let his grades slip, and Nicole was flunking Spanish. She
brooded about her future, convinced she'd never be loved and never
find someone who'd marry her. Nicole was not only afraid of getting
close to a person, she was afraid of getting close to the "wrong" person
and the secret suddenly becoming very public.

It almost happened twice. The first time it came from outside the
school, just after Nicole had joined a club called A Company of Girls,
or ACOG, an organization that seeks to empower teenage girls primarily
through theater and the arts. Nicole, who already enjoyed drawing, also

wanted to explore acting. At one of the meetings, out of the blue, another student asked her if she was transgender.

"What?" Nicole responded.

Her heart was pounding so loud she was certain everyone in the room could hear it, but she tried to remain low-key and reacted as if she didn't understand what the girl was talking about. How had she found out? Nicole tried to be as blasé as possible, and prayed the other girl would drop the subject, which she did, but not before Nicole had spent a few anxious moments worrying her cover had been blown. Another time, in the girls' locker room, a girl asked Nicole why she always dressed and undressed for gym in a stall, not out in the open like the others. Before she could answer, though, another student distracted the girl and she wandered off without waiting for Nicole's reply.

Eighth grade was not much better than seventh. The twins had each other, and that was about it. Jonas watched TV. Nicole played video games. Sometimes she closed the door at the bottom of the staircase to the attic and curled up on one of the lower steps to read a book. Her favorites were *Luna* and *Almost Perfect*, two young adult novels about transgender youth her father had given her.

Nicole had been miserable her final two years at Asa Adams when she was out of the closet, and she was miserable her first two years at King when she was in it. It was all so bewildering and depressing, like never having a sense of balance. How could she, when she and Jonas felt as isolated as they did and were actively hiding a part of their lives from people who might otherwise have become their friends? Friendships, in fact, were more tease than reality. Just when Nicole seemed on the verge of making a good connection with someone, she'd ask her mother, "Can't I tell anyone?" And every time her mother said, "No." When Nicole balked once and asked why she couldn't at least tell just one person, since it was *her* life after all, Kelly answered her in no uncertain terms.

"It's not just about you. It's about the whole family, Nicole. If you tell someone and it all goes downhill, we'll all have to move again."

After the ACOG incident, there was really only one other close call, and it came on one of those rare occasions when Nicole invited someone over to the house after school. On the stairway leading up to her bedroom, Nicole had lined the walls with drawings and photos. One of the photographs was a still from *The Wizard of Oz*, autographed by one of the Munchkins. The twins' uncle Andy had gotten it for Nicole years earlier, and it was inscribed "To Wyatt."

"Who's Wyatt?" the friend from King asked Nicole as she passed the photo on the staircase.

"Oh, that's my uncle Wyatt. He gave me the picture because he didn't want it anymore."

Nicole barely missed a beat, but her heart was pounding. When her classmate left she took the photo down and hid it in a drawer.

The oddest part about being in the closet at King was that anything even remotely related to being transgender felt threatening. One day, Kelly received a call from Nicole's teacher, who wanted her to know that the following week there was going to be a bullying-awareness day and a film shown to all students that included transgender issues. Nicole might feel uncomfortable during the discussion afterward, the teacher said, so she was being given permission to call in sick that day if she wanted. She did.

Even when things were going well, it wasn't about the danger of slipping up so much as the sense of always having to hold back. Eventually Nicole and Jonas developed a small, select group of friends, but they were always held at an emotional distance. For Nicole, it wasn't about shutting people out so much as shutting herself down. It felt especially hard one weekend when she and about five others gathered at a friend's house and built a campfire in the backyard, then watched movies. Everyone was so relaxed and the conversations often veered toward the intimate. These were people who knew Nicole, and yet didn't. She knew them well enough to know she could probably trust them, but not saying anything was a promise she'd made to her mother—to her whole family—and she couldn't break that.

———

IN FEBRUARY 2010 EVERYTHING seemed at a breaking point for Wayne. They were still paying $1,500 a month in mortgage on a house the family no longer lived in, and for which they'd eventually take a $28,000 loss. They were paying another $1,200 in rent for the duplex in Portland. Then there were the utilities for two households, books and clothes for the kids, and the cost of Wayne traveling hundreds of miles every weekend, sometimes by car, often by bus. He estimated that over the course of the first seven years in Portland, the family took on an additional $105,000 in expenses. On top of that he and Kelly also owed $33,800 in lawyer's fees to their first attorney, whom the family had just dropped. He just didn't seem to be on top of the case, and it didn't help that his own teenage son had acted disparagingly toward Nicole. The incident happened outside school when the boy pointed her out to a friend and Nicole heard him say, "There's that kid my father is representing" in a tone that could only have been called disgust. When Kelly called the attorney that night to complain, he actually seemed irritated.

"What do you want me to do?" he said.

Kelly was worn down with worry, and losing weight, but she was determined not to let Nicole and Jonas see her anxiety. She rarely cried, but she did one night, watching, of all things, an episode of the reality series *Cops*. The story that night was about a transgender child, male to female, like Nicole, who lived on the streets and worked as a prostitute. In the episode the police were giving her a hard time, even though she wasn't a runaway. Her parents had thrown her out of the house. The thought of rejecting Nicole had never crossed Kelly's mind and, as difficult a time as Wayne had understanding their daughter, she was sure it hadn't crossed his, either. In fact, Kelly was used to telling her mother, her friends—anyone who would listen—that Nicole would always have a home with her. She'd never be abandoned by her family, and she would never be left to be harassed by the police, or anyone else for that matter, as long as Kelly had anything to say about it. If Nicole couldn't make it in the outside world, she would live with her mother the rest of her life, and that was that.

A bit of good news arrived in March 2010, when Kelly and Wayne received word that attorneys for Boston-based GLAD would represent them in their legal battles, along with Maine private attorney Jodi Nofsinger. The biggest relief: The GLAD lawyers would be paid only if they won the case.

CHAPTER 31

Puberty Begins

NICOLE WAS ELEVEN YEARS OLD AND SHE WANTED BREASTS. ANYone can grow their hair long and wear makeup and feminine clothing, but if she had breasts, there would be no mistaking her for who she really was. Before she could begin taking estrogen, however, Dr. Spack had to make sure she didn't enter male puberty. He'd promised her that when the signs were there, they'd begin her on puberty-suppressing drugs.

At Nicole's appointment in September 2008, Spack had told Kelly and Wayne that he would begin to carefully monitor her gonadal hormone level and that if it started to rise high they would move quickly, because beginning male puberty would be terrifying for her. In early January 2009 he noted that Nicole had not had a growth spurt and had not developed adult body odor or chest hair. Two months later, however, her hormone levels had risen, there was evidence of a bit of coarse pubic hair, and she had experienced some unwanted erections. It was clear she was on the cusp, and Spack didn't want to miss the window. The puberty-suppressing drug Lupron can sometimes take as long as three to four months to begin working, so the decision was made: Nicole would begin monthly injections right away. She was thrilled.

When Nicole next saw the psychologist at the gender clinic for a periodic checkup, Dr. Laura Edwards-Leeper asked her what it felt like to still have a penis.

"I'd like to cut it off," she said, before quickly realizing how melodramatic that sounded and added, "Not seriously."

"Is that how you really feel about your penis?" the therapist pressed.

"I just try not to care about it because there's nothing I can do about it at this point. Not until I'm older."

With her friends beginning to bud small breasts, a flat-chested Nicole still looked childlike in many ways. When she pleaded with her parents for a bra and a set of falsies, Wayne left the decision up to Kelly, and Kelly finally relented. But where do you get falsies for a prepubescent trans girl? Kelly was on her own. She began by buying A-cup bras at Target and at a local sewing shop picking up gel packs worn inside a bra to enhance what's naturally there. What was "there" for Nicole, however, was nothing, so Kelly sewed little pockets into the bras to hold the gel packs in place. The "enhancement" wasn't very satisfactory. Nicole's first boobs, as Kelly called them, were just a bit underwhelming. After more Internet searching, Kelly learned she could buy silicone breast prostheses and bras with built-in pockets designed for women who have had mastectomies. That's how she bought Nicole's first real set of "falsies," the smallest ones available, online. Nicole thought they were perfect. They were squishy and felt substantial in her hands and they even had nipples. Nicole threw away the awkward gel packs and slipped the two, teardrop-shaped silicone breasts into the pockets of her new bra. Wearing them was altogether transformative. Nicole walked around school with a newfound confidence. She was even able to be playful about her "breasts" with her friends back in Orono, once tossing them at another girl while they tried on clothes in a dressing room at the mall.

Kelly always looked in on the twins on her way to bed, and in the first few weeks after Nicole received her new breasts, she would find her daughter all tucked in, but still wearing her bra and prostheses under her pajamas. It made Kelly smile, remembering all the times Nicole had felt embarrassed about her body. Once, when Kelly opened the door to the bathroom while Nicole was taking a shower, she realized she was washing herself in the dark, just so she didn't have to look at herself.

On another night, feeling lonely and a bit down, Nicole wandered into her parents' bedroom and asked if she could sleep with them. Kelly was watching *The Tonight Show,* and Wayne was almost asleep. Out of the corner of his eye, he watched Nicole tiptoe carefully over to his side of the bed, trying not to wake him. Then, just before sliding in under the covers, she carefully placed her new breasts on the nightstand next to the bed.

About a year after moving to Portland, Kelly was hired to be the executive assistant to the city's sheriff, where she quickly learned the department had one of the best transgender prisoner policies in the nation. Staff was trained to make sure transgender female prisoners were assigned cells with other females, not males. There were no incidents of harassment, no derogatory comments. Rather, there was a simple, even dignified acceptance that started at the top, with the sheriff.

Life at home, however, was anything but simple. Once, on a weekend afternoon, with Kelly and Wayne doing chores and the kids on their own, a thunderous crash sent them all running toward the sound, which appeared to be coming from outside the house. Kelly thought she'd seen Nicole moments before going up to her attic bedroom, so the horrifying possibility that her daughter had just plunged through her bedroom window and was lying in a heap by the side of the house seemed all too real. Jonas and Wayne dashed outside while Kelly grabbed her phone and tried to dial 911. She didn't have her contact lenses in and her reading glasses weren't nearby. Blindly she pushed at the buttons. Just then, Nicole sauntered up from the basement where she'd been playing video games.

"Hi, guys, what's up?" she asked breezily.

"Oh my God," Kelly said.

She grabbed Nicole and hugged her close just as Wayne and Jonas, confused, wandered back inside.

"I thought you were dead!" said Kelly.

"Thank God you're okay," said Wayne.

Without hesitating, he and Jonas joined Kelly and Nicole in one big family embrace and they laughed with relief. The noise turned out to be someone moving furniture next door, but it was clear from their initial reactions just how much strain they were all under, especially Kelly. They'd been through so much, and trouble seemed never to be more than a few minutes or feet away. It was almost like they all had post-traumatic stress disorder, always expecting the worst, always in "what next" mode.

WHEN THE ORONO PROPERTY finally sold, Wayne moved into cheap graduate student housing. Kelly and the kids, who were now in the eighth grade, were also able to move into a new home several blocks and a world away from the duplex. It was a street of modest, single-family houses and stately trees. The backyard wasn't huge, and a commuter train ran by several times a day, just beyond the fence. But it had more room, including a patio, and there were no police sirens in the middle of the night.

In the spring, Nicole had an appointment to see Dr. Spack at his Boston clinic. He told her he might start the estrogen sooner than age sixteen, as originally planned. Nicole could have kissed him she was so excited. When she'd first met the doctor she'd been a bit intimidated, but he gave off an aura of assuredness that always seemed to put her at ease. In fact, after the first couple of visits, Nicole began to think of Dr. Spack as family. So whatever he needed to do to make her fully female, it was all right with her. Spack started Nicole on estrogen right away. She was thirteen. She would also need to continue taking the male hormone blockers until she underwent sex reassignment surgery. Everything was moving ahead at the right pace, he assured the family, just as he'd expected.

After the appointment, the family had lunch at a dim sum restaurant in Boston, then rode the elevator up to the eighth floor of the building that housed GLAD's main office in Boston. They were greeted by several GLAD staffers, including their lead lawyer on the lawsuit, Jennifer Levi, the director of GLAD's Transgender Rights Project. After twenty years as a litigator at GLAD, she was a nationally recognized expert on transgender issues. This was the first time the legal team had met the family face-to-face, and they were eager to tell them how strongly they believed in the case, but that not counting appeals, it could take as long as two years before it was all over.

At a reception for the family that night, held at the home of a GLAD board member, Nicole was a whirlwind of energy. She was clearly the star of the show. Afterward, Wayne was moved to write a long thank-you note. He needed to explain to all the people he'd just met how grateful he was.

> In the past we have openly discussed the difficulties and rewards that exist for transgender children with those who are willing to listen. We attempted to answer any questions and work with teachers and staff to help provide a positive learning environment. . . . However, the continued concerns that we face on an almost daily basis have placed us in a position that requires we speak out from behind a curtain.

It was impossible for the Maineses not to feel the importance of their case among these hardworking people, and they realized that their lawsuit wasn't just about Nicole or their family. It wasn't even just their story anymore. The lawsuit, even though it was just a state case, had meaning and significance for many others. And now Wayne, Kelly, Nicole, and Jonas would carry the hopes of those others with them as they sought affirmation from the courts.

CHAPTER 32

Born This Way

WORRIED ABOUT WHAT THE KIDS WOULD DO DURING THE SUM-mer, Kelly made arrangements for Nicole and Jonas to spend time with their father in Orono, but she also had a surprise for Nicole. She'd heard from someone in Dr. Spack's office about a transgender camp in Connecticut, one of the first of its kind. Nicole was signed up to attend for a week at the end of August.

Camp Aranu'tiq (the name comes from the Chugach indigenous people of Alaska and means "two spirit," or "half man, half woman") is part of Harbor Camps, founded in 2009 by Nick Teich, a trans man. As an avid former camper, he recognized the need for the more marginalized members of society, especially children and adolescents, to have their own summer camp experience. Although Harbor, a nonprofit, would eventually be able to buy, renovate, and equip their own 112-acre wilderness camp in New Hampshire, in its inaugural year it leased a rustic lakeside campsite in Old Lyme, Connecticut.

After a sleepless night, Nicole jabbered nervously to her parents and Jonas on the ride down from Orono to Old Lyme. Mostly she didn't know what to expect. She'd never been to a sleepaway camp, much less one with other transgender kids. There were forty-one of them in total, all eight to fifteen years old. Beneath the name tags they wore around their necks were written the preferred personal pronouns. After reaching the camp and stepping for the first time inside Robeson cabin, the one set aside for the younger campers, Nicole wasn't impressed. The bunk beds were okay, but the dirt floor, the cobwebs—it was all a bit shabby, she thought. But the campgrounds included a rec hall, an art center, and a cafeteria. There was a volleyball court, yoga, and kayaking. There were also campfires, games of capture the flag, a talent show, and skit night, when they doused one another in blue glitter. Within forty-eight hours Aranu'tiq felt like a home away from home, and Nicole loved everything about it.

One of the best parts of the day were meals because you were required to switch your seating so you were never next to the same person. At lunch one day, after downing quesadillas and rice, one of the counselors led the group in singing the camp song, which they'd just written— "Aranu'tiq, a great place to be. I love this camp because I can be me"—which led to other rousing, more traditional camp songs, such as "Rigabamboo," "The Moose Song," and "Little Red Wagon," which for some reason segued into Lady Gaga's "Born This Way."

> I'm beautiful in my way
> 'Cause God makes no mistakes.

On one of the last evenings, Nicole wrote, directed, and acted in a three-act play with her cabin mates based on the board game and movie *Clue*. Nicole camped it up playing Mrs. White, but instead of the sexy widow, memorably and melodramatically portrayed by Madeline Kahn in the 1985 film, Nicole performed the role as a cranky old lady, a routine she'd developed a couple of years earlier. She'd named her character "Muriel," and she was a classic curmudgeon, even misanthrope, with a Long Island accent. The audience at Camp Aranu'tiq lapped it up. One of her camp friends played the role of Mrs. Peacock, brash, obnoxious, and loud—just the kind of person Muriel disliked. When another character announces that Mrs. Peacock has been murdered and they all stand around looking at her body, Nicole ad-libbed.

"I know, it's a miracle. Her mouth is shut."

The campers and counselors convulsed in laughter.

At the end of the week, before they all went their separate ways, the campers gathered in the cafeteria and passed a ball of yarn from one table to the next until every person in the room was connected by a single spool. She'd spent only a week among these other transgender kids, but Nicole felt she'd made fast friends with at least two other trans girls. They hadn't talked that much about being transgender; they'd just laughed and gossiped and swapped details about their favorite music, games, and TV shows. Cellphone numbers and email addresses were exchanged. Most of the campers tied the yarn around their wrists. Nicole wore hers until it finally fell off about six months later. She would return to Camp Aranu'tiq two more summers. When she attended the camp for the third and last time, after which she was too old, the final ceremony included a gift for all the graduates: a compass, so that they could always find their way back.

CHAPTER 33

A Time for Change

A FEW WEEKS AFTER THE START OF EIGHTH GRADE, NICOLE learned a celebrity was coming to Portland to speak out against the military's "don't ask, don't tell" policy. At five in the afternoon thousands of Mainers, including Nicole and Wayne, stood shoulder to shoulder in a downtown park to hear pop music icon and political activist Lady Gaga. She was there to sing and speak at a rally organized by the Servicemembers Legal Defense Network.

"My name is Stefani Joanne Angelina Germanotta. I am an American citizen," she told the crowd, before urging Maine's lawmakers to pressure the Obama administration to repeal DADT. She offered a new law she called "If you don't like it, go home," which would remove homophobic straight soldiers from the military instead of gay soldiers.

At one point, the singer recited the oath of enlistment, words spoken by every member of every branch of the military when they pledge their service to their country. Wayne had spoken these words some thirty years earlier when he entered the air force at a time when the military was very unpopular in the United States.

I, _____, do solemnly swear (or affirm) that I will support and defend the Constitution of the United States against all enemies, foreign and domestic. . . .

As a brand-new recruit, Wayne had been both scared and proud when he swore the oath to his country. He and Kelly had raised their children to respect the military.

Lady Gaga, of course, was there to make a point, and so at the end of the oath, she added three words: "Unless you're gay." For a moment Wayne felt anger toward the military, but mostly the politicians who had allowed the military, for so long, to dismiss honorable men and women from its ranks because of their sexual orientation. All that hiding and the secrecy, the lying and the shame—it was corrosive. The Maineses probably knew that better than most. Wayne hoped a time would come soon that all four of them could stand up and declare themselves. But until then, they'd continue living undercover.

Wayne and Kelly constantly worried that Nicole or Jonas would slip up, or that the news from Orono would somehow catch up with them, but it didn't. In fact, after two years in Portland, few people other than schoolteachers and staff knew that Nicole was transgender. They'd all stayed closeted, until suddenly, in April 2011, toward the end of the eighth grade, something happened that made the whole family question whether they could continue to live in hiding.

Wayne and Kelly learned the Maine legislature was considering a new bill, LD 1046: An Act to Amend the Application of the Maine Human Rights Act Regarding Public Accommodations. If passed, the new law would allow the owners of any business to decide who could use their restrooms. Furthermore, if someone was denied access to the facility of their gender identification, they would be unable to claim discrimination under Maine's Human Rights Act.

Kelly, Wayne, Jonas, and Nicole all felt disgusted. They'd moved their primary residence, given up friends and jobs, spent their savings, and lived in secret, all because of harassment and discrimination over

Nicole's use of the gender-appropriate restroom. Now the state of Maine was looking to roll back civil rights even more, to codify discrimination. Wayne boiled over inside. For so long it had been just Kelly fighting for Nicole. He knew his wife must have felt exquisitely alone. He understood that better—albeit in a different way—now that he was forced to live away from his family. For the past two years, from the outside, they'd looked and acted like any average American family, except that they weren't. Something needed to change. Something had changed. And Wayne knew exactly what it was.

CHAPTER 34

We Can't Lose

A MIDDLE-AGED MAN WEARING READING GLASSES STOOD SILENTLY at the microphone before the House Judiciary Committee of the 124th Maine legislature. Then he cleared his throat and began:

> My name is Wayne Maines, I live in Old Town. I have a thirteen-year-old transgender daughter. In the beginning, I was not on board with this reality. Like many of you I doubted transgender children could exist, I doubted my wife, and I doubted our counselors and doctors. However, I never doubted my love for my child. It was only through observing her pain and her suffering and examining my lack of knowledge about these issues did I begin to question my behavior and my conservative values. . . .
>
> When my daughter lost her privileges at school and both children and adults targeted her, I knew I had to change and I have never looked back. . . . When she was told she could no longer use the appropriate bathroom her confidence and self-esteem took a major hit. Prior to this my daughter often said, "Dad, being transgender is no big deal, my friends and I have it under control." I was very proud of her. It was only when adults became

involved with their unfounded fears that her world would be turned upside down. . . . This bill tells my daughter that she does not have the same rights as her classmates and reinforces her opinion that she has no future. Help me give her the future she deserves. Do not pass this bill.

Trembling, Wayne wiped away the tears streaming down his face. It was Tuesday, April 12, 2011, and he felt like he'd just come out of his own closet. He had spoken openly and honestly about his transgender daughter, about himself and his family, and now there was no turning back.

State representative Ken Fredette was the conservative legislator sponsoring the bill with the support of the Republican governor, Paul LePage. The Maine Civil Liberties Union and several other organizations had gone on record opposing it. The hearing before the Judiciary Committee was a chance for the public to speak, and it was an overflow crowd. Before Wayne addressed the committee, Jennifer Levi, one of the Maineses' lawyers in their suit against the Orono school district, spoke:

The only way a business could enforce LD 1046 in a consistent and nondiscriminatory fashion without resorting to gender profiling would be through physical inspections, which raises serious privacy and medical confidentiality concerns and, again, risk of litigation. Not to mention that a person's anatomy is personal, private information that nobody would want to be required to disclose (or worse, viewed) before being given access to a public facility.

Levi set out not only the reasons why transgender people should be allowed to use the bathroom of their gender identity, but logically, pragmatically, and legally why enforcing a biological-sex accommodation rule would not work. Everything Nicole, Kelly, Wayne, and Jonas had fought for, sued for, been harassed for, was suddenly at stake, and not just for Nicole, but for every transgender person in the state of Maine.

Before he spoke, Wayne wasn't sure how he was going to do it, or even if he could. Now he knew there had never been any other option. For years Kelly had quietly borne the family burden of protector and provider for Nicole's needs. Now it was Wayne's turn to step up and speak out. He was oddly ebullient, as if he'd finally rid himself of some suffocating weight, and it was all he could do to keep himself tethered to the ground. All those values he'd been taught growing up—defending the defenseless, helping the downtrodden—he'd always thought they meant standing up for a friend or a neighbor or a stranger in need, not his own child.

No one, however, was confident LD 1046 would be defeated. In fact, Wayne was worried enough it might pass that just days after he spoke at the hearing he called Kelly from work and said he'd been thinking about the state legislators and the upcoming vote.

"I think they have to meet Nicole," he told his wife. "We can't lose."

Wayne liked to write things down. Partly it was an organizational habit. He had many thoughts running through his mind. In a way, he talked more to himself than to Kelly, but it was how he worked things out. When he first began to do his own searches on the Internet he was stunned to find so little information for fathers of transgender children. Being the self-starter he was, he realized that maybe he could fill the void. It wasn't that he knew any better than anyone else how to raise a transgender child; he just thought it could help other fathers if he shared his own questions and experiences. Maybe he'd even hear back from someone. Every few months he wrote a piece for the Huffington Post blog called *Gay Voices*. At first he posted anonymously, but, encouraged by responses from other bloggers and readers, he began to write more personally. The responses were often a means for further discussion, such as the column he wrote about allowing Nicole to wear dresses. After reading the post, one person wrote:

> You may be correct. However, is it not a parent's job to show a kid some direction in life and not just giving in to what they say?

Sorry, I would never let my son wear a dress at five because I would not have given up on him so early in the process, but that is the manly side of me talking. Whatever he develops into later, I would accept, but it wouldn't be because I decided to throw him over the fence to the other side at an early age.

Wayne and Kelly had heard all this before. It had taken them both time to realize that it didn't matter how much they'd encouraged or discouraged Nicole's feminine behavior. The truth was going to win out no matter what. Wayne was reminded of something Kelly had said when a friend "kindly" suggested that perhaps Nicole was transgender because her parents had given her dolls at such a young age.

"Are you kidding?" Kelly asked. "So what you're saying is, every man is just one doll away from being a woman?"

NICOLE NEVER FLINCHED. For two days, along with her father, she walked around the statehouse, a thirteen-year-old kid, knocking on doors and stopping representatives in the hallways.

"Hi, my name is Nicole Maines, and I really want your support to defeat this bill," she'd tell each person she met.

A few walked away when they saw her coming, but most were polite and listened. Of the 151 state representatives, she spoke with 60 or 70. What bothered Nicole wasn't simply the injustice of the bill; it was the stupidity of it. She asked the politicians, "How are you going to know if a person is transgender in order to stop them from using the bathroom of their choice?" For the past two years, she'd been just another teenage girl at Helen King Middle School. No one knew her story, no one knew she was transgender, and so no one thought twice about her using the girls' restroom.

Accompanying Nicole to the statehouse, Wayne made his own personal pleas, distributing leaflets that began with a single, simple declaration:

Today I am announcing I am the proud father of identical twins. One is a boy and one is a girl.

Included in the handouts were photographs of Nicole in her sparkly tutus, with scarves over her head or wearing her princess costume.

Wayne went on to describe how, as a child, when Nicole first began talking she tried to tell her parents she was a girl, not a boy. He asked others to imagine how painfully hard that must have been for a toddler.

> We have tried to live our lives privately, but the stakes are now too high to sit on the sidelines. . . . Nicole is not alone. Children as young as age four will experience severe consequences [if the bill is passed]. . . . These children deserve better. They deserve unconditional love and support. . . . Transgender children deserve the same level of safety and same basic human rights that their friends and their parents often take for granted. If each of us does our part, other children, like Nicole, will not have to say, "Daddy, what did I do wrong?"

Kelly was proud of both her husband and her daughter. Public speaking was not something she was comfortable doing, and she didn't like her family's life suddenly being pried open, but it was all worth it if they could help defeat the proposed restrictions on public accommodation.

There was one positive development for both Jonas and Nicole, and that was the prospect of starting over at a new school in ninth grade. The experience of going stealth at King had drained them both, and Kelly and Wayne knew they couldn't keep it up. They still needed to be protected, but they also needed to be in an environment where they could be themselves, freely and without reservation. Casco Bay, a public high school in Portland, appeared to be a good fit. Kelly met with the principal and found the school was both progressive and welcoming. But because there were never enough slots for the number of kids who wanted to attend, a lottery was held every year. Jonas and Nicole put their names in, but only Jonas was offered a slot. Kelly and Wayne had assumed the twins were entered into the lottery together, as a family unit, but when they contacted the school and asked them how they could accept one and not the other, they were told those were the rules. The options were dwindling. There was another public school in Portland as well as a Catholic school, but the former did not have as good a reputation as Casco Bay, and neither Kelly nor Wayne was particularly religious, so their last best hope was Waynflete, a private school, pre-K through twelfth grade, of fewer than six hundred total students. Nicole and Jonas passed the entrance tests easily and were accepted as ninth graders for the 2010–11 school year.

Waynflete, named by its two female founders after a British educator, opened in 1898 with forty-nine students. The curriculum was based on the progressive educational ideals of American philosopher John Dewey, who emphasized the need for a balance of physical, social, emotional, and intellectual development in young people. Its mission, according to the school's website, is to "engage the imagination and intellect of our students, to guide them toward self-governance and self-knowledge, and to encourage their responsible and caring participation in the world."

Waynflete's mission embodied ideals that had become the family's watchwords. At King, Jonas and Nicole had arrived as strangers and, for the most part, stayed that way for the next two years. But they arrived at Waynflete on the first day of classes having already made friends during Wilderness Week, an outing held every year for incoming students. Chewonki is an environmental education camp on a 400-acre peninsula in Wiscasset, fifty miles north of Portland. The incoming ninth graders canoed, kayaked, played games, and hiked for miles.

"Hi, how are you?" more than one person asked Jonas as he walked down the path to the campsite with a book under his arm. One kid even stopped to ask him what he was reading. It took Jonas a moment to compute what had just happened. At King no one went out of their way to talk to you, unless it was to make fun of you. Jonas had nearly forgotten how to socialize. There had been the harassment in the fifth and sixth grades, then the depression of the seventh and eighth grades, when he and Nicole couldn't tell their friends why they'd moved to Portland. It was tiring keeping secrets, and it had exhausted everyone in the family. Sometimes it had been so hard Jonas didn't want to get out of bed in the morning. Now, all that seemed to vanish. Life didn't feel like a battle anymore.

Nicole's biggest worry was no longer about keeping a secret, but about how to finally share it, now that she and Jonas were in a small, progressive school. She'd forgotten how to talk about herself, something that had always come naturally to her, growing up as an effusive, self-confident child who thought there was nothing unusual about saying she was a boy-girl. But as a teenager, especially after two years of burying her identity, she didn't know how to resurrect it, to let people back in. Nicole desperately wanted to, but she bottled it in, looking for an opening that didn't come until the class was on its way back to Portland. She'd bonded with another girl on one of the first nights at Chewonki when they both broke out in song, singing Lady Gaga's "Bad Romance." So the two sat next to each other for the hour-long bus ride home. Nicole was feeling comfortable; her worries about being at a new school were slowly melting away. There was just this one last hurdle. That was when her new friend told her she was pansexual. Yes! Nicole thought to herself. She smiled and nodded and told the other girl she was transgender.

"Cool."

And that was it. Relief, joy—every good feeling she'd ever had about herself, poured right back in. When classes began the following week, Nicole came out to someone nearly every day. No one had an issue; no one turned away. One classmate did ask her if that meant she was now going to start dressing like a boy. Nicole laughed so hard she almost cried.

CHAPTER 35

First Kiss

WHEN THE NINTH GRADE HAD BARELY BEGUN, NICOLE MADE her first scripted public remarks at the 2011 GLAD Spirit of Justice Award Dinner, where she introduced her father. Standing on a step stool behind a lectern, she wore a sleeveless lavender-patterned chiffon dress with matching scarf around her neck. Confidently, if still a bit shyly, she began to speak to an audience numbering in the hundreds.

My name is Nicole Maines. I am fourteen years old. I would like to introduce you to my amazing family. My twin brother, Jonas, is kind, funny, and one of my strongest supporters. My mom has always encouraged me through everything. And my dad has lobbied with me at the statehouse in Maine and given speeches on my behalf. And we're not even through high school yet, people.

The crowd chuckled. Nicole smiled bashfully.

I am a transgender girl. I was born a boy but I've always known I was a girl. I changed my name and wore my first dress to school

in the fifth grade. I was a little worried what my friends would say,
but they said it was about time.

It was an emotional moment, and while the main honorees that
night were the governor of Massachusetts, Deval Patrick, his wife, and
two daughters, Wayne and Nicole were recognized for their recent activism. The accolades were appreciated, but the family knew they weren't
close to finishing the job. For better or worse, they were all now part of a
public story, one they wouldn't always be able to control. Nicole enjoyed
the attention, but she squirmed at the loss of privacy, and that loss was
connected to her discomfort over dating. How would she know now,
when she met a boy, if he knew her as just Nicole, or as Nicole the transgender teenager in the news? A romance was something she desperately
wanted for herself, but how do you tell a boy you're a girl, and yet different from other girls? That challenge became very real in the middle of
the ninth grade.

The sheriff's office periodically conducted training exercises for law
enforcement in how to respond to a school shooting. For the purposes of
verisimilitude, the Active Shooter program, as it was called, liked to have
teenagers play the parts of school shooting victims. It was a chance to
act. Nicole, of course, volunteered. She'd have preferred to play someone injured so she could at least scream and cry a bit, but a part was a
part, so she was determined to play the best dead body ever.

A few teenagers at the school where the exercise was taking place also
volunteered to be victims. One of them was a boy who attended the
school. When he and Nicole found themselves lying close to each other,
supposedly dead, they couldn't help whispering during the long exercise.
He was cute, Nicole thought. He had romantic eyes, dirty brown hair, and
was very attentive. At one point, they touched hands. Toward the end of
the training, when they were all picking up spent gun cartridges—the
ammunition was blank—the boy leaned into Nicole and gave her a
quick kiss. She was surprised, embarrassed, and delighted all at the same
time, and she probably blushed to her roots. It was thrilling.

Afterward, at a reception for the volunteers, he sought out Nicole. She knew he had no idea she was transgender, and she panicked at the thought of him finding out. She just wanted to go home. While they waited for their rides, they stood with the other student actors outside, chatting. As Kelly pulled up to the school, she noticed Nicole being very animated with a young boy. A sheriff's deputy, whom Kelly knew well, sidled up to the car and told her he'd seen Nicole and a boy exchange a quick kiss.

"They were so cute!" he said.

Kelly frowned. She knew Nicole badly wanted a boyfriend. But any romantic relationships before she made her full physical transition were complicated—especially if it was someone Nicole had just met. All he saw was a beautiful girl.

"What's wrong?" the deputy asked Kelly.

"She's transgender."

"Oh, yeah, that's right."

Just then, Kelly spotted Nicole in the distance, still talking to the young boy, who was snuggling up to her. Nicole looked up and caught Kelly's eye. Her face fell. Both knew what the other was thinking. This boy had no idea who Nicole was and maybe didn't even know what it meant to be transgender. This brief romance wasn't going anywhere.

When Nicole got in the car, she slumped down in the front seat.

Kelly knew it wasn't the right time to ask her anything, so they drove home in silence. Eventually, though, she knocked on Nicole's bedroom door and said she wanted to talk.

"What happened?"

"There was a boy there, and I think he really liked me."

She started to cry.

"What am I going to do?"

"Honey, you're not going to do anything," Kelly said. "You're not going to marry him. But you did just get your first kiss!"

As a child, Nicole wanted more than anything to be seen as a girl and accepted as a girl; it was enough at that age. But all through adolescence, her greatest fear hadn't been about others knowing who she was; it had been about someone not loving her for what she was. Could any boy truly want her, knowing she was transgender? She looked like a girl, she felt like a girl, and she yearned to be kissed like the girl she really was, but what would a boy say if he knew that technically she was not 100 percent female?

A few days later the boy from the training exercise tried to reach Nicole through Facebook. She wasn't at all sure she was ready to share her innermost secrets. With Nicole's agreement, Wayne blocked him.

CHAPTER 36

Small Victories

Two weeks after Nicole lobbied hard against LD 1046, which would have amended Maine's Human Rights Act to remove protections for transgender people, the bill was defeated in both the state senate and house, where more than a dozen Republicans joined the Democrats in voting down the measure. It was a significant victory for Maine but also for the Maines family. So it felt like a kind of bonus when, the following day, a new bill was introduced to the Maine legislature seeking to strengthen the state's anti-bullying laws. At the time, most schools in the state relied on their own individual student conduct policies when it came to harassing behavior. The new legislation sought to turn those policies into one statewide standard. Less than a year later, Paul LePage, Maine's conservative governor, signed the bill into law with overwhelming bipartisan support. Broadly but explicitly defined, bullying was strictly prohibited in every school in the state. Had the law been in place when Jacob, at the insistence of his grandfather, harassed Nicole in the fifth grade, the administrators at Asa C. Adams Elementary School might well have reacted differently.

With the defeat of the proposed public accommodation restrictions and the adoption of stricter standards regarding bullying, the Maines family felt a small sense of vindication. They'd given up their privacy for the cause. They'd been written about in the local press and interviewed on the Maine Public Broadcasting Network, and now LD 1046 was soundly rejected by the state legislature. A transgender blogger announced the victory this way: "Score one for Nicole and the Maine trans community."

The two years of living "stealth" at King had done a lot of harm. Nicole had withdrawn from many social activities, and one of them was sleepovers. She hadn't been on one, or invited kids over for one, since she was eleven years old. From the age of seven, the issue of sleepovers, with girls in pajamas and nightgowns, had been fraught with anxiety for Nicole.

As Wyatt, his girlfriends wanted him to be a part of all their activities, in and out of school, but Kelly and Wayne had known that the parents of those kids might not all be on board. As each sleepover approached, they'd carefully inquire about the parents of the hosting friend. What were their politics, their religion, their values? How open-minded were they? Once Kelly explained the situation—that Wyatt considered himself a girl with boy parts he felt didn't belong to him and never wanted anyone else to see—the majority of parents were fine with it.

Sleepovers may have seemed a minor detail of growing up—games, movies, s'mores, and very little sleep—but Kelly and Wayne had come to realize they were deeply validating for their child. Having to go stealth in middle school essentially ended the sleepovers. They were too risky, and their loss for Nicole further underscored her sense that she was living a lie. Being a girl wasn't just something she was in isolation and at home. It was who she was with others all the time.

So it was a big step in December when Nicole invited a group of girls over to the house and they ate, watched movies, and chattered all night long. Kelly and Wayne didn't mind the lack of sleep because of all the noise. It was happy noise, and as they lay in bed, exhausted and awake, they were happy, too. The next day, as parents arrived to pick up their children, the Maineses quietly thanked them for helping to make the sleepover such a success for Nicole.

A couple of months later, a reporter from *The Boston Globe* contacted the family. She wanted to write a feature about them and everything they'd been through. A page-one article in the Sunday *Boston Globe* meant a whole lot more publicity, but they all agreed the time was right to tell their story. Kelly had had so few resources when she first began trying to figure out what to do for her child. In those early years, she'd had to grope along, finding help and support where she could. There was so much more that other people needed to know. This was a chance to show them what it means to have a transgender child.

The article appeared two weeks before Christmas, 2011, with a huge photograph of Nicole and Jonas sitting side-by-side on the front page, above the fold. The headline read "Led by the Child Who Simply Knew."

It was an unprecedented story for a major American newspaper, and the *Globe* was flooded with calls and emails, the large majority from people moved by the details of the Maineses' journey. Then came a tsunami of media requests. Kelly didn't want her family's life to become a circus. She just needed to buy them some time, she thought to herself, time for both her children to experience life as average teenagers, with all the normal obligations, expectations, dreams, and problems. She wanted to keep them as close to her as possible and give them as much of their childhood as she could, before the world took them away. She'd waited for these children. If she could just hold on to them a little bit longer.

CHAPTER 37

Someone Else's Brother

Just when Nicole seemed to be finding her footing, Jonas appeared to be losing his. If he was not entirely failing, he was certainly floundering. He'd already dropped jazz band, so he picked up lacrosse, but mostly as a bench warmer. He was a strong science student, but he also enjoyed writing poetry and song lyrics. He couldn't exactly put his finger on why he felt angry and depressed, he just knew he felt less and less in control of his emotions. Kelly took him to see a therapist, and over the summer he improved. But with the start of sophomore year, depression and anxiety seemed to paralyze him.

It was hard being Jonas, hard being Nicole's brother—the other child, the other twin, the one without the unusual story. *The Boston Globe* had made Nicole a minor celebrity, and the article was now framed and hanging in Wayne's office at work. In fact, Nicole had received more than a dozen letters from public officials, including Olympia Snowe, U.S. senator from Maine, all congratulating her on her effort to educate the public and advance transgender rights. Sometimes, when the kids came home from school, there was a camera crew or a reporter waiting outside the house wanting to talk to Nicole. It wasn't that Jonas was jealous of his sister. He was proud of her. It's just that an awful lot of the time he felt like a bit player in the theater of his own life. He didn't have his own story—his own narrative. His life revolved around Nicole's.

Wayne and Kelly started to receive invitations to give talks. Kelly, as usual, had no interest in public speaking, but Wayne embraced the role, perhaps in part to make up for all the time he'd spent ashamed, embarrassed, and confused about having a transgender daughter. When Jonas occasionally attended one of his father's talks, he'd watch Wayne get emotional when he spoke about Nicole; as a result, Jonas felt sort of invisible. There was nothing special about his life. No singular talent or achievement. My biggest role, he sometimes said to himself, is being someone else's brother. When things were at their worst, when his thoughts got the better of him, they tended to be a lot more negative, like, If I was gone, everything would still go on without me, as if I'd never existed.

Sometimes Jonas found solace in music, like the Icelandic band called Of Monsters and Men and its song "Little Talks." It was the story of a girl losing her mind and a boy who's known her all his life and who tries to take care of her:

> *Your mind is playing tricks on you, my dear. . . .*
> *Though the truth may vary . . .*

Other times, Jonas tried to channel his despair into his own poetry:

> *There's an evening haze settling over town,*
> *That nest in the old maple tree . . .*

> *None of them are special when looked at from across the plain,*
> *That will never be repeated. . . .*

It wasn't easy for Jonas to talk to either of his parents, but he was more like his mother than his father. Neither he nor Kelly were as verbal as Wayne and Nicole, and both were more on the introverted side. Like

Jonas, Kelly didn't need or want to be in the limelight. And like Kelly, Jonas was steadfast and loyal to a fault. He had his sister's back, and he wanted—needed—to be a part of her life. He just didn't want to always be known as the twin brother of a transgender sister.

Sometimes, of course, it was more than okay being Nicole's brother. In June 2012, Wayne and the twins joined dozens of other activists at the White House to help the Obama administration celebrate LGBT Pride Month. Only Wayne and Nicole had been invited, and when Wayne called to see if he could arrange for two extra tickets, only one was available. There was no way Kelly was going to let Jonas miss out on the experience, so though the whole family went to Washington, D.C., Kelly stayed behind in the hotel the afternoon of the White House event. They'd already toured the city and Kelly had been part of the family's visit to Capitol Hill where they met with officials at the Department of Education and the Department of Justice to talk about transgender issues.

For the twins, the White House event was exhilarating, standing with their father, shoulder to shoulder with other path breakers in the East Room, listening to President Obama:

> After decades of inaction and indifference, you have every reason and right to push, loudly and forcefully, for equality. . . . So we still have a long way to go, but we will get there. We'll get there because of all of you. We'll get there because of all of the ordinary Americans who every day show extraordinary courage. We'll get there because of every man and woman and activist and ally who is moving us forward by the force of their moral arguments, but more importantly, by the force of their example.

All of them were overwhelmed by the event, by seeing and hearing the president in the flesh, and by being invited into one of America's most sacred places. Wayne wished Kelly could have been there, too, but he knew how proud she was—how proud they both were—of their children. Nicole, in particular, was awed by the circumstances. Here she was, barely a teenager, being treated like a celebrity, and really all because she was transgender. She'd lobbied hard for the defeat of the restrictive public accommodation bill, but no harder than many others had. The invitation to the White House would always be part of her personal story, but it was also part of the country's story. She felt as if she were standing in for all transgender kids seeking, and speaking out about, their rights.

When it was time to leave the White House grounds Nicole lingered to take one more photograph. Jonas said, "Dad, should I go get her?" It was always his instinct to shepherd his sister. Wayne and Kelly had asked a lot of their only son, and sometimes they forgot the sacrifices he'd had to make being Nicole's brother. Wayne hugged him and told him how proud he was of him for looking out for Nicole all these years, for worrying about her, and for stepping up whenever and wherever he was needed.

CHAPTER 38

One Step Back

O N A RAINY DAY IN SEPTEMBER 2012, BENNETT KLEIN ARRIVED at the Penobscot Judicial Center in Bangor a half hour early. Superior Court judge William Anderson wasn't scheduled to hear arguments in *Doe v. Clenchy* until nine o'clock, but Klein and Jennifer Levi, both from GLAD, wanted to go over their notes. After a couple of dozen visitors, including the four Maines family members, took their seats in the small courtroom, the judge asked to see both the defendant's and plaintiff's lawyers in his chambers. In a rare move, the *Bangor Daily News* had asked the court if it could videotape the proceedings. Judge Anderson wanted to know if anyone had an objection. No one did.

The case was unusual from the start. When Klein and Levi wrote their court brief they decided to do something neither had ever done—include photos of their client. Referred to as "Susan Doe" in all the legal documents, Nicole never appeared on a witness stand or sat at a counsel's table, because the issue at stake was legal, not personal. This was a suit to decide a question, really two questions, of law: Did a transgender girl have a right in the state of Maine to use the bathroom of her gender identity? And by forcing her to use a unisex bathroom, did the school discriminate against her? Neither Levi nor Klein was sure what judge Anderson knew about "Susan Doe," or, for that matter, what it meant to be transgender. Everything, however, rested on that understanding, so included in the twelve-page statement that opened the plaintiff's brief were six color photographs of Nicole in the fifth and sixth grades.

It was Levi's idea to include the photos, and it was based on an observation she had made years earlier in one of the first transgender discrimination lawsuits she'd litigated. Accompanying Levi that day in court was a legal intern, a woman who eventually would transition to being a man. At the time, the transgender intern looked more masculine than feminine, but was still using a female name. The trans woman Levi was actually representing looked extremely feminine, but she was seated, like Nicole now was, in the gallery. The press that day made a wrong assumption. They identified Levi's legal intern, sitting at the plaintiff's table, as being the transgender woman involved in the case. Appearances, Levi learned, mean everything in transgender litigation. People will call to mind whatever the word means to them. For the media, back then at least, "transgender" meant the masculine-looking woman sitting beside Levi.

Although the Maines family would be sitting in the courtroom to hear the arguments, Levi and Klein knew they couldn't count on the judge recognizing Nicole, so adding photographs to the statement was crucial. The lawyers in the GLAD office in Boston debated long and hard about the choice of pictures, their size, order, and arrangement. Should they lead with the one of Nicole holding the family cat? And if so, how large? They did lead with it, and medium sized. It was a candid shot of Nicole, dressed simply in jeans and a blue blouse, with the family's gray cat in her lap. In the photo she is looking up at the camera with a half smile, her hair spilling over her shoulders. It's a snapshot of a sweet-faced, ordinary nine-year-old girl, except that Nicole wasn't an ordinary nine-year-old girl, and Klein and Levi were able to make both points early and succinctly in their brief. Beneath the photograph with the cat was another picture of Nicole, in the sixth grade, posed outside and wearing a pink top and pink plaid skirt. Under the photo, the statement began with these two sentences:

Susan Doe is a girl. She is also transgender.

Nine words—but those two sentences were the heart of the matter.

Judge Anderson, a balding, avuncular man, was, like most judges, difficult to read, in terms of how he might be leaning. Klein gave the main argument for the plaintiff's side, taking up about fifteen minutes of his allotted time. This was the second case he'd litigated in Bangor. Fourteen years earlier, he had been a senior attorney in the case of *Bragdon v. Abbott*, representing a woman with HIV who was denied dental care because of the dentist's written policy of refusing to treat anyone with AIDS. Klein took the case all the way to the U.S. Supreme Court, where he prevailed in an historic 1998 victory that established protections against discrimination for people with HIV and AIDS under the Americans with Disabilities Act.

During Klein's argument in *Doe v. Clenchy*, Anderson appropriately interrupted him with questions, but none that gave any indication as to how he would eventually rule. Barely two hours later, the proceedings had concluded and the courtroom was adjourned. It was unclear when a decision would be rendered or announced, since it depended on several things, including how complicated the case was, and how busy the judge. Six months was about average, and that's what Klein and Levi hoped for. This would be an important ruling, but both lawyers knew it would not be the last. No matter who won, there would be an appeal to the state supreme court, which would have the final say on the matter.

Levi didn't know if it was an omen or not, but earlier that morning, she'd noticed a familiar face on the front page of the *Bangor Daily News*: Bob Lucy, the acting principal at Asa Adams who had forbidden Nicole from using the girls' restroom after she was harassed by Paul Melanson's grandson. Lucy was in the news because the Bangor paper had found out he'd allowed some students at Orono Middle School, where he was principal both before and after he temporarily took over the same job at Asa Adams, to change answers on a standardized exam after the allotted time was up. When the Orono school district found out, it eliminated his position. He had recently accepted a job as assistant superintendent for the Bangor School Department, but when Bangor got wind of the controversy, it promptly launched its own investigation. Ultimately, in March 2013, Lucy resigned from the district.

The Maineses and the GLAD lawyers didn't have to wait six months. Two months after Judge Anderson listened to the arguments of both sides in *Doe v. Clenchy*, his decision was announced. The Orono school system, he ruled, had not violated Maine's Human Rights Act when it prohibited Nicole from using the restroom that matched her gender identity.

"The court is not unsympathetic to [the girl's] plight, or that of her parents," the judge wrote in his twenty-six page opinion.

> It is no doubt a difficult thing to grow up transgender in today's society. This is a sad truth, which cannot be completely prevented by the law alone. The law casts a broad stroke where one more delicate and refined is needed. . . . Our Maine Human Rights Act only holds a school accountable for deliberate indifference to known, severe and pervasive student-on-student harassment. It does no more.

Anderson concluded the school neither harassed Nicole by its action nor was deliberately indifferent to the harassment she experienced from Jacob. Anderson granted the school district summary judgment. It was a victory for the Orono board of education and Kelly Clenchy. Wayne and Kelly felt crushed, but they mostly worried that Nicole and Jonas might hear about the loss from a reporter before they heard it from them. Wayne told his boss he needed to leave work early, then drove two and a half hours to Portland. Speeding down the interstate, he wondered how he was going to break it to his kids—that after five years of the family's work, sacrifice, and worry, a judge had said the school had done nothing wrong, that it was Nicole's problem. He thought of all the people who had helped them in the past, especially Lisa Erhardt, the school counselor at Asa Adams, who had been Kelly's confidante and adviser and with whom Wayne was occasionally still in touch.

When Nicole and Jonas were given the bad news, they were disappointed but then asked, "What's the next step?" They didn't want the fight to end there, and Kelly reassured them it would not. Klein and Levi and the other lawyers had all said they'd immediately appeal to the state supreme court. Win or lose there, though, that would be it. That was fine with the family. They'd been on this ride so long and there had been so many ups and downs. If it meant another few months to possibly turn things around, it would be well worth the wait.

In April 2012, Wayne and Nicole visited a satellite campus of the University of Maine in the coastal town of Machias, the site of an annual LGBT youth and allies conference. The highlight every year was the Rainbow Ball, when scores of gay and transgender kids dressed up for a raucous night of dancing. Sometimes they even dressed as their favorite superheroes. The kids slept in campus dormitories, with chaperones in adjoining rooms. Wayne didn't get a wink of sleep. Instead, he found himself continually amazed at the diversity around him. He'd met gay people in college but he'd never really gotten to know them. Right next door, talking and laughing all night long, were gay boys, trans girls, trans boys—some of them Wayne had no idea what their gender was, but none of it seemed to matter, least of all to them. That's what struck Wayne. Everyone was different and no one cared how or why. Some, like Nicole, watched anime on Wayne's laptop; others ate pizza.

For so long Wayne had tried to analyze kids, including his own child, looking for the right descriptions, the right terms, to explain it all, but here in Machias, in this dormitory suite, he finally gave up. It didn't matter to these kids whether someone was called gay, transgender, genderqueer or whatever, so why should it matter to him? He remembered a year earlier all the people he'd met at a transgender conference in Albany where he was giving his first major keynote address. Wayne met so many attendees just sitting in the lobby working on his speech. One night he went out for dinner and drinks with two transgender couples—four women—and spent two hours talking with them. At the end of the conference one of the women he'd been out to dinner with approached him and said, "I have to tell you this, Wayne. When we first saw you, I said that man is the best put together trans man at the conference."

It was quite the compliment, and Wayne was both amused and moved. He'd spent a lifetime developing his communication skills through safety training, but he hadn't really taken those lessons to heart, certainly not with his wife or his kids. He'd learned more about connecting with people deeply and honestly at that Albany conference than he had in any of his thousands of hours of safety training. For some reason, he knew these kids in the dorm, and the whole LGBT community they represented, had his back. It's all about who you can count on, he thought to himself. He had not been that person for Kelly in the beginning, but Kelly had been that person for Nicole. Thank God for that. Now, Wayne knew he needed to be that person, too.

IN EARLY AUGUST 2013, Wayne found something Nicole had written on her Facebook page:

> Just watched an episode of Family Guy where Brian had sex with a trans person and when he finds out he screams and pukes everywhere. And then I think: forever alone.

Three people "liked" her post. Other friends commented:

> Transphobia in television is utterly appalling. I was just starting to enjoy Ace Ventura when I discovered the highly insensitive

transphobic scene (much like the family guy episode), and I got really mad.

Eh . . . its a show that appeals to the mass of functional morons out there . . . your future holds bigger n better . . . where there is love, attracts love . . . I have no worries I'll be invited to your wedding one day.

Wayne's heart bled. He knew there was no such thing as total protection from insults and ignorance, no way to insulate a child from, or fend off, every odd look, insensitive comment, or slur. He needed to let Nicole know he understood, so he posted his own comment on her Facebook page:

To my beautiful daughter, I love you with all my heart. My life mission is to protect you from harm and to help you grow. I worry about you every day, but I have seldom worried that you will be alone. You have never been alone. You are admired by so many. You are beautiful, amazingly smart, strong beyond your years and funny. I know that someday someone will take you away from me. I say someday because I am not ready for you to grow up.

CHAPTER 39

Imagine

KEEPER OF THE HOUSE

> *I remember back to the warm summer afternoon.*
> *In the massive forest that I called my backyard.*
> *It seemed so huge, unthinkably huge*
> *Perhaps because I was so small.*
> *I remember the acres being painted with light and*
> *Infinite shades of greens and yellows.*
>
> *My father would stand among a pile of stumps and logs,*
> *The crisp smell of sawdust still lingered.*
> *His grey sweatshirt decorated with wood-chips and paint.*
> *His hands were scraped at the knuckles, and the sun*
> *Bore down on his neck, leaving a bruise of red heat.*
>
> —Jonas

KELLY AND WAYNE CONTINUED TO BE AMAZED AT THE PACE OF maturity in Jonas after a difficult period of emotional highs and lows.

Yes, he'd spent nearly the entire previous year holed up in his bedroom, reading, listening to music, or playing his guitar, but he was slowly coming out of his teenage shell. During the summer after his freshman year of high school, he took four weeks of college-level classes in ocean studies, won a poetry contest, and was part of the school's winning Model United Nations team. Jonas had become a deeply reflective person. He loved and respected his parents for all their hard work, but he wondered how it all added up. He knew he wanted his own life to mean something substantial, and he couldn't yet see that meaning in having a wife or raising children or working at some job every day. Instead, he was in love with big ideas and exploration, and had a yearning to travel. His life to this point had been largely circumscribed by the travails of his sister, and he was just now beginning to feel the contours of his own individual being.

In May 2014, Jonas wrote a short story about the former gangster Legs Diamond, imagining him confronting his own mortality. In it, Diamond sits and talks with the character of Death, who can't take his eyes off the Depression-era thug. But when Diamond asks what his life meant, Death is not at all obliging.

> People, nowadays, always expect others to solve their problems and answer their questions. It's juvenile. . . . Who would know more about your life's ultimate meaning than you? Think about it. Every choice you make, every thought that runs through your head, they are all yours. Every instant of your life is determined by you.

So much of life is unpredictable—Jonas, like Nicole, Kelly, and Wayne, knew that all too well—and everything is earned. Meaning was something to be sought, struggled with, fought for, and ultimately found. And it was precious.

When Wayne was asked to be a keynote speaker for a Civil Rights Day program at Memorial Middle School in South Portland, he asked

Jonas if he wanted to come along as his "roadie." Jonas looked sharp in a tie, and as he set up his father's laptop for the PowerPoint presentation, he couldn't help noticing a gaggle of girls loitering nearby. They were actually Googling his name on their smartphones. It was flattering. Wayne spoke for half an hour, then took questions from the students. One girl raised her hand.

"Can we ask your son some questions?" she asked.

"If he wants to, that's fine with me," Wayne answered.

Normally Jonas didn't like taking part in these presentations. He was entirely supportive of Nicole, but like his mother, public speaking wasn't his thing. Nonetheless, he politely obliged.

"What was it like growing up with a transgender sister?" the girl asked.

Jonas took a moment to reflect.

"Imagine," he said, "what it's like for kids, teachers, adults asking you about your sister being transgender and you're trying to explain it all with a sixth-grade vocabulary."

Wayne was struck by Jonas's self-awareness, his ability to parse an experience so finely, to see it and understand it so acutely. It was uncanny. Jonas had a preternatural ability to understand not only his own mind, but the thoughts and feelings of others. He was exquisitely sensitive in that way, which is perhaps why it was inevitable he would rediscover acting. It had been one of his and Nicole's chief pastimes as children. Nicole loved being on a stage, the center of attention. Jonas, though, shied away from school theatricals, especially after the sixth grade. That's when he'd landed the lead in *Charlie and the Chocolate Factory*, but he'd messed up, fooling around onstage during a performance. Wayne had been so embarrassed by his son's behavior that night he apologized to the play's director. Jonas couldn't explain why he'd been disruptive. Maybe he just wasn't ready for the responsibility or public attention. Whatever it was, he swore off theater.

Now he was feeling different, more confident, and he auditioned and won roles in productions each year at Waynflete, both comedy and drama. He played Reverend Hale in Arthur Miller's *The Crucible* and Vice Principal Douglas Panch in the musical *The 25th Annual Putnam County Spelling Bee.* He was one of the two stars in Tom Stoppard's *Rosencrantz and Guildenstern Are Dead* and played the part of Will Shakespeare in William Gibson's *A Cry of Players.* He loved the language, he loved moving an audience, but above all he loved the storytelling, immersing himself in a role. It was, in some ways, the best kind of therapy for a kid whose biggest role in life so far had been being someone else's brother. All the major events in Jonas's life had been framed by Nicole's experiences, but onstage, as part of an ensemble, *he* defined the experience. He was in control. "Theater works for me," he liked to say.

ON JUNE 12, 2013, Jennifer Levi, representing the Maines family, argued the appeal of the Superior Court's summary judgment in front of Maine's Supreme Judicial Court, referred to as the Law Court in its appellate role. She'd driven up from western Massachusetts in her Nissan hybrid the day before, which was a good thing because it was cold, windy, and rainy the morning of the hearing—the same weather she and Ben Klein had encountered in Bangor nine months earlier. They hoped their luck would be better this time. It was Levi's turn to make the argument before six justices of the Law Court—the seventh had recused himself for unknown reasons. Levi wasn't used to arguing a lot of cases because her work is so specialized. As a transgender rights lawyer, she covered a wide range of issues, from healthcare access to employment discrimination to rejection of bank loan applications, but it wasn't often that those cases made it to court. This was different. Only one other bathroom accommodation discrimination case involving a transgender person had ever reached a state supreme court, in Minnesota in 2001, and the plaintiff lost. If Levi and Klein prevailed, they would set a precedent.

When she opened her bright yellow legal folder to begin her argument, Levi looked over her typewritten, highlighted list of facts taped to the left side of the folder, and, taped to the right side, questions she anticipated the judges might ask. She'd spent more than a thousand hours on this case and had made countless trips to Maine to visit the family. She'd even researched the biographies of each of the judges, hoping to gain an insight or an edge. Levi wanted to make sure the judges understood that Nicole had been forced to use a separate restroom and that even the school's own staff had deemed the boys' restroom inappropriate for her. Most of all, it was important for the court to see Nicole as the girl she was.

Levi and a member of the Maine Human Rights Commission spoke first. Then the defendant's attorneys. There were questions from the judges as well as rebuttals by both sides. After the hearing, Levi told the media, "We have a strong case here of a young girl trying to go to school and learn, and the school failing to protect her. I feel confident that we got a fair hearing from the court, and I look forward to their decision." Outside the courthouse, in a driving rain and standing next to her parents and brother, Nicole spoke to the press as well:

> I want all transgender kids to be able to go to school and not have to worry about being treated unfairly or bullied. I've been very lucky to have a family that's stood by me and stuck up for me, and I'm really grateful for them.

On August 12, 2013, California's governor Jerry Brown signed into law AB 1266, and in doing so, broke new ground as California became the first state to establish a law aligning bathroom use not with sexual anatomy but with gender identity.

> A pupil shall be permitted to participate in sex-segregated school programs and activities, including athletic teams and competitions, and use facilities consistent with his or her gender identity, irrespective of the gender listed on the pupil's records.

Brown's signature came after months of public controversy and attempts by various conservative and right-wing religious groups to stop the bill's passage. Even afterward, one of them, Privacy for All, launched a petition drive to repeal the legislation, writing on its website that it was wrong to use

> laws to frustrate and deny great natural and moral truths. One such truth is that men and women offer unique and complementary contributions to human flourishing. Society is better served when those contributions are encouraged, not when the uniqueness of being male and being female are stripped from societal norms and we're guided into a genderless future.

One vocal opponent of California's AB 1266, as well as other state and federal attempts to expand civil rights protections to transgender people, was Brandon McGinley, the field director of the western region for the Pennsylvania Family Institute. In October 2013, he argued in an online essay that relying on "disgust, discomfort, or another visceral reaction to carry the day in opposing such progressive legislative innovations" was a fool's errand.

> We could affirm that gender is distinct from sex, and even that its contours are complex, fluid, and partially socially-construed, without affirming the radical view that our biology is irrelevant to our gender. . . .
> We need not go into detail to observe that men and women have different experiences in restrooms, locker rooms, and other sex-segregated places because of the differences in their anatomy. Separating the sexes in these facilities allows for distinct physical accommodations proper to the needs of men and women, but more importantly it allows for camaraderie among those who share the whole life experience of manhood or womanhood— among those who are the same.

For Kelly, Wayne, Nicole, and Jonas, the theory simply made no sense. They argued that the female experience, the "life experience of manhood or womanhood," was exactly what had been denied to Nicole by Orono Middle School. Using the girls' restroom, combing her hair, and gossiping with friends: These seemed like small things, but they were all a part of being a teenage girl and *that's* what was being denied to Nicole. She didn't want a genderless society; she just wanted to be recognized for the gender she knew she was, the one that allowed her to have all the same experiences of being female that other teens girls enjoyed. No one could argue that equal rights for all religions would result in a religionless society. It was about the law, and the law should be blind to differences when it comes to handing out rights and privileges. The experience of who we are is a celebration of what makes us human, and one of those experiences is being male or female—or something in between.

CHAPTER FORTY

Our Story

THINGS THAT I'D LIKE TO SEE HAPPEN

September (2013)—Start eleventh grade
October—Turn 16
2014:
September—Start twelfth grade
2015:
GRADUATE!!!
turn 18
Be accepted into a fantastic Acting school
Have [sex reassignment] surgery
2018:
Turn 21 and party hard!
2019:
Graduate from College with a masters degree in acting . . .
    move to the west coast to better my acting career . . .
    buy a pretty house.
2020–2030:
Find someone who loves me and get married

—Nicole's journal, 2012

THE MAINESES WERE AN AVERAGE, MIDDLE-CLASS FAMILY—AND AT
the same time they were not. They were acting as they believed families
should. They loved and supported one another. And Wayne and Kelly
did everything they could so that their children would flourish and live
long, productive lives.

In December 2013, Wayne decided to send out the family Christmas
card with a letter inside for the first time since 2006. He'd given up
shortly before Wyatt became Nicole, at a time when he couldn't face the
fact that his child was transgender. When he announced his intention to
Kelly, she simply laughed and said, "Have fun!" He did.

Nicole has had a very full year and is growing into a beautiful
young lady who is still interested in the Performing Arts, video
games and civil rights work. She was in *Cinderella* and *The Crucible* at Waynflete. She again spent time volunteering at Equality-
Maine and watched our state become the first state to bring
marriage equality to our friends by popular vote.

Jonas is a tad taller than Dad, has a size 12 shoe and is typically impeccably dressed, just like his dad (NOT). He was a
member of the Model United Nations Team that competed at
Harvard, a member of the Mock Trial Team and he also joined
the Performing Arts Club this year. He also played "Reverend
Hale" in *The Crucible*.

He still loves history and was also selected to represent Waynflete in the state poetry contest. He continues to play the guitar
and keyboard and drive his sister nuts! He was a guest performer
at "Open Mic Night" in Orono this summer.

Kelly had a very busy year at work, solving problems, developing new partnerships for the Sheriff's Office, while taking on
many new duties. Of course the rest of the time she was keeping
track of, organizing and driving the kids to their many events.

It is still a big challenge for us to find time together. Living in two towns is not easy. . . . Outside of work I continue to teach others about transgender youth and how to support equal rights. Every time I speak I can see that I am breaking down barriers that have existed for generations. It is always emotional and often healing. Our story is a good story and hearing it in person is a powerful tool.

ON THURSDAY MORNING, JANUARY 30, 2014, shortly before noon, Wayne picked up the phone at work. It was someone from GLAD, and she had a message: "You won!"

"What are you talking about?" Wayne, not sure who was on the other end of the line, was confused.

"You won and we want you to go to Portland right away!"

Then it clicked. Wayne was nearly speechless and as soon as he hung up he called Kelly to confirm it wasn't all a joke—or a dream.

"We won?" he asked her. "Are you sure? I don't believe it."

Kelly had just gotten off the phone with GLAD, too, and she'd already texted the news to Nicole and Jonas. At that moment both of them were sitting in the school auditorium at an assembly, and Nicole didn't hesitate when she saw the exclamation points on her phone: She dashed to the front of the auditorium and shouted out the news to the whole school.

"Everyone was clapping!" Nicole texted excitedly back to her mother and father.

Wayne excused himself from work and drove eighty miles an hour down the highway to Portland. It would take him longer than the usual two and a half hours, because he had to stop a couple of times to do phone interviews.

"This is a momentous decision," Michael Silverman of the Transgender Legal Defense and Education Fund said in a press release. "It sends a message to transgender students that their lives are valuable, that their education needs are important, and that schools have to provide them with equal educational opportunities," attorney Jennifer Levi said.

The opposing counsel said the Orono school district would take every step to comply with the law, and that the court "provided helpful guidance about how to handle this issue that is becoming more and more common in schools around the state and the country."

As Wayne pulled up to the house he was met by a TV crew and asked to make a statement.

"I haven't even talked to my wife yet!" he told them. "As parents, all we've ever wanted is for Nicole and her brother, Jonas, to get a good education and to be treated just like their classmates, and that didn't happen for Nicole. What happened to my daughter was extremely painful for her and our whole family, but we can now close this very difficult chapter in our lives. We are very happy knowing that because of this ruling, no other transgender child in Maine will have to endure what Nicole experienced."

In other parts of Maine there was consternation. Michael Heath had resigned his top position at the Christian Civic League in 2009. Later he would write that others in the organization thought he'd become too "radioactive," too opinionated about fighting homosexuality and what he referred to as transgenderism. In 2012, as the head of Helping Hands Ministries, Heath wrote on his blog that others at the league had questioned his "relentless advocacy to keep the 'gay' fight as the League's number one priority," which is why after leaving the league he turned his attention full-time to sexual orientation and transgender issues. In 2013, he wrote on his blog that he was continuing to try to hold back the "pro-sodomy" movement, because the "vile tide of perversion which these forces unleashed is now at a high-water mark, as sodomy and transgenderism have encroached on every institution in our state, in particular our public schools."

When Paul Melanson heard the Supreme Court had decided against the Orono public school district, he was philosophical. He knew there'd be more fights about other issues, and he was determined to keep speaking his mind. That's all he could do, win or lose, and he would keep doing it no matter what.

As for Melanson's grandson Jacob, the legal fight had receded from his life after the sixth grade when he moved back to live with his mother in the town of Gilead. She worked as a hostess at a local restaurant, and he hoped to get a job in the metals trade, perhaps someday become a welder. When he thought about the case—and he didn't much—it wasn't about rights or bathroom politics or, frankly, even Nicole. He still believed it was wrong for someone born a boy to "pretend" he was a girl, but he did wonder what it was like for Jonas. He knew Jonas didn't like him, but Jonas was the only person involved in the whole thing he could really understand. Jonas was a boy just like him. He knew who he was and was happy being male. What must it have been like, Jacob wondered, to be the brother of a transgender twin? He barely knew his own brothers, and he wondered if it had disappointed Jonas that Wyatt had become Nicole, that his brother had become his sister. It hadn't, of course. Jonas was very clear about that.

"I never had a brother," he once said to Nicole. "You were always a sister to me."

IV

Breaking Barriers

Stories are about the dropped stitch. About what happens when the pattern breaks. . . . Why is this moment different? What has changed? And why now? . . . They mark the turning points of our lives.

—DANI SHAPIRO

CHAPTER 41

Commencement

In March 2015, seven years after Kelly and Wayne had urged Orono Middle School to do the right thing, a school board in Millinocket, Maine, about an hour north of Orono, announced the creation of a transgender student policy. The Maines case had forced school systems all over the state, indeed all over the country, to examine their rules and regulations to ensure they wouldn't be legally liable in the way the Orono school district had been found to be. The four pages of new policy recommendations were written in direct response to the court order that enjoined the Orono School Department from discriminating against transgender students.

Under "Purpose," the document stated that the new guidelines were meant to "foster a learning environment that is safe and free from discrimination, harassment, and bullying" and "to assist the educational and social integration of transgender students" in the schools. Two important items were also addressed in the Millinocket memorandum:

Restrooms:

A student who has been identified as transgender under these guidelines should be permitted to use the restroom assigned to the gender which the student consistently asserts at school.

Locker rooms:

The use of locker rooms requires schools to consider a number of factors, including but not necessarily limited to the safety and comfort of students; the transgender student's preference; student privacy; the ages of students; and available facilities. As a general rule, transgender students will be permitted to use the locker room assigned to the gender which the student consistently asserts at school. A transgender student will not be required to use a locker room that conflicts with the gender identity consistently asserted at school.

When the *Bangor Daily News* ran the story about Millinocket's response to the Maineses' state Supreme Court victory, many of the online comments were surprisingly unsympathetic.

They didn't discriminate in Orono. They said they didn't know what to do . . . so they provided a faculty bathroom. Those poor administrators in Orono getting a bad rap over this.

This is oh so wrong.

My kids better never have an opposite sex in their restroom. I've told my daughter if you see an Adam's apple, scream and keep screaming. She knows how.

At nearly the same time as the Millinocket debate, Boston University School of Medicine released the results of the first comprehensive review of the scientific evidence regarding gender identity as a biological phenomenon, and concluded, according to one of the authors of the report, that it provides:

> one of the most convincing arguments to date for all medical pro-
> viders to gain the transgender medicine skills necessary to provide
> good care for these individuals. . . . Clinical experience with
> treatment of transgender persons has clearly demonstrated that
> the best outcomes for these individuals are achieved with their
> requested hormone therapy and surgical sexual transition as op-
> posed to psychiatric intervention alone.

In a March letter to Nicole, the University of Maine, whose insurance is managed by Cigna, begged to differ.

> After reviewing the information we have, we determined we
> cannot approve this request. . . . We found the service requested
> is not a covered benefit.

In other words, Nicole's sex reassignment surgery was considered cosmetic, and therefore not a medical or health necessity. Wayne and Kelly
were not entirely surprised. Cigna had approved sex reassignment surgery
and other transgender medical procedures in December 2014, but the
University of Maine's health management system had not adopted them.
Still, after all they'd been through, to be told that Nicole's final transition
was cosmetic was laughable. Wayne and GLAD talked to the University
of Maine management team, and Wayne submitted a second appeal. It
worked. A little more than two months later, the University of Maine
made a complete reversal—and not just for Nicole, but for all its health
insurance beneficiaries. It was yet another battle won by the Maineses,
and in the process they smoothed the way for others who would follow.
That night Wayne wrote to Jennifer Levi about the family's sense of relief. "I don't know about you, but we needed a break from the battlefield."

244 AMY ELLIS NUTT

———

IN THE SPRING OF 2015, high school was coming to an end for both Nicole and Jonas. They'd been accepted into colleges, with Jonas opting to study theater and psychology at the University of Maine in Farmington and Nicole pursuing theater and art at the University of Maine in Orono. Wayne and Kelly would get a break on tuition because Nicole and Jonas were the children of a university staff member. Instead of the $10,000 in-state tuition for each, for the year, the family would pay half that.

By the time the twins graduated from Waynflete, Wayne and Kelly had laid out nearly $120,000 dollars for their four years at the private academy. Without scholarships from the school, it would have been twice that much. To save more money, for the twins' senior year Wayne once again downsized his living situation, moving from his graduate student housing to Orono's Wilson Center, a nondenominational church, which, much like a mini YMCA, provided rooms for renters. At $450 a month, it nearly cut in half Wayne's rent for his student apartment. He also had the advantage of belonging to a community. On Wednesday evenings, dinner was free and everyone pitched in to cook. On Monday there was meditation and yoga; on Tuesdays the Quakers held services. Wayne took pleasure in being an all-around handyman and was quick to befriend the two students with whom he shared close living quarters, an engineer from China and a sociology major from New Jersey. Wayne had enough room for a sectional couch, a bed, and a small refrigerator. There were shared shower facilities. "It's like living in a tiny frat house," he told visitors. "A co-ed frat house."

At the beginning of the year, Wayne received an email from a transgender staff person at the Los Angeles offices of GLAAD, formerly the Gay and Lesbian Alliance Against Defamation (and distinct from GLAD, the organization that had represented the family in their legal battle). The GLAAD staff person had an offer for Nicole: Would she be interested in auditioning for the guest role of a transgender teen in an upcoming episode of *Royal Pains*, an hour-long series on the USA Network? The show follows the character of Hank Lawson, a reluctant "doctor for hire" to the rich and famous of Long Island's Hamptons. In May, after her second callback, Nicole was offered the part.

The following month, Wayne drove his daughter down to New York for a week of rehearsals and taping. USA Network provided a limo every day to take them from their Manhattan hotel to the set. On the second day of shooting, their driver chatted about how he'd twice voted for Obama as president but was now a Republican. When Wayne asked why, he said, "They're even screwing up college mascots." Wayne asked what he was referring to and the driver told him that he'd just heard that Rutgers University in New Jersey announced it was going to try and create different versions of its mascot: the Scarlet Knight.

"They want a transgender mascot!" the driver said.

Wayne and Nicole immediately turned to each other and smiled. When they got back to the hotel room, they said, "What the hell was that all about? And what's a transgender scarlet knight, anyway?" Transgender was the theme of the day. Toward the end of the week the driver asked Nicole about her role on the show. When she told him she was playing the part of a transgender student and that she herself was transgender, the driver seemed surprised and embarrassed, but Wayne engaged him in more discussion. He told the man that being transgender was a medical condition and that transgender rights weren't about being a Democrat or a Republican. They were about being true to yourself.

Sometime after the sixth grade, Nicole wrote a poem called "Disequality." It expressed sadness, frustration—and defiance.

> *What do you call a girl with a head*
> *who regrets what she heard that equality said?*
> *That you deserve the same*
> *as your peers without blame?*
>
> *Feeling the townspeople's stares can't even compare*
> *to being watched by the dogs whose eyes are aflair.*

Waiting for you to slip
for you to make one wrong move,
when their brains may flip
and their screams disapprove.

They have you sit alone,
away from friends
in hopes that your difference will come to an end.
What do you call a girl with a head
who regrets what she heard that equality said?
That you deserve the same as your peers without blame?

You call her Nicole.
And her difference makes her whole.

Before Nicole could express herself, before she was able to claim her own identity, Kelly had to do it for her. Wayne liked to say that the most important thing parents can do is make sure they have confidence in themselves. Only then can they give their children what they need without fear of what others might think. It had taken Wayne a long time to attain that confidence. For some reason, Kelly had always had it. There were self-doubts, of course—how could there not have been, especially when she had to piece together her own lesson plan on how to raise a transgender child? She and Wayne had sacrificed so much just to keep their kids safe. It was never easy. It was often painful. Kelly had set aside so much in her life. She'd pushed her love of painting into the background to raise two kids virtually alone. Wayne had missed much of the twins' childhoods. And yet he'd be the first to say it had all been worth it.

Kelly knew that, too, although she sometimes felt she had to apologize to Jonas and Nicole. With all the worries, the planning, and the self-educating, she hadn't had much time to actually play with her children as they were growing up. "I'm sorry if it hasn't been much fun," she sometimes said to the twins, but Jonas and Nicole would have none of it. This was how it was supposed to be. Jonas told his mother and father it would be cool if someday someone said, "Hey, have you heard about the transgender person?" and the response would simply be, "Yeah, so what?" It should just be a normal thing, he said, the way it had always been for him growing up. He'd always seen his brother as his sister. It just took a while for everyone else.

In the first week of June 2015, Nicole and Jonas took part in their last high school prom. Nicole's date was Alex, a boy she'd met at an anime convention in Portland the year before, and with whom she'd been keeping in touch mostly through email since his home was about an hour away. He was a year ahead of Nicole in school, a rising sophomore at the University of Maine in Orono, where he was studying computer science. Jonas was between girlfriends, so his date was a close friend of both his and Nicole's.

It was a warm night under a full June strawberry moon. Nicole wore a formal black gown and four-inch high heels, and along with Jonas and his date and their friend Austin and his boyfriend, they all piled into a rented limo for the trip to the Falmouth Country Club, ten miles north of Portland. It was a big step up from their freshman year prom, held at a local church. At the country club, the Waynflete seniors danced under white tents and colorful strobe lights to the music of a DJ. It was romantic, much like a wedding, and nearly perfect. When the limo dropped them all off at Austin's house at the end of the night everyone was so exhausted they collapsed on various couches, fully dressed, and didn't stir till dawn.

A week later, Waynflete held its 117th commencement. Jonas Zebediah Maines and Nicole Amber Maines were among the sixty-eight graduates who received diplomas and congratulations from the president of the board of trustees, the head of the school, and the director of the upper school. Jonas strode confidently across the stage in a tie and blue blazer that was a half size too small, then promptly bear-hugged each school official in turn, with the audience laughing in approval and the head of the school shrugging his shoulders in amusement. Next, Nicole, in a short white dress and tan high heels, skipped across the stage, curtsied ever so slightly to the three school officials, then, just as she was about to descend the steps of the stage, struck a pose: hands on hips, one leg bent behind her, head tossed back. They were identical twins, they were brother and sister, and they were, each of them, unmistakably their own person.

Watching from the audience, Kelly couldn't quite believe any of it. It had taken so long to get here, and yet it had all gone so fast. After all those hours encouraging her kids to study, she still couldn't believe they'd gotten all their work in on time. If it was possible—and she'd never thought so in the past—she was going to miss the "old times," but since she was someone who was also always looking ahead, she couldn't wait to see what her children would do with their futures.

As usual, Wayne tried not to cry. He kept thinking about the decision to send the kids to Waynflete, the worry over how they were ever going to pay for it, his doubts about why they even needed to attend a private school, a place that seemed so foreign to what he and Kelly had known growing up. If they hadn't felt pushed into a corner by the dismal experience of King Middle School and the lottery split decision at Casco Bay, or if the decision had been his alone, he'd probably not have opted to send his kids to Waynflete. And he would have been so wrong.

Wayne knew he could teach Jonas and Nicole only so much—how to skin a moose, track a deer, maybe even play poker. He hoped he'd been able to pass on his and Kelly's work ethic and their strong survival instincts, maybe even a bit of his own penchant for storytelling. But he knew Waynflete had exposed his kids to much more than he and Kelly had ever experienced as teenagers. A lot of people had helped them to get to this place, from schoolteachers and doctors to lawyers, activists, and politicians, friends, and family. Lisa Erhardt, the school counselor at Asa Adams, even sent the twins graduation presents.

Jonas and Nicole were ready for college. All on his own, Jonas had even won a major acting scholarship by performing a monologue from *Macbeth*, a part he'd never played onstage. When Jonas hugged the dean of the school, Wayne finally let the tears flow. It was the old Jonas, the happy, funny, clever child. And Nicole, mincing across the stage and striking that pose—yes, she was sassy, and she'd done exactly what he'd expected her to do, totally engaging in the moment and having fun with it. He hoped he and Kelly had provided the right foundation. He also hoped all the scars wouldn't impede their ability to flourish. He didn't think they would, and he knew a lot of the reason was Kelly. They'd learned so much from her, about honesty, the power of self-confidence, and the importance of standing up for their beliefs. As Jonas and Nicole sat back down with their diplomas in hand, Wayne thought again about how much his wife had done to get them to this place, this exact spot. They were all going to be okay.

The philosopher Charles Taylor once wrote:

Each of us has an original way of being human: Each person has his or her own "measure." . . . There is a certain way of being human that is *my* way. I am called upon to live my life in this way, and not in imitation of anyone else's life. But this gives a new importance to being true to myself. If I am not, I miss the point of my life; I miss what being human is for *me*.

No one could accuse the Maines family of missing what it meant to be human. And they were certainly living in imitation of no one. But for Nicole, there was at least one more step, one more task to complete so that she, too, could claim her most authentic self. Wayne had spent most of Nicole's life trying not to think about the surgery, the final procedure that would take away the last physical reminders of the gender that never belonged to her. He thought about all those male bonding memories from his youth.

He remembered in particular the black bear hunt on Montague Island off the coast of Alaska he'd made with several of his buddies. One of them had a motor home, and they'd driven it four hundred miles from Fairbanks to Valdez, drinking, playing cards, and talking about hunting.

Somewhere on a mountain pass outside Valdez they needed a bathroom break, but with no facility for miles, they simply pulled over. There, all six men lined up, a heavy snow falling, to relieve themselves by the side of the road. Wayne actually stepped back and took a quick photo of the scene: five friends, standing in the headlights, in the middle of the Alaskan wilderness, with their "manhood" hanging out. He'd thought of that photo as the ultimate male bonding picture. That was something he'd wanted for Wyatt and he'd given up on for Nicole, and it hadn't been easy. Then he thought about how far he'd come, how far the world had come, in just a few years. In half a lifetime, really.

Nicole and Jonas hadn't even lived a quarter of their own lives yet. It was all still too close for them. The memories they'd already laid away were for events that had barely passed. In the confusion and sometimes chaos of the past few years, none of them had had much time to be reflective, but a year or so earlier they'd all had the chance to do it, together, on a long afternoon.

The family had been contacted by StoryCorps, the oral history project that records the conversations and memories of ordinary people. Some of those stories are highlighted on National Public Radio's *Morning Edition*. The producers of StoryCorps had heard about the Maineses' unusual journey and wondered if they could come up to Portland to record the family interviewing one another. Kelly and Wayne liked the idea of their voices being held in perpetuity in the archives of the Library of Congress, so they agreed. The StoryCorps staff lugged their recording equipment to Portland, and the family sat down for several hours. Kelly and Wayne interviewed each other, then Nicole and her father, then Nicole and Jonas. Prompted by the facilitator to ask certain questions, Jonas asked Nicole where she saw herself in ten years. She said, hopefully in acting school, but also visiting Jonas and going to his wedding.

"Your wife will throw the bouquet and I'll plow down several people trying to catch it," she said. "I see myself probably still single. Probably working my hardest to get my acting career going."

Jonas probed some more. "Obviously being twins shaped our lives a lot," he said. "If we hadn't been twins, where do you think we'd be?"

It was a question Nicole couldn't answer. For that matter, neither could Jonas. "No one knows us as 'Jonas,' and as 'Nicole,'" he said. "They know us as 'Jonas and Nicole.' We're the classic never-apart twins." It was true. They were so close, and yet they'd each fought so hard to have their own lives.

"You're so closely knitted together and when both of you are struggling for that independence, there's so much clashing," Jonas said. "So much wanting to be your own person."

Yet, when it came down to it, when Jonas asked Nicole what was her most special memory of being an identical twin, Nicole said she remembered a time that seemed like it could only have come *before* memory. Jonas seemed to remember it, too.

"We were babies, we were sort of like a tag team," Nicole said. "Our parents would set us down for naps. We didn't want to sleep, so we'd climb up over the bars [of our cribs] and, of course, I got up and over and you kept falling back down. So I climbed yours and helped you over."

Of course: One helping the other, up and over whatever obstacles lay in their way, always together.

CHAPTER 42

Transformation

W HO WE ARE IS THE STORY WE TELL ABOUT OURSELVES. THE self, says philosopher Daniel Dennett, is the center of narrative gravity, "an abstraction that is, in spite of its abstractness, tightly coupled to the physical world." Nicole knew that she was more than the sum of her parts—that her heart and mind defined who she was, but her body gave her context. Bodies hold our stories. They connect us to the world because they are the instruments by which we experience the world. Nicole finally needed to make that connection right. She regretted that people who don't understand what it means to be transgender focus so much on the surgical part of transitioning. It was for her just a final step, but a necessary one, and the chance, finally, to be conscious of her own body in a good way.

HEADING INTO HER SENIOR YEAR in high school, Nicole was eager to have her surgery the following summer, before she started college. Dr. Spack recommended a Philadelphia plastic surgeon. The operation would be expensive, about $20,000, but Wayne and Kelly had set aside the money from their portion of the $75,000 that had been awarded the family in its lawsuit against the Orono School Department. After paying GLAD and the remainder of the money they owed their first attorney, the Maineses had about $44,000 left.

A couple of weeks before the operation, a miscommunication between the surgeon's office and the Maineses regarding presurgical protocols put the entire operation on hold. The family hadn't realized Nicole needed to stop taking her estrogen a month earlier, a necessary precaution because hormone treatments increase the risk of blood clots. The clock for the operation would now have to be reset, but in order to still complete the surgery in time for Nicole to heal before heading off to college, the family had to find a different surgeon. Luckily, there was one just outside Philadelphia, Dr. Kathy Rumer, a nationally recognized transgender surgical specialist, and she had an opening in her schedule at the end of July.

Months before the operation, Nicole underwent numerous laser treatments for the removal of all her pubic hair, since a portion of her scrotal and penile tissue would be used to form her new vagina. It was an excruciating process she likened to someone flicking a rubber band against her skin, then injecting the spot with a hot needle.

Wayne and Nicole had both met Dr. Rumer a year or two earlier at a transgender conference in Philadelphia, so there was already a good rapport with the doctor. She explained the procedure to the entire family, telling them that although Nicole would be losing her penis and testicles, sensitive parts would be retained to create a clitoris, enabling sexual arousal. She'd have to learn how to position herself differently to urinate, and over a period of months would need to use a device to expand and maintain the shape of her new vagina. Most reassuringly, when Nicole was fully healed, it would be almost impossible to tell, from outward appearances, that she hadn't been born with female anatomy.

A week before the scheduled operation at Pennsylvania's Delaware County Memorial Hospital, Nicole was in a state of nervous anticipation, part fearful, part excited, knowing that the upcoming surgery was a kind of light at the end of a very long tunnel, and yet understanding there would be real-world differences, and complications, with this new body. She worried especially that the surgery would reignite old feelings of dysphoria. Over the last seventeen years, she'd become accustomed to what she called her "boy parts," and now, having made peace with them, she was going to replace them with new, unfamiliar "girl parts." What if the disorientation about her body came back? She wrote down some of her thoughts:

> I've been having realizations that surgery isn't going to be the magic fix to everything like I thought. I think that I already knew that, but it's still a hard feeling to accept. I've always been afraid of dating, with the way my body is now—but it's still going to be scary because of the way my body used to be. I'm also still going to be unable to have a child—which is something that has always intensely bothered me. Even if I change my body and even if I look like I was born a natural woman—there is always going to be that reminder that I wasn't—and I think that that's something that I'll always have bad blood with.

Despite her worries and concerns, Nicole also knew this was the only option, and the only way to complete her transition: a final piece of the puzzle finding its rightful place.

> If not for me, I feel like I need to do this for Wyatt. I need to do this to make up for everything that he had to put up with. I need to do this to apologize to him. I need to do this to show him that it was all worth it. I need to do this to thank him for not giving up and for giving me a chance. . . . He always remembered that there was something to be gained from putting up with everyone else's nonsense—he was going to have the body that he always felt like he deserved and was meant to have. And that made it all—the harassment and the bad feelings and the discomfort and the awkwardness—worth it.
> I feel like I need to have surgery because I promised him.

A few days before the operation, Jonas was also thinking about the significance of this moment for his sister and wrote on his Facebook page:

> So we leave tomorrow for Philly where Nicole will undergo the Sex Reassignment Surgery that she has been waiting to have her whole life. Chances are the next couple of posts I make are gonna be sappy and long, but I can't help it. This is the conclusion to a very long struggle and very enlightening journey for Nicole and I want to thank all of you guys (you're all probably Nicole's friends, since you're my friends, and the whole twin thing, you get it) for being there to support her and show her love and kindness. . . . I'll try and keep you all posted. It's going to be a VERY exciting week for us, and a little emotional, so before you ask I'm not crying I'm just allergic to touching moments.
>
> P.S. If you have any ideas of what I should write on a cake let me know because there is SO much potential there.

On July 28, 2015, on a humid, foggy morning, the entire Maines family arrived at the hospital outside Philadelphia in the dark. It wasn't quite six yet, but Nicole already looked wrung out. She was wan and her hair hung limply across her face. In a loose-fitting pale blue shift and canvas slip-ons, she shuffled down the hospital corridor supported by her parents. She hadn't eaten solid food for forty-eight hours and had had to endure an enema that morning, all in preparation for the operation.

The night before she'd felt so weak, in fact, she'd laid down on the bathroom floor in one of the patient apartments above Dr. Rumer's office, where up to four sex-reassignment patients at a time stay as part of their recovery. She would live there with Kelly for a week after her own surgery, and that's where they checked in the day before the operation. Wayne and Jonas were staying at a nearby Hilton Hotel, but they were all there in the apartment, just twelve hours before the surgery, and Nicole was dizzy, hungry, and feeling vulnerable.

"I can't do this," she moaned from the bathroom floor, just a bit melodramatically.

"You don't have to," Kelly told her. "We can cancel the surgery right now if you want."

"No! No! I have to have the surgery!"

There was never really any doubt that she would. She knew it; Kelly and Wayne knew it; Jonas knew it. But neither twin had ever even been in a hospital before. The most serious medical procedures they'd had were getting their wisdom teeth extracted. But Nicole was going to have a four- or five-hour surgery, and she would be recuperating for several weeks. It was a long walk to the elevator, so a hospital attendant retrieved a wheelchair for Nicole, and Jonas took over, pushing his sister through the serpentine halls, then up to the sixth floor. Once there, Nicole seemed to relax a bit, but admitted her worries to her mother.

"I wonder if it will come back," she said.

Kelly understood. Nicole was concerned, again, about the dysphoria, the sense of her body not belonging to her. She'd pushed back against her male body for so long, not wanting it, not recognizing it as her own. Kelly reassured her the feelings were natural. A lot of changes were in store, and what's unknown is always scary.

A nurse asked Nicole to change into a hospital gown and then went over some forms with her and her mother. As she closed the door on Wayne and Jonas, she told the two men they could find the waiting room down the hall and around the corner.

"I'm staying right here," Jonas said, as he sat down outside his sister's hospital room and leaned his back against the wall.

Over the next hour or so a steady stream of hospital personnel went in and out of the room: the duty nurse, the operating room nurse, the nurse anesthetist, the anesthesiologist, and finally the surgeon, Kathy Rumer. Before she left to prep for surgery, Rumer asked Nicole if she had any questions or concerns.

"Let's get this thing done!" Nicole said. "I'm hungry!"

A long-sought relief settled over Kelly and Wayne as their daughter was wheeled into the operating room at 7:35 A.M. They were almost over this last big hurdle. In retrospect, Kelly thought Nicole's meltdown the night before had, in a way, broken the tension. Her own emotions had been so high she'd been afraid of grabbing Nicole and telling her, "No! Don't do this." It wasn't that she didn't think her daughter wanted or needed the surgery. She did. It was that she hated the idea of one of her children being cut open. But this day had been out there so long, had been anticipated and planned for and dreamed about. Now she just wanted it over so that everyone could move on.

All that was left was the waiting. Wayne had brought a kind of tool-box and worked on his new hobby, weaving small baskets from pine tree needles; Kelly checked work email on her laptop; and Jonas fiddled with his smartphone. He also posted to Facebook:

Nicole is goin under!! It has begun.

All during the surgery—and actually for days before and after the surgery—messages for Nicole had poured in through social media. She received "good luck" texts from family members, from Asa Adams school counselor Lisa Erhardt, even from the dean of students at the University of Maine. Lexie, her best friend from Waynflete, texted, "ARE U PSYCHED FOR SURGERY?" Nicole texted back, "SUPER PSYCHED—nervous—BUT PSYCHED," to which Lexie replied, "U gonna look SO GOOD."

At 11:06 A.M., Dr. Rumer appeared in the waiting area.

"She did great," she told the family.

The operation was completed in under four hours, and Nicole was just fine, she said. The surgeon was able to construct a five-inch long vagina and did not have to do a skin graft to find extra tissue, which was a huge relief. Kelly and Wayne embraced each other.

Referring to the surgery, Wayne said, "This part was a good thing. It's like a present, after everything we've been through."

Nicole was in the recovery room almost longer than the OR. The nausea from the general anesthesia was getting the best of her.

"Can I just peek in to give her a kiss?" Kelly asked.

No, it was against hospital privacy rules, since the beds in the recovery room were not partitioned. Kelly would have to wait a bit longer. Finally, at 2:35 in the afternoon, Nicole's bed was wheeled down to the inpatient surgical unit, room 504. There was some irony to the room number: It was the same as the policy at Asa Adams that had both protected Nicole and then become a kind of albatross. Now it would designate the room where she'd recover from her final transition.

Nicole slept most of the day, and Kelly, Wayne, and Jonas lingered in her room keeping a watchful eye over her. On Facebook, Jonas posted another update.

> With Nicole! She's sleepy, but she's feeling good! She'll be awake and kicking soon so I'll enjoy the quiet while I can.
>
> I just want to thank you all again for all of your support. This is a huge day for Nicole and my family and you've all been so kind throughout our journey. Those of you who know me (hopefully all of you) know that this publicity "family story" stuff isn't my jam. This week I'm making an exception. She has fought incredibly hard for her rights and the rights of others, and you all played a part in that, too. Pat yourselves on the back, champs. You earned it. She loves all of you and so do I. Thank you again and I'll see if she's up for a selfie when she wakes up.

Two days after the surgery, Nicole ate a hamburger, made phone calls—to her grandmother Donna, to other relatives and friends—and received visitors. One of them was a trans woman she'd met at a convention and who lived nearby. They talked animatedly to each other while Kelly and Wayne and Jonas lingered in the room. At one point, Nicole said to her friend, "I kinda like having a twin brother, because now I can see I would have looked awesome as a man, too!"

Her good friend Lexie texted, "HOW U FEELIN?" And then, "YOU'RE LIKE ARIEL," the little mermaid who emerged from the sea in the form she'd always longed for.

Nicole's transition was now complete. She would still need to take female hormones the rest of her life, and she would never be able to have her own children, but she knew she wanted to marry a man someday and adopt. Everything else was still to be decided, which is how it's supposed to be when you're just seventeen years old.

For Nicole, for Jonas, for Wayne and Kelly, nothing, of course, would ever really be over because nothing ever is until we take our last breath. We are, all of us, always crossing borders. Everything seems to happen all at once when we're young, but as we get older we see that we are always moving away from one thing and toward another, never still, never without motion. We live in liminal time, each moment sliding into the next, the future into the present, the present into the past. We believe all things are possible, and that there are always more stories to be written.

"Stories move the walls that need to be moved," Nicole told her father recently. Nicole's story had started before she was even born. So had Jonas's—in atoms and molecules, in liquid beginnings. One DNA, two souls, and a billion possibilities. "I believe we don't choose our stories," the poet and author Honor Moore once said. "Our stories choose us. . . . And if we don't tell them, then we are somehow diminished." Kelly and Wayne and Jonas and Nicole were still in the middle of their stories, but they hadn't backed away from sharing them.

Nicole had searched for hers in mirrors, in her brother, in the world around her—and she'd found it with her family's help. Nicole's truth had always been impatient to make itself known. It was, in those first few years of life, unnameable. Kelly, Jonas, and Wayne helped her words find "a local habitation and a name." There was no confusion anymore when she looked in the mirror. She'd solved her own great riddle and in the process helped her family solve theirs. They'd spun the stories of their lives. And when it was all unspooled it all made sense, and the knots in their hearts were freed.

As Long as She's Happy

E VEN IN THE TIME IT HAS TAKEN TO WRITE THIS BOOK, THE RIGHTS of transgender people continue to be recognized. The push for marriage equality in the past few years helped to galvanize the transgender movement, and there is clearly no going back. In a 1966 survey of medical and psychiatric professionals in the United States, an overwhelming majority believed transsexuals were "severely neurotic." Today, eighteen states and the District of Columbia as well as more than two hundred U.S. cities and counties bar discrimination against transgender people. Worldwide, seven countries legally recognize more than two genders. And in July 2015, the Obama administration moved to lift the restriction from transgender people serving in the military.

How far we have come—though there is a great deal more still to be done—is a testament to the acceptance of young people who are now growing up with marriage equality as the law of the land. How children spontaneously understand fairness and equality and accept differences in others was illustrated in a conversation among three third-grade students at Asa C. Adams Elementary School a few years ago. Lisa Erhardt, who meant so much to the Maines family during Nicole's odyssey at the school, was giving a lesson about sticking one's neck out for friends and classmates in bullying situations. At the end of the hour the third-graders were asked to draw a picture based on the lesson. Walking among their desks while they worked, Erhardt overheard several students who had taken a creative approach to the concept of sticking one's neck out. That night, she wrote to the Maineses.

Hi, Wayne & Kelly—

I just had to share this conversation that happened in one of my third grade classrooms today. It made me smile and when I had a moment, it brought a tear to my eye. I know you have been on this long hard journey, and at times schools have been a pain in your ass. But the struggles are worth it—not just for Nicole, but for the lives she has touched.

Boy: "I'm coloring my giraffe both teal and pink because he's transgender."

Girl: "What's that?"

Boy: "You know, when a person is a boy, but it really is a girl. You know, it's having two genders."

Girl: "Oh, I think frogs can do that, have more than one gender."

2nd Boy: "Yeah, you're right. But how can a person have that?"

Boy: "I don't really know, but we have a girl in our school who is transgender."

Girl: "Really? What's her name?"

Boy: "Oh, man, I can't remember! Well, maybe she's in middle school now."

Girl: "That's cool."

2nd Boy: "I didn't know that. How is she a boy and a girl?"

Lisa Erhardt: "Well, she has the brain of a girl, and her body is

like a boy body. But she lives like a girl, and when she is
grown up she will have surgery to change her body to match
her brain."

2ND BOY: "You mean like plastic surgery?"

LISA ERHARDT: "Exactly! Just like plastic surgery."

BOY: "I remember her name. She's Nicole."

GIRL: "Oh, I know Nicole. She's cool. I didn't know she's transgender."

BOY: "Yeah, but it isn't a big deal, you know."

GIRL: "Oh, I know. It doesn't really matter. As long as she's
happy."

Acknowledgments

I T GOES WITHOUT SAYING THAT THIS BOOK COULD NOT HAVE BEEN
written without the extraordinary collaboration of the Maines family. I
am grateful for their time, their honesty, and their friendship. Wayne's
detailed records of the lawsuit and Kelly's collection of the twins' art-
work, journals, and school records were invaluable. This was never easy
for any of them, but especially Nicole and Jonas, whom I watched grow
up into kind, intelligent young adults. Lisa Erhardt at Asa C. Adams
Elementary school also provided much insight, as did Dr. Norman
Spack, and GLAD attorneys Jennifer Levi and Ben Klein, who helped
me understand the nuances of the legal case. I especially want to thank
Jennifer for acting as a liaison and bringing the story of the Maines family to my attention. Guidance and information from my very dear friend
Dr. Jane McInerny was also key to helping me understand transgender
issues. My sister Eva Nies provided an invaluable last look at the manuscript, and Cyndi Togans advised me on Papua New Guinea culture.

The privilege of being published by Random House is deep and
abiding, as is my respect for, and immense gratitude to, my editor David
Ebershoff. His talents as a mentor, editor, author, and intellect are boun-
tiful, and without him this book would have been the poorer. My thanks
also to the second and third Random House "eyes" on the manuscript,
Caitlin McKenna (who also juggled multiple duties and guided me
through many a computer malfunction) and Annie Chagnot, and to the

extraordinary staff of Random House, who worked long hours under great time pressure, including Susan Kamil, publisher and editor in chief; Tom Perry, associate publisher of nonfiction; Benjamin Dreyer, managing editor; Sally Marvin, publicity director; Leigh Marchant, marketing director; Paolo Pepe, the art director for the jacket; Evan Camfield, production editor; Michelle Daniel, copy editor; Jennifer Backe, production manager; Carolyn Foley, associate general counsel; and cover photographer Kelly Campbell. Contributions were much appreciated from Nick Adams, director of transgender media at GLAAD; and especially Dr. Joshua Safer, endocrinologist and associate professor of molecular medicine at Boston University School of Medicine, and Dr. Curtis Crane, a reconstructive urologist and plastic surgeon in San Francisco.

Thank you also to Marty Baron, executive editor of *The Washington Post*, who allowed me a crucial two months of writing before I joined the newspaper in September 2014. Finally, thank you to my agent, Wendy Strothman, who always goes above and beyond, and to my parents and the rest of my large extended family and friends, but especially Jane Wulf, who started me out on this whole writing thing twenty-five years ago. Thanks, Bambi.

Sources

M UCH OF THE MATERIAL FOR THIS BOOK WAS DRAWN FROM hundreds of hours of interviews with the Maines family, doctors, lawyers, friends, Asa Adams school counselor Lisa Erhardt, and others. The research also included extensive personal papers, journals, medical records, court depositions, photographs and videos, and an unpublished memoir by Wayne Maines, all courtesy of the Maines family. Some of the events in this book also were witnessed firsthand by the author.

BIBLIOGRAPHY

Boag, Peter. *Re-Dressing America's Frontier Past*. Berkeley: University of California Press, 2011.

Bornstein, Kate. *Gender Outlaw: On Men, Women and the Rest of Us*. New York: Routledge, 1994.

Bornstein, Kate, and S. Bear Bergman. *Gender Outlaws: The Next Generation*. Berkeley: Seal Press, 2010.

Boylan, Jennifer Finney. *She's Not There: A Life in Two Genders*. New York: Broadway Books, 2003.

Brooks, Peter. *Enigmas of Identity*. Princeton, N.J.: Princeton University Press, 2011.

Burr, Chandler. *A Separate Creation: The Search for the Biological Origins of Sexual Orientation*. New York: Hyperion, 1996.

Burt, Stephen. *Belmont.* Minneapolis: Graywolf Press, 2013.

Colapinto, John. *As Nature Made Him: The Boy Who Was Raised as a Girl.* New York: Perennial, 2001.

Davis, Elizabeth Gould. *The First Sex.* New York: Putnam, 1971.

Dorsey, James Owen. *A Study of Siouan Cults.* Charleston, S.C.: Nabu Press, 2011.

Erickson-Schroth, Laura, ed. *Trans Bodies, Trans Selves: A Resource for the Transgender Community.* Oxford: Oxford University Press, 2014.

Fine, Cordelia. *Delusions of Gender: How Our Minds, Society, and Neurosexism Create Difference.* New York: W. W. Norton, 2010.

Francis, Richard. *Epigenetics: The Ultimate Mystery of Inheritance.* New York: W. W. Norton, 2011.

Garcia-Falgueras Alicia, and Dick F. Swaab. "A Sex Difference in the Hypothalamic Uncinate Nucleus: Relationship to Gender Identity," *Brain* 131 (2008): 3132–46.

Green, Richard, and Robert J. Stoller, et al. "Attitudes Toward Sex Transformation Procedures." *Archives of General Psychiatry* 15, no. 2 (1966): 178–82.

Hines, Melissa. *Brain Gender.* Oxford: Oxford University Press, 2004.

Krieger, Irwin. *Helping Your Transgender Teen: A Guide for Parents.* New Haven, Conn.: Genderwise Press, 2011.

Kuklin, Susan. *Beyond Magenta: Transgender Teens Speak Out.* Somerville, Mass.: Candlewick Press, 2014.

Leger, Tom, and Riley MacLeod, eds. *The Collection.* New York: Topside, 2012.

Mahlsdorf, Charlotte von. *I Am My Own Wife: The True Story of Charlotte von Mahlsdorf.* San Francisco: Cleis, 1995.

Meyerowitz, Joanne. *How Sex Changed: A History of Transsexuality in the United States.* Cambridge: Harvard University Press, 2002.

Morris, Jan. *Conundrum.* New York: New York Review of Books, 2005.

Norton, Aaron T., and Gregory M. Herek. "Heterosexuals' Attitudes Toward Transgender People: Findings from a National Probability Sample of U.S. Adults," *Sex Roles* 68, nos. 11–12 (2012): 738–53.

Parravani, Christa. *Her.* New York: Henry Holt, 2013.

Prosser, Jay. *Second Skins: The Body Narratives of Transsexuality.* New York: Columbia University Press, 1998.

Reis, Elizabeth. *Bodies in Doubt: An American History of Intersex.* Baltimore: Johns Hopkins University Press, 2009.

Rudacille, Deborah. *The Riddle of Gender: Science, Activism, and Transgender Rights.* New York: Anchor Books, 2006.

Salamon, Gayle. *Assuming a Body: Transgender and the Rhetoric of Materiality.* New York: Columbia University Press, 2010.

Segal, Nancy. *Entwined Lives: Twins and What They Tell Us About Human Behavior.* New York: Penguin Group, 1999.

Solomon, Andrew. *Far from the Tree: Parents, Children, and the Search for Identity.* New York: Scribner, 2012.

Spector, Tim. *Identically Different: Why You Can Change Your Genes.* London: Weidenfeld and Nicolson, 2012.

Stryker, Susan, and Stephen Whittle, eds. *The Transgender Studies Reader.* New York: Routledge, 2006.

Tarttelin, Abigail. *Golden Boy.* New York: Atria, 2013.

Tolbert, T. C., and Tim Trace Peterson, eds. *Troubling the Line: Trans and Genderqueer Poetry and Poetics.* Callicoon, N.Y.: Nightboat, 2013.

Walton, Eda Lou. *Turquoise Boy and White Shell Girl.* New York: Thomas Y. Crowell, 1933.

Williams, Walter L. *The Spirit and the Flesh: Sexual Diversity in American Indian Culture.* Boston: Beacon Press, 1986.

Wittlinger, Ellen. *Parrotfish.* New York: Simon and Schuster, 2007.

Zhou, Jiang-Ning, Michel A. Hofman, Louis J. G. Gooren, and Dick F. Swaab. "A Sex Difference in the Human Brain and Its Relation to Transsexuality." *Nature* 378 (1995): 68–70.

Resources

SUICIDE PREVENTION

THE TREVOR PROJECT

thetrevorproject.org

For transgender people in crisis, call the Trevor Lifeline, 866-4-U-TREVOR (866-488-7386), or ask for help through TrevorText (text "Trevor" to 1-202-304-1200), TrevorChat, the Trevor Project's online messaging service, or the National Suicide Prevention Lifeline at 1-800-273-TALK (8255).

EQUALITY ADVOCATES

NATIONAL CENTER FOR TRANSGENDER EQUALITY

transequality.org

A social justice advocacy organization based in Washington, D.C.

GLAAD

glaad.org/transgender

Empowers LGBT people to tell their stories, and works with the media to shape the narrative about LGBT issues.

HUMAN RIGHTS CAMPAIGN

hrc.org/resources/category/transgender

A national civil rights organization.

TASK FORCE TRANSGENDER CIVIL RIGHTS PROJECT

thetaskforce.org/tcrp

Dedicated to the expansion of transgender rights in legislative and policy arenas.

THE AUDRE LORDE PROJECT—TRANSJUSTICE

alp.org/TransJustice

Political group created by and for trans and gender-nonconforming people of color, mobilizing community action on pressing political issues, including access to jobs, housing, and education.

TRANS PEOPLE OF COLOR COALITION

transpoc.org

Nonprofit social justice and advocacy organization based in Washington, D.C.

I AM: TRANS PEOPLE SPEAK

transpeoplespeak.org

A website dedicated to empowering transgender people by giving them a place to share their own stories and speak for themselves.

THE TRANS 100

thetrans100.com

An overview of the work being done in, by, and for the transgender community in the United States.

WE HAPPY TRANS

wehappytrans.com

A website devoted to sharing positive stories from trans people everywhere.

LEGAL HELP

TRANSGENDER LAW CENTER

transgenderlawcenter.org

Organization dedicated to changing law, policy, and attitudes toward transgender people.

SYLVIA RIVERA LAW PROJECT

srlp.org

Legal advocacy organization based in New York City.

TRANSGENDER LEGAL DEFENSE AND EDUCATION FUND

tldef.org

Provides public education, test-case litigation, direct legal services, community organizing, and public policy efforts.

NATIONAL CENTER FOR LESBIAN RIGHTS—TRANSGENDER LAW

nclrights.org/explore-the-issues/transgender-law

Social justice and advocacy organization.

GAY AND LESBIAN ADVOCATES AND DEFENDERS

glad.org

GLAD is New England's leading legal rights organization dedicated to ending discrimination based on sexual orientation, HIV status, and gender identity and expression.

LAMBDA LEGAL

lambdalegal.org

The oldest national organization pursuing high-impact litigation, public education, and advocacy on behalf of equality and civil rights for lesbians, gay men, bisexuals, transgender people, and people with HIV.

YOUTH AND FAMILIES

PARENTS, FAMILIES AND FRIENDS OF LESBIANS AND GAYS

pflag.org

PFLAG is a national nonprofit organization for parents, family, friends, and allies of LGBTQ people that also provides resources and support for transgender children.

GAY, LESBIAN AND STRAIGHT EDUCATION NETWORK

glsen.org

GLSEN focuses on education support for K–12 schools.

GENDER SPECTRUM

genderspectrum.org

Gender Spectrum helps to create gender-sensitive and inclusive environments for all children and teens.

TRANS YOUTH FAMILY ALLIES

imatyfa.org

TYFA empowers young people and their families through support, education, and outreach about gender identity and expression

CAMP ARANU'TIQ

camparanutiq.org

Summer camp for transgender kids, teens, and families who might not fit in at other camps, or who want to be at camps with kids like them.

TRANSKIDS PURPLE RAINBOW FOUNDATION

transkidspurplerainbow.org

TKPRF is committed to enhancing the future lives of trans children by educating schools, peers, places of worship, the medical community, government bodies, and society in general in an effort to seek fair and equal treatment of all trans youth.

TRANS STUDENT EDUCATIONAL RESOURCES

transstudent.org

A youth-led organization providing trans-related information on school issues in support of creating policy changes in school districts.

LAURA'S PLAYGROUND

lauras-playground.com

This site has weekly online chat support group meetings every Thursday night at 8 P.M. EST.

MERMAIDS

mermaidsuk.org.uk

London-based family and individual support site for teenagers and children with gender identity issues.

TRANSPARENTCY

transparentcy.org

Founded by a transgender parent and dedicated to transgender parents and their children, TransParentcy is committed to the fight to protect and honor the relationship between the two.

TRANSACTIVE GENDER CENTER

transactiveonline.org

Provides a wide range of services and expertise to transgender and gender-diverse children and youth, as well as their families.

TRANS YOUTH EQUALITY FOUNDATION

transyouthequality.org

Provides education, advocacy, and support for transgender and gender-nonconforming children and youth and their families.

Glossary

UNDERSTANDING SEX, GENDER, AND SEXUAL ORIENTATION

SEX. The classification of people as male or female. At birth infants are assigned a sex, usually based on the appearance of their external anatomy. (This is what is written on the birth certificate.) However, a person's sex is actually a combination of bodily characteristics, including chromosomes, hormones, internal and external reproductive organs, and secondary sex characteristics.

GENDER IDENTITY. One's internal, deeply held sense of one's gender. For transgender people, their own internal gender identity does not match the sex they were assigned at birth. Most people have a gender identity of man or woman (or boy or girl). For some people, their gender identity does not fit neatly into one of those two choices. Unlike gender expression (see below), gender identity is not visible to others.

GENDER EXPRESSION. External manifestations of gender, expressed through one's name, pronouns, clothing, haircut, behavior, voice, or body characteristics. Society identifies these cues as masculine and feminine, although what is considered masculine and feminine changes over time and varies by culture. Typically, transgender people seek to make their gender expression align with their gender identity, rather than the sex they were assigned at birth.

Sexual Orientation. Describes an individual's enduring physical, romantic, and/or emotional attraction to another person. Gender identity and sexual orientation are not the same. Transgender people may be straight, lesbian, gay, or bisexual. For example, a person who transitions from male to female and is attracted solely to men would identify as a straight woman. Some people are asexual, meaning they lack a sexual attraction to either men or women.

OTHER TERMINOLOGY

Transgender (adj.). An umbrella term for people whose gender identity and/or gender expression differs from what is typically associated with the sex they were assigned at birth. People under the transgender umbrella may describe themselves using one or more of a wide variety of terms—including *transgender*. Some of those terms are defined below. Use the descriptive term preferred by the individual. Many transgender people are prescribed hormones by their doctors to change their bodies. Some undergo surgery as well. But not all transgender people can or will take those steps, and a transgender identity is not dependent upon medical procedures.

Transsexual (adj.). An older term that originated in the medical and psychological communities. Still preferred by some people who have permanently changed—or seek to change—their bodies through medical interventions (including but not limited to hormones and/or surgeries). Unlike *transgender, transsexual* is not an umbrella term. Many transgender people do not identify as transsexual and prefer the word *transgender*. It is best to ask which term an individual prefers. If preferred, use as an adjective: transsexual woman or transsexual man.

Transgender man. People who were assigned female at birth but identify and live as men may use this term to describe themselves. Some may also use *FTM*, an abbreviation for female-to-male. Some may prefer to simply be called *men*, without any modifier.

TRANSGENDER WOMAN. People who were assigned male at birth but identify and live as women may use this term to describe themselves. Some may also use *MTF*, an abbreviation for male-to-female. Some may prefer to simply be called *women*, without any modifier.

CROSS-DRESSER. While anyone may wear clothes associated with a different sex, the term *cross-dresser* is typically used to refer to heterosexual men who occasionally wear clothes, makeup, and accessories culturally associated with women. This activity is a form of gender expression, and not done for entertainment purposes. Cross-dressers do not wish to permanently change their sex or live full-time as women. Replaces the term *transvestite*. PLEASE NOTE: Transgender women are not cross-dressers or drag queens. Drag queens are men, typically gay men, who dress like women for the purpose of entertainment. Be aware of the differences between transgender women, cross-dressers, and drag queens. Use the term preferred by the individual.

TRANSITION. Altering one's birth sex is not a one-step procedure; it is a complex process that occurs over a long period of time. Transition includes some or all of the following personal, medical, and legal steps: telling one's family, friends, and co-workers; using a different name and new pronouns; dressing differently; changing one's name and/or sex on legal documents; hormone therapy; and possibly (though not always) one or more types of surgery. The exact steps involved in transition vary from person to person. The phrase "sex change" should be avoided.

SEX REASSIGNMENT SURGERY (SRS). Refers to doctor-supervised surgical interventions, and is only one small part of transition (see *Transition* above). Not all transgender people choose to, or can afford to, undergo medical surgeries. The preferred term now is *gender confirmation surgery*.

GENDER DYSPHORIA. In 2013, the American Psychiatric Association released the fifth edition of the *Diagnostic and Statistical Manual of Mental Disorders* (DSM-V) which replaced the outdated entry "Gender Identity Disorder" with "Gender Dysphoria" and changed the criteria for diagnosis. The necessity of a psychiatric diagnosis remains controversial, as both psychiatric and medical authorities recommend individualized medical treatment through hormones and/or surgeries to treat gender dysphoria. Some transgender advocates believe the inclusion of Gender Dysphoria in the DSM is necessary in order to advocate for health insurance that covers the medically necessary treatment recommended for transgender people.

CISGENDER. A term used by some to describe people who are not transgender. "Cis-" is a Latin prefix meaning "on the same side as," and is therefore an antonym of "trans-." A more widely understood way to describe people who are not transgender is simply to say *non-transgender people*.

GENDER NONCONFORMING A term used to describe some people whose gender expression is different from conventional expectations of masculinity and femininity. Not all gender-nonconforming people identify as transgender; nor are all transgender people gender nonconforming. Many people have gender expressions that are not entirely conventional—that fact alone does not make them transgender. Many transgender men and women have gender expressions that are conventionally masculine or feminine. Simply being transgender does not make someone gender nonconforming. The term is not a synonym for *transgender* or *transsexual* and should only be used if someone self-identifies as gender nonconforming.

GENDERQUEER A term used by some people who experience their gender identity and/or gender expression as falling outside the categories of man and woman. They may define their gender as falling somewhere in between man and woman, or they may define it as wholly different from these terms. The term is not a synonym for *transgender* or *transsexual* and should only be used if someone self-identifies as genderqueer.

INTERSEX Replaces the outdated term "hermaphrodite." Someone who is intersex is born with one of several medical conditions that leads to the person's biological sex being ambiguous. Their external sex organs and/or reproductive anatomy may have characteristics of both males and females. Intersex advocates are urging the medical establishment to stop performing surgeries on intersex infants to force their bodies to conform to convention. Often the choice made by the doctor and reinforced by surgeries does not match the gender identity the person ultimately develops.

Adapted from the GLAAD Media Reference Guide

EDITION 9.1, MAY 2015

glaad.org/reference/transgender

ABOUT THE AUTHOR

AMY ELLIS NUTT won the Pulitzer Prize in 2011 for her feature series "The Wreck of the *Lady Mary*," about the 2009 sinking of a fishing boat off the New Jersey coast. She is a health and science writer at *The Washington Post*, the author of *Shadows Bright as Glass*, and the coauthor of the *New York Times* bestseller *The Teenage Brain*. She was a Nieman Fellow in journalism at Harvard University and Ferris Professor in Residence at Princeton, and was for a number of years an adjunct professor of journalism at Columbia University Graduate School of Journalism. She lives in Washington, D.C.

@amyellisnutt

ABOUT THE TYPE

This book was set in Electra, a typeface designed for Linotype by renowned type designer W. A. Dwiggins (1880–1956). Electra is a fluid typeface, avoiding the contrasts of thick and thin strokes that are prevalent in most modern typefaces.